Looking Ahead

Mastering Academic Writing

CHRISTINE HOLTEN
University of California at Los Angeles

JUDITH MARASCO
University of California at Los Angeles
Santa Monica College at Santa Monica

SERIES EDITORS
PATRICIA BYRD
Georgia State University

JOY M. REID
University of Wyoming

Video notes in Instructor's Manual by
Elizabeth Mejia
Washington State University

Heinle & Heinle Publishers
I(T)P An International Thomson Publishing Company

Pacific Grove • Albany • Bonn • Boston • Cincinnati • Detroit • London
Madrid • Melbourne • Mexico City • New York • Paris
San Francisco • Tokyo • Toronto • Washington

The publication of *Looking Ahead: Mastering Academic Writing* was directed by members of the Newbury House ESL/EFL at Heinle & Heinle:

Erik Gundersen, Editorial Director
Jonathan Boggs, Market Development Director
Kristin M. Thalheimer, Senior Production Services Coordinator
Nancy Mann Jordan, Senior Developmental Editor
Stanley J. Galek, Vice President and Publisher

Also participating in the publication of this program were:
Project Manager/Desktop Pagination: Thompson Steele, Inc.
Managing Developmental Editor: Amy Lawler
Manufacturing Coordinator: Mary Beth Hennebury
Associate Editor: Ken Pratt
Associate Market Development Director: Mary Sutton
Photo/video Specialist: Jonathan Stark
Media Services Coordinator: Jerry Christopher
Interior Designer: Sally Steele
Cover Designer: Ha Nguyen
Cover Artist: Katherine Stuart

ISBN 08384-7893-X
10 9 8 7 6 5 4 3 2 1

To our mentors:

Donna M. Brinton, Russell N. Campbell,

and Marianne Celce-Murcia

Thank You

The authors and publisher would like to thank the following individuals who offered many helpful insights, ideas, and suggestions for change during the development of *Looking Ahead: Mastering Academic Writing:*

Victoria Badalamenti, *LaGuardia Community College, New York*
Karen Batchelor, *City College of San Francisco*
Cheryl Benz, *Miami Dade Community College*
Pam Butterfield, *Palomar College, California*
Lisa Camp, *Hunter College, New York*
Marvin Coates, *El Paso Community College, Valle Verde Campus*
Carol Culver, *San Francisco State University*
Kathleen Flynn, *Glendale Community College, California*
Barbara Foley, *Union County College, New Jersey*
Byrun Hauser, *Miami Dade Community College*
Gayle Henrotte, *Mt. San Antonio Community College, California*
Mary Hill-Shinn, *El Paso Community College*
Cynthia Howe, *Seattle Central Community College*
Sheila McKee, *University of North Texas*
Lynne Nickerson, *DeKalb College, Georgia*
Norman Prange, *Cuyahoga Community College, Ohio*
Jennifer Ross, *LaGuardia Community College, New York*
Dawn Schmid, *California State University at San Marcos*
Catherine Sessions, *Hunter College, New York*
Bob Shiel, *St. Augustine College, Illinois*
Joe Starr, *Houston Community College*
Christine Tierney, *Houston Community College*
Patricia Weyland, *Ohio State University*

ONTENTS

Chapter 2: Reporting   38

Chapter 3: Investigating   80

• • • • • • • •

Chapter 4: Evaluating   120

Chapter 7: Synthesizing   224

*W*ill your students be ready to meet the academic writing expectations of their instructors and professors outside your ESL program?

*T*hey will if they use *Looking Ahead,* Heinle & Heinle's new 4-level academic writing/grammar series.

SUCCESSFUL WRITING WITH *LOOKING AHEAD*!

Chapter 7

*S*ynthesizing

Business and Responsibility

Will your students be ready . . . to perform various types of academic writing?

Looking Ahead focuses on the various types of writing that successful students must learn to employ: *investigating, explaining, evaluating, summarizing, describing, analyzing,* and others. In practicing these various forms of academic writing, students call upon a host of rhetorical modes such as *classification* and *cause-effect* to support their ideas and opinions. They also develop facility in using a host of academic writing formats such as *paragraphs, essays, and reports.*

Will your students be ready . . . to understand and meet challenging academic expectations?

Each chapter begins with authentic academic assignments from across the disciplines (e.g. sociology, history) for the students to analyze and discuss. These assignments show how writing tasks are used in the "real world" of academic course work.

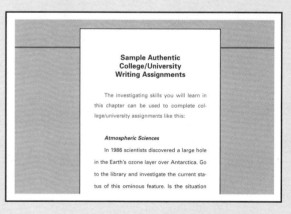

Sample Authentic College/University Writing Assignments

The investigating skills you will learn in this chapter can be used to complete college/university assignments like this:

Atmospheric Sciences

In 1986 scientists discovered a large hole in the Earth's ozone layer over Antarctica. Go to the library and investigate the current status of this ominous feature. Is the situation

Will your students be ready . . . to apply their own writing skills to academic situations?

Each chapter contains several short writing activities and at least one longer writing assignment designed to prepare students for the writing tasks they will encounter in college classes. Throughout the chapters, students practice writing activities that are appropriate for a specific academic setting (e.g., answering exam questions). The writing activities in each chapter end with a writing assignment that guides students step-by-step through the process.

PUTTING IT ALL TOGETHER

FINAL WRITING ASSIGNMENT

Choose two or three general statements about anger made in "The Anger Factor," *The Great Catharsis Debate,* and/or *Manners, Emotions, and the American Way.* Based on your own experiences with or observations about expressing anger, do you agree or disagree with these generalizations? Write a two- to three-page paper in which you agree or disagree with ideas from the readings.

Will your students be ready ... to exploit a variety of academic skills in writing?

Being a successful student means being a successful academic writer. In *Looking Ahead*, students learn essential academic writing skills like *brainstorming, seeking* and *using input from peers, gathering ideas from various sources, giving recognition to sources,* and *editing.*

Will your students be ready ... to exercise key vocabulary acquisition skills?

Special focus is given to developing vocabulary acquisition skills necessary for success in a variety of academic fields. Students gain strategies for learning new vocabulary and the relevant grammar associated with these vocabulary items.

Will your students be ready ... to apply the reflective skills necessary for fluency in academic writing?

Each chapter contains several *Learner's Notebook* activities that accomplish two purposes. First, *Notebook* activities give students an opportunity to gain fluency through reflective writing that will not be evaluated. Second, this type of free-writing helps students generate ideas for the academic writing tasks to come later in the unit.

Will your students be ready ... to look ahead to their academic future?

Chapters end as they begin—with information about authentic academic tasks and assignments. Students can analyze these assignments to learn more about the work that will be required of them when they enter degree programs. These sample assignments motivate students by showing them that they will apply the skills they are learning with their work in *Looking Ahead.*

SUCCESSFUL GRAMMAR ACQUISITION
WITH *LOOKING AHEAD*!

Will your students be ready ... to recognize the different discourse types found in academic writing?

Authentic readings and writing assignments in *Looking Ahead* were selected based on the academic discourse types that students most often need to read and produce in academic settings. These authentic materials give students many opportunities to see and analyze how English grammar and rhetoric "work."

ACADEMIC FIELDS
Business
Economics

Section 2 Past Time Narrative

   A Overview of Past Time Narrative Grammar
   B Past Tense Verbs
   C Proper Nouns, Pronouns, Demonstratives, and Cohesion

Section 3 Informational Writing

   A Overview of Informational Writing
   B Making Complex Nouns Using Relative Clauses
      Steps to Edit Relative Clauses
   C Complex Nouns with Prepositional Phrases
   D Participle Phrases
   E Verbs in Academic Writing
      Steps to Edit Verb Tense Shift
   F Subject-Verb Agreement
      Steps to Edit Subject-Verb Agreement
   G Passive Sentences
      Steps to Edit Passive vs. Active Voice

Will your students be ready ... to apply the grammar of academic writing?

Recent research has shown that specific grammar structures appear in clusters within types of discourse. By concentrating exclusively on one grammar cluster in each chapter, *Looking Ahead* focuses only on the grammar that is essential for the writing typical of a specific discourse type.

Will your students be ready ... to easily access important academic grammar information?

The *Grammar and Language Reference (GLR)* section at the back of the book pulls together all of the grammar explanations and authentic examples for easy student access. An icon **GLR** tells students when to refer to the *GLR*.

3A   Overview of Informational Grammar

Informational writing is found in almost everything you read in academic courses. This type of writing presents generalizations, theories, data, facts, and definitions.

- As the short sample demonstrates, informational writing is characterized by many structures, all of which work together.
- complex noun phrases (in bold)
- long sentences made up of several clauses that a connected with subordination, coordination, transition words and *-ing* participle phrases
- the simple present tense to indicate a generalization
- the present perfect tense to communicate about time relationships
- shifts in verb tense
- passive sentences are used to

Although many firms engage in business abroad, most of the ethical issues in this area arise for the transnational corporation, or TNC, [which is generally defined as a firm that has a direct investment in two or more countries.] The emergence of TNCs in the second half of the twentieth century has had a profound effect on developed and undeveloped countries alike. Their wealth and power have given rise to concern about **the impact on local economies and about the capacity of governments** to regulate them effectively. The pharmaceutical industry, more than any other, has been criticized for its activities abroad. Although prescription and over-the-counter drugs have done much to alleviate suffering and increase the well-being of

SUCCESSFUL ACADEMIC READING
WITH *LOOKING AHEAD*!

Will your students be ready ... to apply essential reading skills for successful writing preparation?

Simply stated, effective reading skills are essential for success as an academic writer. Academic writing requires that you draw on reading sources in a variety of ways—to get ideas for writing, to get background information on a topic, and to use the information you find to support your ideas. Given this, each chapter in *Looking Ahead* has a "reading theme," which allows students to become familiar with the vocabulary, ideas, and issues within that topic. In both content and style, readings reflect the types of selections that students encounter in their academic classes.

ETHICS IN INTERNATIONAL BUSINESS

Although many firms engage in business abroad, most of the ethical issues in this area arise for the transnational corporation, or TNC, which is generally defined as a firm that has a direct investment in two or more countries. The emergence of TNCs in the second half of the twentieth century has had a profound effect on developed and undeveloped countries alike. Their wealth and power have given rise to concern about the impact on local economies and about the capacity of governments to regulate them effectively. The pharmaceutical industry, more than any other, has been criticized for its activities abroad. Although prescription and over-the-counter drugs have done much to alleviate suffering and increase the well-being of people around the globe, the major drug companies are also faulted for many of their practices.

Different Instructions

One of the most heavily criticized practices is promoting drugs in the third world with more suggestions for their use and fewer warnings about side effects than in developed countries. The following are some typical examples.

Diarrhea is a mild inconvenience in developed countries, but it is a life-threatening condition in the third world and the major killer of children under the age of three. One treatment for diarrhea is Lomotil, marketed by G.D. Searle. This drug does not treat the underlying causes of diarrhea, however, but merely relieves the symptoms. Consequently, the World Health Organization (WHO) has declared Lomotil to be of "no value" in the treatment of diarrhea and a waste of time and money. The drug is also dangerous for young children and should not be prescribed to children under the age of two. But Searle has recommended the drug for diarrhea in children as young as one year in Indonesia and in infants between three and six months in Thailand, the Philippines, and Central America.

CNN VIDEO
WITH
LOOKING AHEAD!

Will your students be ready . . . to use a variety of authentic media to prepare for their academic future?
Each chapter in the *Looking Ahead* series has a CNN video clip related to the chapter theme and designed to further stimulate authentic discussion and writing. Appealing to the learning style preferences of auditory and visual students, the videos connect the content of *Looking Ahead* to the real world. An introduction to video use in the ESL classroom by Elizabeth Mejia (see the Instructor's Manual) provides the foundation for sound teaching strategies with video.

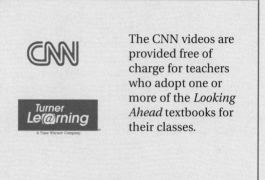

The CNN videos are provided free of charge for teachers who adopt one or more of the *Looking Ahead* textbooks for their classes.

THE WORLD WIDE WEB
WITH
LOOKING AHEAD!

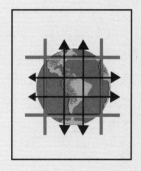

Are you ready . . . to provide all you can for your students' academic preparation?
The authors and editors of *Looking Ahead* have created an on-line system of support for teachers using the series. At **http://lookingahead.heinle.com**, teachers can find expanded versions of the Instructor's Manuals, lesson plans provided by teachers who are using the books, additional materials to supplement the books, and other support materials. In addition, the site offers opportunities to communicate with the editors and authors—to ask questions, share ideas, and make suggestions for improvements in the *Looking Ahead* series and its support materials.

GET READY WITH *LOOKING AHEAD*!

The four textbooks in the *Looking Ahead* series are designed to prepare students to be successful in their academic courses in U.S. colleges and universities. Specifically, *Looking Ahead* teaches students to read academic texts and materials, understand academic assignments, apply effective study skills, and respond appropriately to writing assignments. Each book "looks ahead" to the next in the series, and together as a group they look ahead to the writing students will do in their degree programs.

To the Teacher

Looking Ahead: Mastering Academic Writing is an advanced level writing and grammar textbook for ESL students. The book is divided into the following sections.

Getting Ready: This section prepares students to handle each type of writing assignment with the following activities:

> ***Warm-up Writing and Activities:*** These orient students to the writing and thinking strategies required to complete the type of writing in the chapter.

> ***The Basics of Writing:*** This section thoroughly explains the components of each type of writing assignment. It shows students, step-by-step, how to approach the particular writing task.

> ***Student and Professional Writing Samples:*** The Basics of Writing contains authentic samples of each type of writing, some produced by students, others produced by professionals.

> ***Writing Activities:*** These activities encourage students to practice what they have learned in the Basics of Writing and prepare them for the final writing assignment.

Focusing: This section immerses students in authentic readings that mirror the writing focus of each chapter, provide rich content from which to write their own essays, and serve as a resource for learning about how grammar and vocabulary work in the given type of writing.

> ***Reading for Writing Activities:*** These activities not only help students understand the key ideas in each reading, but help them approach the reading from a writer's perspective. They read not only for content, but learn to understand the decisions that the authors made about content and organization to meet their audience and purpose.

> ***Vocabulary Activities:*** The focus of these exercises is on helping students expand their vocabulary for academic writing.

> ***Grammar Activities:*** Key grammar features found in academic writing are presented to help students complete each writing assignment.

Putting It All Together: This final section asks students to implement what they have learned in previous sections and chapters. It takes students through the steps of producing the final writing assignment from the stage of gathering information for a specific audience and purpose to organizing the piece of writing to self-editing, peer response, and revision.

The Final 2–3 page Writing Assignments: Cumulative writing tasks that build on what students have learned through the authentic readings and the Basics of Writing.

Planning/Drafting Activities and Peer Response/Self-Editing Activities: These activities walk students through the writing process for each writing task.

Special Features of the Book: The book contains the following resources to help students master the writing strategies, grammar, and vocabulary of academic writing:

Looking Ahead and Authentic Writing Assignments: This real academic assignment from a college course allows students to strategize about how to use what they have learned in the chapter to complete real college writing tasks

Grammar and Language Reference: The GLR contains writer-based explanations and authentic examples of grammatical structures common to all types of academic writing. The GLR also contains Steps for Self-Editing to help students edit their own writing.

Learner's Notebook: This writing and language-learning journal gives students the opportunity to record personal experiences and insights related to chapter content, prepare for writing assignments, and reflect on their learning.

Writing and Vocabulary Appendices: These review the "basics" of any piece of academic writing including introductions, conclusions, transition sentences, and paragraph development. They also provide lists and guidelines for how to learn and use essential academic vocabulary.

To the Student

Are You Looking Ahead?

What are your goals for the future? You are probably looking ahead to getting your college degree and entering a satisfying career that allows you to use your skills. One important skill that you can take with you into your future is the ability to write for any audience or purpose. It has been predicted that each of us will change jobs approximately 5 times during our life. This means that we have to transfer skills to a variety of settings. Equipped with solid writing skills, you will be able to approach successfully any new task that involves writing.

How Can You Use This Book?

This book is designed to help you become a more confident writer. It combines writing and language skills—because both are needed to communicate successfully in writing. The material in this book can help you to learn to think as a writer. It contains strategies to help you approach a variety of writing tasks—understanding your audience and purpose, discovering what elements are required in each writing task, seeing the grammar and vocabulary that you can use in a given writing task, and applying editing strategies to accurately convey your meaning.

What Is Special About This Book?

Real College-Level Writing Assignments: Each chapter in this book focuses on a type of writing that you will probably be asked to do in college courses and in your future profession. The sample assignments at the beginning and end of each chapter are actual assignments from college courses.

The Basics of Writing: This section explains each type of writing assignment that you will find in this book. Using a step-by-step approach, we explain how each particular type of writing is constructed, so that you understand all of the 'parts' that make up the final product. In this section and throughout the chapter, guided activities help you to brainstorm ideas and organize the information you gather for each chapter's 2–3 page writing assignment.

Student and Professional Writing Samples: Samples of each type of writing—written by students and professionals—help you see what the final product will look like.

College-Level Readings: These readings will not only interest you and help you to get ideas for the final writing assignment, but they are also models of the type of writing you will do in each chapter. Accompanying activities help you "get inside the writer's head" to understand the writing strategies you need to complete each type of writing.

Vocabulary Activities: Most college students know they need to expand their vocabulary, but they don't always know how to go about doing so. The vocabulary activities in this book focus on words and expressions that are frequently found in academic writing.

Grammar Activities: You have probably spent a lot of time studying English grammar or working in English already. Yet, you also know how challenging it is to use all that you know to write clearly and accurately. The grammar activities in this book are different from what you might find in other textbooks because they help you see how writers use several grammar structures together to complete a particular type of writing task.

The Grammar and Language Reference: This section is a tool to help you review and learn grammar structures that are key to academic writing. It provides both explanations, real examples, and steps for editing grammar in your own writing.

Acknowledgments

For their belief in this project and their professional help bringing it to fruition, we are indebted to many people at Heinle and Heinle/ITP. Ken Pratt, Associate Editor, brought us on board this project, made it possible for us to meet with other *Looking Ahead* team members, and spent countless hours putting together all the pieces of a complex project. For orienting us to the ins and outs of publishing and Newbury House, we would like to thank Erik Gundersen, Editorial Director. Nancy Mann Jordan, Developmental Editor, and Amy Lawler, Managing Developmental Editor, who coordinated the review process and communication between the seven *Looking Ahead* team members, helped us process feedback, and generally kept us on task. Finally, we thank Kristin Thalheimer, Production Services Coordinator, and Sally Steele, Joanne Lowry, and Donna McDaniel at Thompson-Steele for turning our rough manuscript pages into a beautiful book.

We are also grateful to those who piloted our materials or otherwise gave us feedback: Carol Linn-Millar, James Apostolos, J.F. Miller, Ellen Choi, Vicki Blaho, Sharon Jaffe, and Melody Nightingale at Santa Monica College, and Kathy Howard, Tami Kremer-Sadlik, Joe Plummer, Susan Strauss, Galina Bolden, Nathan Carr, Claire Chik, Tosha Schore, and Leah Wingard at UCLA. These experienced ESL professionals pointed out many problems with the manuscript that helped improve the pedagogical quality of the final product. We would also like to thank students enrolled in ESL courses at both Santa Monica College and UCLA for their reactions to our materials.

Additional thanks are due to Mila August of UCLA and Dayle Hartnett of Santa Monica College for providing administrative assistance and program support for our endeavor. Thank you also to Ramona Tan for helping us with obtaining permissions.

Finally, we wish to express our gratitude to our *Looking Ahead* colleagues, Linda Fellag, Sharon Cavusgil, and Elizabeth Byleen whose creativity, hard work, and problem-solving abilities kept us inspired, on task and on deadline (more or less). Our deepest appreciation is reserved for Drs. Patricia Byrd and Joy Reid, without whose vision and guidance this book could not have been written. They spent countless hours reading drafts of our manuscript. Their gentle suggestions and insightful editorial comments improved the book at every turn. Most of all, we thank them for their faith in us and for all they have taught us throughout this process.

Christine Holten
University of California at Los Angeles

Judith Marasco
University of California at Los Angeles
Santa Monica College at Santa Monica

Chapter 1

Academic Reading
and Writing

How We Deal with Anger

GOALS

WRITING
◆ practice various strategies for effective academic reading
◆ write a response to generalizations made in a reading passage

GRAMMAR
◆ practice structures used to write general statements
◆ practice the grammar of past time narrative
◆ practice writing paragraphs that use interactive grammar to emphasize information

CONTENT
◆ learn about the psychological and physical results of anger
◆ learn about the different ways that anger can be expressed by people from different cultures

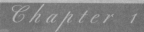

ACADEMIC FIELDS
Psychology
Anthropology
Medicine

Sample Authentic College/University Writing Assignments

The reading strategies and writing skills you learn in this chapter can be used to complete college/university assignments like the ones below.

Political Science

Write a three-page, typewritten book review of any historical topic; see the reading list in the following book for appropriate literature to read: M. McAuley, *Politics and the Soviet Union* (New York: Penguin Books, 1977).

Women's Studies

Read Chapters 1 and 2 in the following book: Sue Ellen M. Charlton, *Women in Third World Development* (Westview Press, 1984). Then write: Is the role of women in development an equity issue or a productivity issue?

 CNN video support is available for this chapter.

GETTING READY

Warm-up Activity: Writing

From the list below, identify five kinds of reading you have done in the past week. Which did you find the most interesting? the least interesting? Why do you find one kind of reading more enjoyable than others? Consider such things as content, vocabulary, level of difficulty, your purpose for reading, and what you get from the reading material.

_____ a newspaper in your first language

_____ a newspaper in English

_____ magazines

_____ a novel in your first language

_____ a novel in English

_____ pages in a textbook

_____ course handouts

_____ lecture notes

_____ an instruction manual

_____ a cookbook

_____ a map/public transportation time schedule

_____ offers in the mail

_____ advertisements (e.g., newspaper, billboards, flyers)

_____ business or financial documents (e.g., a bank statement, a financial aid application)

_____ other: _____

The Basics of Academic Reading and Writing

Audience and Purpose

We all do a variety of types of reading that are designed to communicate something. How they communicate varies according to the writer's purpose and audience. In fact, even when writers write about the same topic, their pieces of writing will contain different kinds of information depending on the audience each author addresses and the purpose for writing.

What do you notice about the difference that audience makes in the way these writers approach the same topic: anger?

Newspaper Article on Anger	Self-Help Book on Anger
Writer: journalist; non-expert on the topic of anger **Audience:** general readers **Purpose:** to inform about recent research	**Writers:** a physician and a Ph.D., an expert on anger **Audience:** general readers interested enough in the topic to buy the book **Purpose:** to help readers understand and deal effectively with their anger
A study by Dr. Murray Mittleman and his colleagues at Harvard Medical School—published this month in the journal *Circulation*—suggests, for instance, that an angry outburst can 5 more than double the risk of a heart attack in some people. And Dr. Redford Williams of Duke University—who has been studying about 100 lawyers for decades in an 10 ongoing look at stress—has found that the attorneys who said their anger levels were high in their years as students were four to five times 15 more likely to die in their 50s than their somewhat calmer colleagues.	Imagine yourself a subject in Dr. Ed Suarez' study on biologic reactivity to stress among hostile persons. You enter the lab, and the experimenter begins describing what's going to happen. After a 5 while a research assistant comes in and says something to the experimenter, but in a rather gruff and abrupt manner. Even after the experiment begins, this same assistant keeps interrupting. 10 How do you feel? Even though this is only an experiment, have you ever encountered such rude people before? And are your feelings—surprise, annoyance, anger, fear, whatever—similar? The feel- 15 ings of the folks in Ed's study are "real."
Source: Jamie Talan, "The Anger Factor," *Los Angeles Times*, September 19, 1995, 3E.	Source: R. Williams and V. Williams, *Anger Kills: Seventeen Strategies for Controlling the Hostility That Can Harm Your Health* (New York: Harper Perennial, 1993, 46–47).

Now look at the writing process of two different writers addressing different audiences on the topic of sleeping disorders. Compare the different types of information that each writer decided to include, and how the choice depends on purpose and audience. Before creating sentences, the writer also chooses the language, tone, and vocabulary that will best communicate the ideas to the audience.

Writing Task: to explain sleeping disorders	**Writing Task:** to explain sleeping disorders
Audience: general readers	**Audience:** students in an introductory psychology course
Purpose: to inform and answer readers' questions	**Purpose:** to teach readers about causes and effects of sleeping disorders
Information included about sleeping disorders: • description of the three most common types of sleeping disorders • common notions about why people have trouble sleeping • case studies of people with chronic sleep disorders • home remedies to relieve sleep disorders • researchers' recommendations about how to deal with sleep disorders	**Information included about sleeping disorders:** • description of the three most common types of sleeping disorders • biological details about each sleeping disorder • who discovered each disorder and when • how each disorder got its name • detailed explanations about the causes of each sleeping disorder • case studies of people with chronic sleep disorders • results of experiments on sleep disorders • researchers' recommendations about how to deal with sleep disorders

Language	Tone	Vocabulary	Language	Tone	Vocabulary
informal colloquial scientific (in quotes from experts)	objective personal	general science terms definitions of terms	formal scientific	objective impersonal	definitions of terms special and general science terms

Written Product	Written Product

LEARNER'S NOTEBOOK

Determining the Influence of Audience

Writers often keep a journal or a notebook in which they write down ideas before or as they draft their papers or write down problems they have while writing. We call this a *Learner's Notebook*. In this first learner's notebook entry, we would like you to reflect on choices that writers make about audience, purpose, and information before they begin writing. Pretend that you are a person who suffers from a sleeping disorder, and you are going to write a short article giving advice to other people who suffer from similar disorders. Write a paragraph describing the kinds of information that you would include in such an article. What questions would you expect to answer in such an article? What information about sleeping disorders would you provide? What language, tone, and vocabulary would you use? Compare the choices you made to another classmate's.

Key Components Shared by Academic Reading and Writing

If writers write to communicate with readers, why do some readings seem so difficult and demand so much work from the readers? Shouldn't the writer be doing the work here? Some of the reading materials listed in the warm-up activity take so little effort that they don't even seem to require "reading," while other reading, such as automobile loan documents, a textbook chapter, or lecture notes, seems like "work."

What is the difference? First, the writer is presenting you with more challenging ideas, and second, you are demanding more from the reading. While you may read a newspaper article quickly to get a general overview of the topic, when you read an academic textbook, you need to read more carefully to understand technical and complex ideas and to select details that you will need to know to pass an exam.

The Basics of Reading	The Basics of Writing
1. Identify the topic	**1. Give your paper a title**
A clear title helps readers to recall what they already know and think about the topic. A clear title also helps identify the author's purpose: to inform; to persuade; or to give advice. Some titles are general and tell only the topic, but not what the writer says about the topic. "The Anger Factor," the title of a newspaper article, is general and indicates that the article has something to do with the topic of anger. Other titles hint at what the author will say. Specific titles indicate exactly what the author says about the topic.	Give your paper a title that indicates the central ideas in your paper. A clear title is more important than a clever one. Most readers are busy people and they want to know if it is worth their time to read the entire article. Here are two clear titles: • "Animal Thinking" • "Anger Kills: Seventeen Strategies for Controlling Anger" The title "To Cherish Life" is intriguing, but vague. It is actually about people who have lived to be 100 years old, but you couldn't guess the content from the title.
2. Understand what unifies the reading	**2. Make sure your paper answers one central question**
What is the central question that the writer is trying to answer in the reading? The author may state it directly in the title, the opening paragraph, or in subheadings. In a psychology text, the subheading "Conditions Affecting Catharsis" signals that the section will answer the question, <u>What conditions affect catharsis (or the expression of anger)?</u> Authors don't always state their questions, which makes your task as a reader more difficult because you must infer it. The answer to the central question unifies or ties all paragraphs in a reading together. After completing a reading, you should be able to complete this sentence: *This reading is about* <u>negative physical effects of expressing anger</u>. A statement such as <u>the reading is about anger</u> is too general.	Good papers are unified because they answer one central question. Usually a paper's central question or argument will be phrased as a *thesis statement*. You should be able to summarize the ideas in your paper in a single, clear, detailed sentence that answers your central question. Here is a sample thesis statement about cross-cultural rules governing anger. It comes at the end of a two-paragraph introduction to the topic: *Often it is this conflict about anger rules, not the rules per se, that can stir up trouble.*

3. Locate and understand the meaning of the author's key terms	3. Define key terms for your reader
Academic writers often use specialized vocabulary to convey their ideas. Some of these terms are technical and will be new to you. These are easy to find. Writers usually put them in **bold** or *italics*. However, some terms may seem familiar, but they have very different meanings in a certain reading. Familiar words often take on special meanings in academic fields. For example, the phrase *anger management* contains the familiar term "management," which means "to oversee" or "organize." In the reading, however, it means "to control."	Don't assume that your readers know all the vocabulary that you use in a paper. Be sure to define technical or scientific terms from your field. If you are giving a new meaning to a familiar word, explain the definition you will give this word. For example, if your audience does not know the meaning of the word *catharsis*, you might state the word and give a short definition in commas after the word. Here is an example. Some people wonder whether *catharsis,* the relief brought about by the open expression of negative emotions, is a helpful way to deal with anger or not. You can also give a formal definition with the words *mean, is called, is labeled,* or *is termed.* The notion that one can purge one's emotions by expressing them **has been labeled** the *catharsis hypothesis.*

4. Find and understand the writer's key arguments and ideas	4. Clearly state your key ideas and support them with evidence and examples
Every reading is composed of key sentences (*the key arguments or ideas*) that respond to the author's central question. These are often stated in headings or in the first sentences of paragraphs. The reading also has less important sentences (*supporting information/evidence*). Active reading requires finding and understanding the writer's key sentences. After this, readers can combine them to understand the author's central idea or argument.	The answer to the question or the explanation of the topic or argument stated in the thesis statement will often be complex and require more than one paragraph to explain. Each paragraph will contain a key, or topic, sentence that states one of the author's central arguments or ideas. The other sentences in the paragraph provide supporting evidence or explanations for the key sentences. See pages 353–354 in Appendix A for more information.

FOCUSING

Introduction to Readings

We've all felt anger and/or observed it in others. A key question about anger is how best to express it. Should we control ourselves when we get angry or show our anger?

From the time we are children, we worry about this issue. Parents must help their children learn to deal with anger appropriately. The readings that follow discuss this issue, but they are written with different purposes and for different audiences.

Pre-reading Activities

Activity 1-1   Key Vocabulary

The authors you are about to read use a variety of verbs and verb expressions to discuss the topic of anger. From the list below, find synonyms for the three verb expressions in the chart and list them in the correct column. If you know any other expressions not listed, add them to the appropriate column. An example is provided.

infuriate	let out one's anger	blow off steam
lose control	arouse	enrage
provoke	express one's anger	repress one's anger
vent hostility	exercise emotional restraint	subdue one's emotions
✓ control one's emotions	discharge	

to make someone angry	**to control anger**	**to show anger**
_____	*control one's emotions*	_____
_____	_____	_____
_____	_____	_____
_____	_____	_____

LEARNER'S NOTEBOOK

Keeping Track of New Vocabulary

Writing new vocabulary in a journal or notebook is a good way to keep track of new words or expressions that will be useful in academic writing. Writers use a notebook to write down new words or expressions including the sentences in which they find them or their own sentence with the new vocabulary. In your learner's notebook, write down five new words or expressions that you found in Activity 1-1. Then, either create your own sentences with the vocabulary or copy a sentence with the vocabulary from the readings in this chapter. For more useful information about learning vocabulary, consult Appendix B: Vocabulary in Academic Writing on page 362.

Activity 1-2   Analyzing an Angry Episode

Read the following scenario. Then discuss the questions that follow with a partner or in a small group.

> Pamela was traveling to a country in Africa on Quantum Airlines, but first she had to take a connecting flight from Denver to Los Angeles. She arrived at the Denver airport only to find that the flight to Los Angeles had been canceled, thereby forcing her to take a later flight.
>
> When the plane arrived in Los Angeles, Pamela ran for the departing flight. As she arrived at the gate, the door was closing. When she asked the gate attendant to let her board the plane, the airline employee said, "Sorry ma'am, we're no longer allowed to board any passengers. You'll have to get the next flight." Pamela usually cried when she was angry, but this time, her face reddened and her rage was visible. The airline employee said, "I can see you're upset. Maybe we can offer you a $25 gift certificate the next time you fly with Quantum." Pamela, even more angry now, replied, "There isn't going to be a next time!" She then threw down her metal luggage carrier.

1. Do you find the way Pamela expressed her anger appropriate to the circumstances? Why or why not?

2. Do the following factors affect your evaluation of Pamela's actions? If so, how? If not, why not?

    a. Pamela had asked the airline to contact people at the gate in Los Angeles and tell them to hold the plane until she arrived.

    b. The plane to Africa sat at the gate for 20 minutes before taking off.

    c. Pamela could not contact her friends in Africa who were planning to meet her at the airport.

    d. Pamela was traveling to Africa to do research and only had seven days there before she had to return to the United States.

    e. Pamela had had other experiences when Quantum Airlines canceled scheduled flights.

    f. Pamela had already postponed the trip once because of the death of her father.

3. Is it positive to vent your anger as Pamela did? Give reasons for your response. Try to use the verbs and verb expressions from Activity 1-1.

LEARNER'S NOTEBOOK

Writing about Anger

Readers and writers also use journals or notebooks to record personal experiences with a topic that they are reading or writing about. In your learner's notebook, write about a situation that caused you to become angry. Include answers to the following questions: How did you express your anger and what factors contributed to the intensity of your emotions? Is this the way you usually express anger? If not, why was this situation different? Share this experience and its causes with your classmates.

Activity 1-3   Considering Purposes for Reading and Writing about Anger

The writers in the left column are writing about the topic of anger to the audience in the right-hand column. From the choices below, circle the writer's purpose for writing and the content that might be included. Then circle the purposes the reader might have for reading the article produced by the writer in the left-hand column. *There is more than one possible answer.* Discuss your choices with a partner or a small group.

The Writer's Task		The Reader's Task
1. <u>A Psychologist</u>	⇨	**1.** <u>A Married Couple</u>
Purpose for Writing		*Purpose for Reading*

Purpose for Writing (left column):
- to inform
- to persuade
- to entertain
- to give advice
- to teach

Purpose for Reading (right column):
- for pleasure
- to learn new information
- to pass a test
- to find solutions to a problem
- to do background research on a topic before writing

Content
- anecdotes about angry people
- findings from scientific studies about anger
- advice about how to deal with anger
- physiological effects of anger
- theories about anger
- how anger affects communication

The Writer's Task	The Reader's Task
2. A Newspaper Reporter	⇨ **2.** A Newspaper Reader
Purpose for Writing	*Purpose for Reading*
to inform to persuade to entertain to give advice to teach	for pleasure to learn new information to pass a test to find solutions to a problem to do background research on a topic before writing
Content	
anecdotes about angry people findings from scientific studies about anger advice about how to deal with anger physiological effects of anger theories about anger how anger affects communication	

READING 1   THE ANGER FACTOR (NEWSPAPER ARTICLE)

This newspaper article challenges the idea that it is healthy to express anger openly rather than keep it inside. The article reviews scientific research studies which show that expressing anger may do physical harm.

Sample Annotation	THE ANGER FACTOR

Main idea of the article
1) *past idea about anger*
 	
2) *NEW proof shows danger of angry outbursts*
 	
• *expert's opinion*
• *evidence of heart attack risk*
 	
• *can die younger*
	Not long ago, letting rage out was, well, all the rage. Now, studies suggest that <u>venting may up the heart-attack risk</u>.
	    In the 1980's, doctors often suggested that waving your anger like a flag was good for the head, and cleansing for the soul.
	    Now, though, the advice is changing: Some recent scientific studies have shown that venting hostility can stir up stress hormones in your body in a way that, ultimately, could damage your heart. 5
	    A study by Dr. Murray Mittleman and his colleagues at Harvard Medical School—published this month in the journal *Circulation*—suggests, for instance, that an angry outburst can more than double 10 the risk of a heart attack in some people.
	    And Dr. Redford Williams of Duke University—who has been studying about 100 lawyers for decades in an ongoing look at stress—has found that the attorneys who said their anger levels were

high in their years as students were four to five times more likely to die in their 50s than their somewhat calmer colleagues.

Richard Friedman, a professor of psychiatry at the State University of New York at Stoney Brook and director of research at the Mind-Body Medical Institute at Harvard, said these studies and others leave little doubt that episodes of anger are dangerous.

"The notion that letting it out is protective," he said, "is not borne out in science."

Once a volcanic kind of guy himself, Williams said he has learned to ask questions about his anger, and now lets steam out in less explosive ways.

"You have to effectively understand your feelings," he suggests, "and find a means of calming yourself down."

At Duke, Williams has studied the long-term effects of hostility for years, but now is also trying to determine the day-by-day events that contribute to heart disease. For one thing, he says he's finding that blood pressure goes up when people are exposed to violence— not just to the real-life kind that's known to cause fight-or-flight hormones to surge, but also to "Rambo"-style movies.

Williams has men and women watch violent and nonviolent clips from movies—"Sleeping With the Enemy"—while hooking them up to blood pressure cuffs and other monitoring devices.

The scientists also drew blood to test stress hormone levels.

With violence, blood pressure moves up from 2 to 6 millimeters. What's more, the dose of violence triggers a higher blood pressure surge when an on-screen argument turns into an arm-swinging wrestle. These cardiovascular changes occur only when people are watching violence carried out by someone of the same sex, suggesting that they identify more with the character.

"When you consider how many people watch a movie, and half the population watching it are having a rise in blood pressure, it is important to worry. Over time, that cumulative extra workload could be contributing to an increased risk for cardiovascular disease," Williams said.

Source: Jamie Talan, "The Anger Factor," *Los Angeles Times,* September 19, 1995, 3E.

Active Reading

Activity 1-4   Reading to Find the "Basics"

Read the article, "The Anger Factor," several times to determine the four basics of the reading. On a separate piece of paper, complete the following:

1. Topic: _____

   Author's purpose: _____

2. The reading's central question and focus (paragraph 2): _____

3. Key terms (circle two or three that you think are most important to understanding the article):

venting	anger level	blood pressure
stress hormones	long-term effects	fight-or-flight
risk	hostility	trigger
cardiovascular changes	cardiovascular disease	

4. The reading's key arguments and ideas: _____

   (*Hint:* See paragraphs 2, 12, and 13.)

Strategies for Academic Reading

Essentially, reading is a way of learning. And, as you probably know, everyone learns differently. Some people learn by doing, others learn by observing, still others learn by reading. Some students have a visual memory; some have an auditory memory. How does this apply to reading? It means that there is no single right way to read an article or textbook chapter. One thing is certain, however: The more complex the ideas in a reading are or the more you need to get from the reading, the more you need to read *actively*. Here are several strategies that you might try, depending on your learning style and the difficulty of the reading.

Strategy 1: Annotating

Annotating consists of highlighting or underlining the author's key sentences. But it goes beyond just highlighting; it includes writing comments or questions in the margin, numbering key points, writing and defining key terms. These "reader-based" comments usually appear in the margin, but can also be done in a notebook.

Your purpose in reading will influence the kind of annotations you will make. If you are reading for information, your annotations will include key terms and definitions, and numbering of key points. If you are reading an argument or opinion piece, your annotations will include your questions and comments about arguments the writer has made. For an example of how to annotate a reading, look at the first four paragraphs of "The Anger Factor."

Strategy 2: Asking and Answering Journalistic Questions

Who? When? Where? What? How? and *Why?* are six basic questions that most newspaper articles answer. These questions can also be useful as you read other types of readings, including academic textbooks. Noting the answers to these questions in the margins, in a notebook, or at the end of a chapter will help you remember the passage more clearly.

Journalistic Questions	Responses from "The Anger Factor"
Who?	scientists and physicians who do research on the physical effects of anger
When?	now
Where?	in the United States
What?	Releasing anger can increase the risk of heart disease.
How?	Anger or violence increases stress hormones and puts pressure on the heart.
Why?	We should know about this topic because people view violence all the time, for example, in films or on TV. Therefore, they run the risk of high blood pressure.

Depending on your purpose for reading, only some of these questions will be important. If you are reading for information, you may need to know the answers to *Who? When? Where? What?* and *How?* If you are reading to respond to an author's argument, the questions *What?* and *Why?* will help you determine exactly what the author is arguing.

We would like to add one question to this list: *So what?* or "why is this information important?" Answering this question will help you understand the *significance* of what you have read—for yourself and as it relates to other course material.

Journalistic Questions	Responses from "The Anger Factor"
So what?	If the research from this article is correct, people should learn to control their anger rather than express it. People should be aware that watching violence has a similar effect to that of becoming angry. For this reason, they should watch fewer violent films or TV shows.

Strategy 3: Writing a Study Summary

The third reading strategy, writing a study summary, entails writing and is an effective way to learn and remember a reading's "basics" or key ideas.

An effective study summary:

- accurately and objectively restates the writer's central idea and the reading's focus
- is concise, but not so brief that it leaves out important and complex ideas
- is balanced; it does not emphasize some ideas in the reading while leaving out other, equally important ideas

Because *you* are the audience for this study summary, the only test of an effective summary is if it helps you to retain the ideas in the reading.

To create an effective study summary:

- Annotate or answer journalistic questions about the reading.
- Carefully look over your annotations or answers to journalistic questions to find the reading's thesis statement, key terms, ideas, and arguments.
- Put your notes aside and try to reconstruct these key elements in the reading.
- Compare your summary to your annotation or responses to journalistic questions. Add information to your summary or rephrase parts of it to be as accurate as possible.

> **Summary:** The article, "The Anger Factor," challenges the idea that it is healthy to release anger. Medical experts and scientists now agree that openly expressing anger increases stress hormone levels and raises blood pressure. These physical reactions can lead to heart attacks. Furthermore, one study shows that watching violence has a similar effect to that of becoming angry. When people watch violence in films or on TV, both their blood pressure and their stress hormone levels go up.

LEARNER'S NOTEBOOK

Considering the Reading Strategies You Use

What strategy or strategies have you used when reading academic course materials? How has this strategy helped your comprehension and retention of information? Are there any drawbacks to the strategy? After learning about the three reading strategies, which of these might you try? How could it help your reading? Record your thoughts in your learner's notebook.

READING 2   THE GREAT CATHARSIS DEBATE
(EXCERPT FROM AN ACADEMIC TEXTBOOK)

This reading, from a chapter in an introductory psychology textbook, challenges the common idea that openly expressing anger, or *catharsis*, is healthy. Like the author of "The Anger Factor," Carlson and Hatfield also summarize research studies about anger, but they present these in much greater detail.

Active Reading

Activity 1-5   Analyzing a Reading for Audience, Purpose, and Tone

Reading the title, headings, and first sentences in each paragraph of a reading to determine the writer's intended audience and purpose—or *skimming*—is useful for any type of reading you do. Skim several paragraphs of *The Great Catharsis Debate* to determine its purpose and audience and the effect of these on the style the writer uses. Circle the answers that best reflect the piece of writing. You may choose more than one answer, but you must be ready to defend your choice with sentences or words from the reading.

	The Great Catharsis Debate		
Audience	general readers	students	experts in psychology
Purpose	to inform	to entertain	to give advice
	to persuade	to teach	
Tone	friendly	objective	concerned
	critical	authoritative	questioning
Point of View How the author addresses the reader	first person (I) third person (it/the problem)		second person (you) first person plural (we)
Evidence/ Information	case studies	anecdotes	statistics
	research results	quotes from authorities	

THE GREAT CATHARSIS DEBATE

Anybody can become angry—that is easy, but to be angry with the right person, and to the right degree, and at the right time, and for the right purpose, and in the right way—that is not within everybody's power and is not easy.

ARISTOTLE

The notion that one can purge one's emotions by expressing them has been labeled the *catharsis hypothesis.* Freudian psychologists, of course, applauded this idea. They assumed that when people shout at someone who annoys them or view a violent film, they are blowing off steam. According to the "pressure-cooker" theory, they should be *less* angry and aggressive than before. 5

In 1979, Thomas Scheff (1979) proposed an updated version of the hypothesis, arguing that catharsis is a therapeutic process for two reasons: (a) Repressed emotions such as fear and anger are discharged by laughing and crying; mood is improved and tension is reduced; and (b) in psychotherapy and drama, people gain a sense of clarity.

Freud's perspective dominated therapeutic practice in the 1960s. Couples were encour- 10 aged to smack each other with foam baseball bats, to give a "primal scream," and to beat on pillows in the expectation that angry feelings so powerfully expressed would spend themselves and disappear.

Does catharsis work? Not really. The evidence makes it clear that the situation is more complex than Freudian psychologists had hoped (Tavris, 1982). Angry people have a dual 15 problem—first, they have to deal with their own emotions and then deal with whatever problems they are facing. When people are enraged and feel dangerously out of control, at first it may seem to help them to cry and pound on pillows until they are exhausted. In that sense, some merit can be attached to the claim that "violent emotional expressions" may have some benefits. 20

But then when we ask, "What next?" we see that things become more difficult. Sometimes an expression of anger helps clear the air; but often, the direct expression of anger is self-indulgent—it begets more anger and aggression. What is probably important is not whether people express anger or withhold it in a single instance, but whether they use their anger to change the things that upset them in the first place. This is what brings about 25 true personal peace in the long run. Let us review some of the voluminous research that leads us to these conclusions.

Catharsis and Frustration

Jack Hokanson and his Florida State University colleagues (1970) conducted a series of studies which provide an understanding of the catharsis process. In an early study, 30 Hokanson and Michael Burgess (1962b) set out to discover (a) the effect that frustration has on general physiological arousal, and (b) the effect that it has when one has a chance to get even.

Students were not told the truth about the purpose of the study. Instead, they were told that the authors were studying physiological responses to performance on intellectual tasks. 35 To aid in establishing this deception, the students were first asked to take a portion of the WAIS (Wechsler Adult Intelligence Scale). Then they were asked to count backward from

100 to 0 by twos, as quickly as they could. (Backward counting is a common laboratory stress inducer, in this case called a "serial twos" task.) During the experiment, heart rate was monitored continuously, and blood pressure was measured every two minutes.   40

During this second task, a critical event happened. In the No-frustration group, the experimenter merely praised students when they reached 0. In the Frustration group, the experimenter repeatedly interrupted and harassed the subjects for counting too slowly. He made them start over three times. Finally, he insisted that the subjects' attitudes made further testing impossible. As you might expect, frustrated men and women were far more   45
aroused than their peers. Their hearts raced and their systolic blood pressure shot up.

The next step was to see the effect that retaliation would have on arousal level. Men and women were randomly assigned to one of the three different conditions: Some subjects had a chance to verbally aggress. (They were asked to fill out, in the experimenter's presence, a brief questionnaire evaluating the experimenter's capabilities as an experimenter, including   50
the way he related to subjects.) Other subjects had to physically aggress against him. (They were given 10 opportunities to shock him. Most of them depressed the shock plunger eight times.) In the No-aggression group, subjects had no chance to aggress against the experimenter, either verbally or physically. In the Fantasy-aggression group, they merely had a chance to conjure up an aggressive story if they wished.   55

This early study found that under the right conditions, retaliation did seem to produce some catharsis. When frustrated subjects were able to aggress either physically or verbally against the source of their frustration, their blood pressures and heart rates returned to normal with surprising rapidity. When they were not able to aggress, their blood pressures and heart rates remained high. (Additional support for the catharsis notion has been secured by   60
Geen, Stonner, & Shope, 1975, and Kahn, 1966.)

Conditions Affecting Catharsis

However, subsequent research, much of it by social psychologists, shows that a catharsis effect can be realized only under very limited conditions:

1. People must be angry and aroused at the time they are given an opportunity to retal-   65
   iate (Bramel, Taub, & Blum, 1968; Doob, 1970).
2. They must have the chance to retaliate against the person who "caused" their problem; if he or she was arbitrary, malevolent, obnoxious, and aggressive, so much the better (Konecni, 1984). Attacking a substitute does not help much (Hokanson, Burgess, & Cohen, 1963).   70
3. The victim must get the retaliation deserved, no more and no less. If one goes overboard, one may feel guilty later (Konecni 1984, Hatfield, Walster, & Berscheid, 1978; Hatfield, et al., 1984).
4. The target must be nonintimidating—so that subjects do not feel anxious afterward (Hokanson & Burgess, 1962a).   75

Of course, such conditions do not occur often, especially in combination.

But more difficulties arise for the catharsis hypothesis than simply that it has limitations. Other research warns that when people express their angry, aggressive feelings, they often get themselves so worked up that the situation may become worse than it was before.

For example, Robert Arms and his colleagues report that Canadian and American football, 80
wrestling, and hockey fans exhibit more hostility after viewing sporting events than before
(Arms, Russell, & Sandelands, 1979; Goldstein & Arms, 1971). Not even a war seems to
purge people's aggressive feelings. In fact, after a war, a nation's murder rate tends to climb
(Archer & Gartner, 1976).

An array of laboratory experiments and correlational studies have come to the same 85
conclusion—anger expressed is often anger/aggression increased. (See Ebbesen, Duncan, &
Konecni, 1975; Feshbach, 1956, for a sampling of such studies.)

Source: J. G. Carlson and E. Hatfield, *Psychology of Emotion*
(Ft. Worth, TX: Harcourt, Brace, and Jovanovich, 1992).

Activity 1-6   Identifying the "Basics" in a Reading Passage

With a partner or in a small group, complete the following tasks for the Carlson and
Hatfield reading. Write your answers on a separate piece of paper.

1. This reading is about _____ _____

2. The central question addressed by the authors is: _____

    _____

3. List three conditions that determine the effectiveness of catharsis. _____

    _____ .

4. Key terms (circle two or three terms that you think are most important to under-
    standing the article). Write a brief definition of each term you select, using the con-
    text of the reading to formulate your definition. Caution: Words that you already
    know may be defined differently by the authors.

    purge   devastating blow   provocation
    catharsis hypothesis   perspective   counteraggression
    catharsis   frustration   aggression

5. The reading's key arguments and ideas: _____

    (*Hint:* See paragraphs 4, 5, and 12.)

Activity 1-7   Choose a Reading Strategy

Using the information about the reading you found in Activity 1-6, choose one of the
three reading strategies: *annotating, answering journalistic questions,* or *writing a study
summary.* Use the strategy you choose to actively read *The Great Catharsis Debate.* Try a

strategy that you want to experiment with or that you think will help you read more effectively. Record your notes in your learner's notebook or in the margins of this book.

Analysis of Language: Using Informational Grammar to Write Generalizations

A. Using the Present Tense to Write Generalizations

A generalization is a general statement, principle, or opinion that is based on a careful consideration of facts or evidence. Academic writing is full of generalizations. These appear in *the present tense*. As you will see later, writers often modify generalizations with words like *could, might,* and *may* or with adverbs such as *generally, possibly.* "The Anger Factor," *Manners, Emotions, and the American Way,* and *The Great Catharsis Debate* contain generalizations.

> For some groups in America, anger *is* an effective way to get your way; for others it *is* the last resort.
>
> "You *have* to effectively understand your feelings," he suggests, "and *find* a means of calming yourself down."

Facts, unlike generalizations, reflect something that has actually happened or an observation that everyone accepts as true. *Generalizations,* which require analysis and critical thinking, are built on facts and appear in the *present tense. Facts* may appear in *present tense* or *past tense.* Facts that were true in the past, but are no longer true or accepted as true, are stated in the past tense. Facts that are currently accurate are stated in the present tense.

> The Japanese practice of emotional restraint, for example, *dates back* many centuries.
>
> At the time of the Samurai knights, these rules had considerable survival value, because a Samurai *could* legally execute anyone who he *thought* was not respectful enough.

> **GLR**   See pages 297–298 in the GLR for more information about verbs in generalizations.

Activity 1-8   Identifying Generalizations

Underline the sentences that make generalizations in the paragraphs below. Circle the verbs in each generalization. What verb tenses do you see in the paragraph? What verb tense is the generalization in? *Note that not all verbs in the present tense are generalizations.* An example is provided.

1. When Anglo-Americans are angry, they tend to proceed in stages from small steps to larger ones: First, they hint around. ("Mort, are you sure that fence is on your side of the property line?") Then they talk to neighbors and friends of Mort. If they get no results, they may talk directly, and calmly, to Mort. Next they will express anger

directly to Mort. Eventually, if they are angry enough, they will take the matter to the courts. And as a last resort, they may resort to violence—and burn the fence down.

2. A culture's rules of anger are not arbitrary; they evolve along with its history and structure. The Japanese practice of emotional restraint, for example, dates back many centuries, when all aspects of demeanor were carefully regulated: facial expressions, breathing, manner of sitting and standing, style of walking. Not only were all emotions—anger, grief, pain, even great happiness—to be suppressed in the presence of one's superiors, but also regulations specified that a person submit to any order with a pleasant smile and a properly happy tone of voice. At the time of the Samurai knights, these rules had considerable survival value, because a Samurai could legally execute anyone who he thought was not respectful enough.

3. Another very recent finding from our research into biologic mechanisms of hostility suggests that hostility can magnify the impact of another important risk factor, blood cholesterol, therefore making a high cholesterol level even worse for a hostile person. Among middle-aged men with high levels of anger, those with higher blood cholesterol levels secreted more adrenaline while performing mental tasks than did those with lower blood cholesterol levels. In contrast, among men with low anger levels there was an inverse association between blood cholesterol levels and adrenaline responses to the mental task—as cholesterol levels rose, the adrenaline responses diminished.

Activity 1-9   Writing Generalizations

Write three generalizations about anger and expressing anger based on the information you learned in "The Anger Factor" and *The Great Catharsis Debate*. An example is provided. Share your generalizations with your classmates.

1. Watching violence on TV or in a film has the same effect on the heart as becoming angry.

2. _____

3. _____

4. _____

READING 3   MANNERS, EMOTIONS, AND THE AMERICAN WAY
(EXCERPT FROM A POPULAR PSYCHOLOGY BOOK)

Carol Tavris asserts that all cultures have different rules about anger. When people from different cultures come together, the rules can collide.

MANNERS, EMOTIONS, AND THE AMERICAN WAY

The class was basic English for foreign students, and an Arab student, during a spoken activity, was describing a tradition of his home country. Something he said embarrassed a Japanese student in the front row, who reacted the proper Japanese way: He smiled. The Arab saw the smile and demanded to know what was so funny about Arab customs. The Japanese, who was now publicly humiliated as well as embarrassed, could reply only with   5
a smile and, to his misfortune, he giggled to mask his shame. The Arab, who now likewise felt shamed, furiously hit the Japanese student before the teacher could intervene. Shame and anger had erupted in a flash, as each student dutifully obeyed the rules of his culture. Neither could imagine, of course, that his rules might not be universal.

Because a major function of anger is to maintain the social order, through its moraliz-   10
ing implications of how people "should" behave, it is predictable that when two social orders collide they would generate angry sparks. It is easiest to see when the colliding cultures are foreign to each other, but we have plenty of such collisions within our society as well. For some groups in America, anger is an effective way to get your way; for others it is the last resort. (Some groups have to learn assertiveness training to deal with others.)   15
You may find your attitudes about anger, and the rules you learned to govern it, in conflict with those of different groups. Often it is this conflict about anger rules, not the rules *per se*, that can stir up trouble.

Each of us is tied to a group—a minitribe, if you will—by virtue of our sex, status, race, and ethnicity, and with countless unconscious reactions we reveal those ties. Anthropologist   20
Edward T. Hall speaks of the "deep biases and built-in blinders" that every culture confers on its members. You can observe them at work every time you hear someone grumble, "I'll never understand women," or, "Why can't he just say what he feels?" or, "The (Japanese) (Mexicans) (Irish) (etc.) are utterly inscrutable."

Hall, who lives in New Mexico, has long observed the clash that occurs between groups   25
when deeply felt rules about the "correct" management of anger are broken. The Spanish are sensitive to the slightest suggestion of criticism, Hall explains. "Confrontations are therefore to be avoided at all costs." The resulting misunderstandings between Spanish- and Anglo-Americans, he says, would be amusing if they weren't so tragic.

When Anglo-Americans are angry, they tend to proceed in stages from small steps to   30
larger ones: First, they hint around ("Mort, are you sure that fence is on *your* side of the property line?"). Then they talk to neighbors and friends of Mort. If they get no results, they may talk directly, and calmly, to Mort ("Mort, can we discuss our fence problem?"). Next they will express anger directly to Mort ("Dammit, that fence is on my property"). Eventually, if they are angry enough, they will take the matter to the courts. And as a last   35
resort, they may resort to violence—and burn the fence down.

These steps, from smallest to largest, seem natural, logical, and inevitable. Actually, they are not only *not* natural, they are not even very common, worldwide. In many societies, such as in Latin cultures and in the Middle East, the first step is . . . to do nothing. Think about it. Brood. This brooding may go on for weeks, months, or even years (some cultures   40
have long memories). The second step is . . . to burn the fence down. Now that matters are back to square one, participants are ready for direct discussions, negotiations, lawyers, and

intermediaries. But notice, says Hall, that the act of force, which is the last step for Anglos, signaling the failure of negotiation, is the start of the conversation to Hispanics.

A culture's rules of anger are not arbitrary; they evolve along with its history and struc- 45 ture. The Japanese practice of emotional restraint, for example, dates back many centuries, when all aspects of demeanor were carefully regulated: facial expressions, breathing, manner of sitting and standing, style of walking. Not only were all emotions—anger, grief, pain, even great happiness—to be suppressed in the presence of one's superiors, but also regulations specified that a person submit to any order with a pleasant smile and a properly happy 50 tone of voice. At the time of the Samurai knights, these rules had considerable survival value, because a Samurai could legally execute anyone who he thought was not respectful enough.

Even today in Japan, an individual who feels very angry is likely to show it by excessive politeness and a neutral expression instead of by furious words and signs. A Japanese 55 who shows anger the Western way is admitting that he has lost control, and therefore lost face; he is thus at the extreme end of a negotiation or debate. In other cultures, though, showing anger may simply mark the *beginning* of an exchange, perhaps to show that the negotiator is serious; a man may lose face if he does *not* show anger when it is appropriate and "manly" for him to do so. 60

Psychotherapy, of course, takes place within a culture and is deeply embedded in cultural rules. Arthur Kleinman, himself both an anthropologist and psychiatrist, tells of a psychiatrist in south-central China who was treating a patient who had become depressed and anxious ever since her demanding mother-in-law had moved in. "She is your family member. It is your responsibility to care for an old mother-in-law," the Chinese psychiatrist said. 65 "You must contain your anger. You know the old adage: 'Be deaf and dumb! Swallow the seeds of the bitter melon! Don't speak out!'"

I am not recommending that Americans learn to "Swallow the seeds of the bitter melon"; in our society, most of us would choke on them. Cultural practices cannot be imported from society to society like so many bits of cheese, because they are part of a 70 larger pattern of rules and relationships. Indeed, that is the reason we cannot avoid the anger we feel when someone breaks the rules that we have learned are the only civilized rules to follow. But we might emulate the Arapesh, who criticize the provocateur; or the Inuit (formerly called the Eskimo), who settle in for a good round of verbal dueling; or the Mbuti, who have a good laugh, understanding as they do the healing power of humor. We might 75 also retrieve the old-fashioned standard of manners, which is, as small tribes teach us, an organized system of anger management.

Good manners melt resentment because they maintain respect between the two disagreeing parties. Someone steps on your toe, you feel angry, the person apologizes, your anger vanishes. Your toe may still hurt, but your dignity is intact. 80

Without rules for controlling anger, it can slip into emotional anarchy, lasting far longer than its original purposes require. Observe how friends and family react to someone undergoing a bitter divorce: They extend sympathy and a willing ear to the enraged spouse for a while, but eventually they expect the person to "Shape up" and "get on with it." What these friends and relatives are doing is imposing unofficial rules of anger management. The 85 victim may grouse and mutter about the loss of sympathy, but actually the friends and relatives are doing what any decent tribe would do: keeping anger in bounds after it has done its job and making sure the victim stays in the social circle. Well-meaning friends and therapists who encourage a vengeful spouse to ventilate rage for years are doing neither the spouse nor the tribe a service.   90

People in all cultures, even the pacifistic !Kung and the Utku, do occasionally feel irritable and angry. But they do not *value* anger. They strive for a state of mind that philosopher Robert Solomon calls "equanimity under trying circumstances," the worldview of small societies that live in dangerous environments. "The Utku," says Solomon, "much more than any of us, are used to extreme hardship and discomfort. Their philosophy, there- 95 fore, is that such things must be tolerated, not flailed against."

In this country, the philosophy of emotional expression regards self-restraint as hypocrisy. The cultures of the Far East do not have this conflict; a person is expected to control and subdue the emotions because it is the relationship, not the individual, that comes first. Here, where the reverse is true, some people express their emotions even at the 100 expense of the relationship, and manners seem to be rare.

Consider the gentle, forgiving environment of Tahiti, where people learn that they have limited control over nature and over other people. They learn that if they try to change nature, she will swiftly destroy them, but if they relax and accept the bounty of nature—and the nature of people—they will be taken care of. Anthropologist Robert Levy calls this 105 resulting worldview among the Tahitians "passive optimism."

The American philosophy, however, produces "active pessimists": people who assume that nature and other people are to be conquered, indeed must be conquered, and that individual striving is essential to survival. But a universe defined as the Tahitians see it is intrinsically less infuriating than a universe in which almost everything is possible if the 110 individual tries hard enough. The individualism of American life, to our glory and despair, creates anger and encourages its release; for when everything is possible, limitations are irksome. When the desires of the self come first, the needs of others are annoying. When we think we deserve it all, reaping only a portion can enrage.

Source: Carol Tavris, *Anger: The Misunderstood Emotion*
(New York: Touchstone/Simon Schuster, 1989, 65–69).

Activity 1-10   Determining a Writer's Audience, Purpose, and Tone

Skim several paragraphs of the Tavris reading to determine its purpose and audience and the effect of these on the writer's style. Then, in the following chart, circle the answers that best reflect the piece of writing. You may choose more than one answer, but you must be ready to defend your choice with sentences or words from the reading.

	Manners, Emotions and the American Way		
Audience	general readers	students	experts in psychology
Purpose	to inform to persuade	to entertain to teach	to give advice
Tone	friendly critical	objective authoritative	concerned questioning
Point of View How the author addresses the reader	first person (I) third person (it/the problem)	second person (you)	first person plural (we)
Evidence/ **Information**	case studies research results	anecdotes quotes from authorities	statistics

Activity 1-11   Identifying the Basics in a Reading Passage

With a partner or in a small group, complete the following for the Tavris reading (you may write your answers on a separate piece of paper):

1. This reading is about _____.

2. The central question addressed by the author is: _____

3. Give some examples of how the rules for expressing anger differ across cultures.

4. From the list below, agree on the three or four most important key terms from the reading. Write a brief definition of each key term you select, using the context of the reading to formulate your definition. Caution: Words that you already know may be defined differently by the authors.

collision	cultural practices	emotional expression
universal	break the rules	self-restraint
management	emotional anarchy	manners
regulations	release	rules of his culture

5. The reading's key arguments and ideas: _____

    (*Hint:* See paragraphs 2, 7, 10,12, 16.)

Activity 1-12   Choosing and Applying a Reading Strategy

Reread *Manners, Emotions, and the American Way* using one of the three reading strategies. Try to use a different strategy than the one you used in Activity 1-7. Compare your results with a partner.

Analysis of Language: Using Interactive Grammar to Emphasize Information

A. Questions and Fragments in Written English: Using a Variety of Sentence Types to Emphasize Information

Good writing "flows"; in other words, writers construct paragraphs in such a way that the audience is able to read from sentence to sentence smoothly. One of the ways writers create flow is by using a variety of sentence types and lengths in paragraphs. Look at the following paragraph to see the different types of sentences writers can use. The different sentences are numbered to match the annotation on the right column.

> ¹Does catharsis work? ²Not really. The evidence makes it clear that the situation is more complex than Freudian psychologists had hoped. ³Angry people have a dual problem. ⁴First, they have to deal with their own emotions and then deal with whatever problems they are facing. ⁵When people are enraged and feel dangerously out of control, at first it may seem to help them to cry and pound on pillows until they are exhausted. In that sense, some merit can be attached to the claim that "violent emotional expressions" may have some benefits.

Sentence 1: Question

Sentence 2: Fragment

Sentence 3: Simple sentence

Sentence 4: Complex sentence: one independent clause + one dependent clause

Sentence 5: Complex sentence: one dependent clause beginning with *when* + one independent clause

The writer uses three types of sentences to emphasize key points in the paragraph:

- *Questions* establish the key question that the paragraph will answer.
- *Simple sentences*, which consist of one clause only, emphasize key information. The key point in the preceding paragraph is that anger is complex and requires a complex response. Most of the rest of the sentences in the paragraph consist of more than one clause.
- *Fragments*, or sentences that are missing some grammatical parts, also emphasize key information. Sentence 2 emphasizes the idea that catharsis is not a helpful way to deal with anger.

Fragments are used frequently in speaking. We use them all the time to give short answers, to finish someone else's thought, and to make jokes. You may have learned, however, that you should avoid fragments in writing. This may be an overgeneralization.

Writers do sometimes use fragments in at least two specific ways. Both ways allow the reader to guess what grammatical parts are missing. Writers use fragments to:

- answer a question that they have just asked

  Why did people die in such great numbers of Black Death? *Because they were weakened by malnutrition.*

- elaborate on a previous word, sentence, or idea

  In many societies, such as in Latin cultures and in the Middle East, the first step is ... to do nothing. *Think about it. Brood.*

Questions are also frequent in speaking and less frequent in writing. Speakers and writers use questions in different ways.

How Speakers Use Questions	How Writers Use Questions
They ask questions to get information.	They ask questions to create reader interest.
They may not answer some questions.	They rarely ask questions that they will not answer in the following sentences or paragraphs.
The answers may be as short as one or two words.	The answers to questions usually require a paragraph or even an entire essay.
They ask questions to keep the conversation going.	They ask questions to raise key points. The questions appear near the beginning of an essay or as the first sentence in some paragraphs.

GLR   See page 333, Section 6, and pages 258–260, Section 1, in the GLR for more information on questions and types of sentences.

Activity 1-13   Analyzing How Writers Use Sentence Variety to Create Flowing Paragraphs and Emphasize Information

Read the following paragraphs and label the type of sentences the writer has used in the paragraph. Label only the numbered sentences. Decide whether the sentence is:

- a question
- a fragment
- a simple sentence
- a compound sentence
- a complex sentence

If you are not sure about the structure of the types of sentences listed above, see pages 258–260 in the GLR GLR for more information. An example is done for you.

Paragraphs	**Types of Sentences**
1. [1]But then when we ask, "What next?" we see that things become more difficult. [2]Sometimes an expression of anger helps clear the air, but often, the direct expression of anger is self-indulgent. [3]It begets more anger and aggression. What is probably important is not whether people express anger or withhold it in a single instance, but whether they use their anger to change the things that upset them in the first place. [4]This brings about true personal peace in the long run.	Sentence 1: Complex sentence Sentence 2: Compound sentence Sentence 3: Simple sentence Sentence 4: Simple sentence
2. [1]During this second task, a critical event happened. [2]In the No-frustration group, the experimenter merely praised students when they reached 0. [3]In the Frustration group, the experimenter repeatedly interrupted and harassed the subjects for counting too slowly. [4]He made them start over three times. Finally, he insisted that the subjects' attitudes made further testing impossible. [5]As you might expect, frustrated men and women were far more aroused than their peers. [6]Their hearts raced and their systolic blood pressure shot up.	Sentence 1: Sentence 2: Sentence 3: Sentence 4: Sentence 5: Sentence 6:
3. [1]Imagine yourself a subject in Ed's study. [2]You enter the lab, and the experimenter begins describing what's going to happen. [3]After a while a research assistant comes in and says something to the experimenter, but in a rather gruff and abrupt manner. "He sure got up on the wrong side of the bed this morning," you probably say to yourself. [4]Even after the experiment begins, this same assistant keeps interrupting. [5]How do you feel? [6]Surprised? Annoyed? Angry? Afraid?	Sentence 1: Sentence 2: Sentence 3: Sentence 4: Sentence 5: Sentence 6:

Activity 1-14   Analyzing How Writers Use Sentence Variety to Emphasize Information

To practice using a variety of sentences to emphasize information and create flowing paragraphs, write your own paragraph that asks and answers a question that will provide the following information about *why people deal with anger in a certain way* and *if it is effective to deal with anger in that way.* (You specify the "way" that you are discussing.) Before you write your paragraph, analyze the example to determine the types of sentences this writer has used.

> Is yelling an effective way to get rid of your anger? Not always. Although some people find that the only way to deal with anger is to yell at someone, they do not always get the results they hope for. Yelling may make them feel better, but ruin their relationship with the person who they have yelled at. Breaking a relationship is just too high a price to pay. Because they have put a higher value on emotional release than on solving the original problem, people who yell seldom get to the core of the issue. They may just start a cycle that they can't get out of.

Analysis of Language: Using the Grammar of Narrative to Give Examples and Report Experiments

A. Language Features of Past Time Narrative

One of the first types of writing we all learn is storytelling (narrative). Academic writers also use this powerful writing tool in examples, case studies, and even in reports of events and experiments. Narratives usually include:

- past tense verbs (underlined)
- time words and phrases to show the order of events (italicized)
- proper nouns and personal pronouns (he, she, they) to refer to the characters in the story (in bold)

Look at these features in a narrative you have already read.

Pamela, a young college student, was traveling to a country in Africa on Quantum Airlines, but *first* **she** had to take a connecting flight from Denver to Los Angeles. **She** arrived at the Denver airport only to find that the flight to Los Angeles had been canceled *earlier*, thereby forcing **her** to take a later flight.

Upon arriving at the Los Angeles airport, **Pamela** ran for the departing flight. As **she** arrived at the gate, the door was closing. *When* **she** asked **the gate attendant** to let **her** board the plane, **the airline employee** said, "Sorry ma'am, we're no longer allowed to board any passengers. You'll have to get the next flight." **Pamela** *usually* cried when **she** was angry, but this time, **her** face reddened and **her rage** was visible.

GLR   See Section 2, pages 285–289, of the GLR for more information.

Activity 1-15   Identifying the Grammar in Past Time Narratives

Look at the following past time narratives from the readings in this chapter. Complete the following tasks:

- Circle the names of the characters. Who is involved in the story?
- Underline all the personal pronouns that are used to refer to the characters (persons).
- Put all the time words and phrases in brackets.
  An example is provided.

A. The class was basic English for foreign students, and an(Arab student), [during a spoken activity], was describing a tradition of his home country. Something he said embarrassed a(Japanese student)in the front row, who reacted the proper Japanese way: He smiled. The Arab saw the smile and demanded to know what was so funny about Arab customs. The Japanese, who was now publicly humiliated as well as embarrassed, could reply only with a smile and, to his misfortune, he giggled to mask his shame. The Arab, who now likewise felt shamed, furiously hit the Japanese student [before the(teacher) could intervene]. Shame and anger had erupted [in a flash], as each student dutifully obeyed the rules of his culture. Neither could imagine, of course, that his rules might not be universal. (Paragraph 1, *Manners, Emotions, and the American Way.*)

B. Jack Hokanson and his Florida State University colleagues (1970) conducted a series of studies which provide an understanding of the catharsis process. Students, who did not know the true purpose of the experiment, were asked to count backward from 100 to 0 by twos, as quickly as they could. During the experiment, heart rate was monitored continuously, and blood pressure was measured every two minutes. During this second task, a critical event happened. In the No-frustration group, the experimenter merely praised students when they reached 0. In the Frustration group, the experimenter repeatedly interrupted and harassed the subjects for counting too slowly. He made them start over three times. Finally, he insisted that the subjects' attitudes made further testing impossible. As you might expect, frustrated men and women were far more aroused than their peers. Their hearts raced and their systolic blood pressure shot up. (Paragraphs 7 and 8, *The Great Catharsis Debate.*)

Activity 1-16   Examining the Purpose of Past Time Narratives

Writers use past time narratives for several purposes:

- to provide examples as support for a generalization
- to "hook" readers' interest in a topic (usually in an introduction)
- to report research experiments

With a partner or in a small group, determine the authors' purpose in using the past time narratives in Activity 1-15. If you need to, go back to the reading where the narrative is used. Which of the two narratives do you find the most interesting? Why?

PUTTING IT ALL TOGETHER

FINAL WRITING ASSIGNMENT

Choose two or three general statements about anger made in "The Anger Factor," *The Great Catharsis Debate,* and/or *Manners, Emotions, and the American Way.* Based on your own experiences with or observations about expressing anger, do you agree or disagree with these generalizations? Write a two- to three-page paper in which you agree or disagree with ideas from the readings.

Audience and Purpose

Write to a classmate. Your purpose is to tell your reader what generalizations about anger you agree or disagree with.

Reviewing the Readings on Anger

Before you write, go back and look at your annotations, answers to journalistic questions, or summaries of the three readings in this chapter. Write down two generalizations about expressing anger from each reading. Compare these with a partner or in a small group.

"The Anger Factor"

1. _____

2. _____

The Great Catharsis Debate

1. _____

2. _____

Manners, Emotions, and the American Way

1. _____

2. _____

Include in your paper at least two generalizations you wrote. Make sure to include the author and title of the article in which the generalization is found. Here are some sample phrases you can use:

- The author of "The Anger Factor" reports that . . .
- In *The Great Catharsis Debate*, Carlson and Hatfield suggest that . . .
- As discussed in *Manners, Emotions, and the American Way* by Carol Tavris, rules about anger . . .

Preparing to Write

Before writing your draft, review the task, audience, and purpose for the writing assignment.

Writing Task: To compare my experiences with anger to the generalizations in the readings

Audience: My classmates

Purpose: To tell readers what generalizations about anger I agree or disagree with

The following diagram will help you gather information for your paper and organize this information. To think about what and how to write, complete the following diagram. Fill in information where you see blanks. Where you are given choices, circle the most appropriate answer. For additional help in writing your paper, see pages 350–354, Appendix A.

PLANNING THE INTRODUCTION

Background about the Topic

Thesis Statement: *(Here are some sample thesis statements. You may also write your own.)*

- My own experiences show that many of the generalizations researchers have made about anger are true.
- My experiences tend not to support the generalizations that Hatfield and Carlson made about cathartic anger.
- My experiences in the United States and in my home country, Taiwan, support Tavris' view that every culture has a unique way of expressing anger.

PLANNING THE BODY PARAGRAPHS

The following are *examples* of generalizations about anger from the readings, a statement of agreement or disagreement, and details and evidence from personal experiences and observations. Choose generalizations from the readings that you want to respond to and write your own statements of agreement/disagreement and find supporting details/evidence.

Generalizations about Expressing Anger	Agree/Disagree: Your Opinion	Details/Evidence: Your Experiences with Anger or Observations of Others
It is better for your health to understand your feelings and try to change what bothers you. ("The Anger Factor")	I disagree that we can always change what bothers us. Instead, I think what is really important is to choose what to get angry about. A lot of things just aren't very important in the long run.	*Details/Evidence:* My teenage son and I have had many arguments because he won't pick up his room. I decided recently that it wasn't worth it for me to get angry about it because he doesn't see the mess as a problem.
Under the right conditions, showing anger can be cathartic. (*The Great Catharsis Debate*)	I agree that, under the right conditions, showing our anger can be good. The "right conditions" seem to be those that lead to a better situation for both parties. But, it is often difficult for this to happen.	*Details/Evidence:* I had a boss once who often got angry at the employees. It seemed to make him feel better, but it didn't help the employees. All of us either were afraid of him or resented him. This created a stressful working environment.
Language (circle one or two) formal informal colloquial scientific	**Tone** (circle one or two) objective subjective personal impersonal	**Vocabulary** (circle one or two) specialized scientific terms general scientific terms definitions of terms

Self-editing Activity

1. Before giving your draft to a peer, read it again to make sure that it says what you intended and is organized in the best way for this particular writing task. Make any changes needed to improve meaning and organization.

2. From the list of language features below, choose two that may need more careful review in your writing and edit your draft. You might want to review the grammatical explanations given in the GLR ⒼⓁⓡ for the structures you choose.

☐ use of the present tense when writing general statements

☐ use of past tense verbs, time expressions, proper nouns, and personal pronouns to give examples or to report on experiments from the past

☐ use of a variety of sentences to emphasize information in paragraphs and to make a paragraph flow

Peer Response Activity

The following first draft is a reaction to the readings on anger written by a student in a community college ESL composition class. First, use the following questions to respond to the student sample. Then exchange drafts of your own paper with a partner and answer the same questions about your peer's paper. Write your comments on a separate piece of paper.

1. What generalizations from the three readings does the writer include?

2. What do you want to know more about? Ask one to three journalistic questions to help the writer give more information.

3. What personal experiences with or observations about expressing anger did the writer include? Which were the most interesting and why?

4. Make one suggestion to help the writer revise the draft.

READING REACTION PAPER
(Student Sample)

Anger is one of a variety of expressions of feelings in human beings. Anger is different from joy, sorrow, etc. Sometimes anger can ease our emotions or sometimes it can have an opposite effect such as making things worse. I would like to compare my personal experiences with and opinions about anger with two generalizations about anger that I read in studies of anger in order to discover whether these generalizations are true in my experience and opinions.

Many laboratory experiments and studies have concluded that "Anger expressed is often anger and aggression increased" (Carlson & Hatfield). I believe this generalization. I think that anger brings a tremendous explosion of feelings. I am disappointed with myself that I can't be more patient and keep myself under control. Continually I have to yell, scream, and even use foul language. And it seems the more I get angry, the more I feel angry. We even see headlines in the newspaper about people killing one another because they weren't able to keep their anger in control.

In another generalization about anger, Carol Tavris maintains that "a culture's rules of anger are not arbitrary: they evolve along with its history and structure" (*Manners, Emotions, and the American Way*). She gives the example of the ways in which the Japanese restrain their emotions and this has been in their history for centuries. The same is true in my culture.

Jonghoon Park

LEARNER'S NOTEBOOK

Reflecting on Your Learning

Report what you have learned about writing a reaction to generalizations made about a topic in textbooks or articles. Consider how you wrote the paper as well as how the sample paper and your peer's paper were written.

Revise

On your draft, list one thing you will add to or delete from your summary of the articles. Rewrite your paper including this change.

• •

LOOKING AHEAD

Every chapter in this textbook has a section entitled "Looking Ahead." This section gives you a chance to apply what you have learned in the chapter to authentic academic assignments. The point here is *not* to write the assignment, but to *analyze* how you might deal with the assignment by using the skills that you have learned in the chapter.

Accounting 4303

1. For the six-week period beginning February 1, collect three to five current articles per week on various news items that may be related to governmental or nonprofit accounting. Clip these articles. Highlight the important points of the articles.

2. Select one issue from your articles and write a five- to seven-page paper in which you:

   a) summarize the issue,

   b) discuss the social, political, and economic implications,

   c) relate the above discussions to accounting aspects of the issue. (Suggestions: What accounting information is presented as support of the issue? How may accounting information be used in analysis, control, or further planning?)

   The paper should be typed and double-spaced. It will be graded for proper form, spelling, and grammar.

DISCUSSION

With a partner or in a small group, analyze the assignment. Use the following questions for your discussion.

1. What academic reading strategies learned in this chapter will help you complete this assignment?

2. What questions might you need to ask the professor to complete this assignment successfully? Formulate one specific question.

3. What problems do you anticipate for the person doing this assignment? What solutions can you offer?

Chapter 2

Reporting

Animal Thought and Behavior

GOALS

WRITING
◆ focus a report and organize the
information by chronology
or classification
◆ present general ideas and support
them with examples

GRAMMAR
◆ practice structures writers use
when presenting information
passive voice in report writing
subject-verb agreement with
complex noun phrases
◆ practice how writers use count
and noncount nouns when
presenting information
◆ practice the use of narratives in
research reports

CONTENT
◆ learn about one aspect of animal
behavior—how animals play
◆ learn about conscious thinking in
animals

ACADEMIC FIELDS

Biology
Psychology

Sample Authentic College/University Writing Assignments

The reporting skills you learn in this chapter can be used to complete college and university assignments like these:

Class: Nutrition, introductory course

Write a **report** for a local newspaper that *explains* the law requiring food manufacturers to list nutrient contents (e.g., calories and fat per serving, vitamins and minerals per serving, etc.) on the packaging of consumer foods.

Class: Chemistry, 2nd year

Write a **report** about the experiment you did today. Use the following sections to organize your report:

Introduction: **Describe** the background of the experiment, what is to be found, and how you went about it

Experiment: **Present** the various observations, measurements, or other results that your experiment yielded. **Present** some of this information in the form of graphs or figures.

GETTING READY

Warm-up Activity: Writing

As part of class assignments, you have probably had experience writing reports that explain, describe, or present information about a topic. In your daily life, you have also probably had experience reporting information to people so they could take action or make decisions.

Activity 2-1   Thinking about Reports

Identify three kinds of reporting that you have done from the list below. Answer the questions below about the report. An example is provided.

- Was the report given orally or was it a formal written report?
- Who was the audience?
- What purpose did the report serve?

Type of Report	Oral/Written	Audience	Purpose
1. A report about an accident	oral written		
2. A report about stolen property	oral (written)	A credit agency that writes you a warning letter because one of your checks has recently bounced	To explain that your wallet was stolen and that someone has been using your checks without your permission
3. Information about yourself to gain admission to a school or program or to get a job	oral written		

Type of Report	Oral/Written	Audience	Purpose
4. A report about a special project that you have been involved in (e.g., a science lab report)	oral written		
5. A report to a government agency to change visa status or get citizenship	oral written		

The Basics of Writing a Report

When you finish your education and find a job, your most frequent on-the-job writing task will probably be report writing. Your employers might ask you to write a report about a task or project you have completed or about some specialized knowledge that you have. Report writing entails gathering, organizing, and sharing information with others who need it to take action or make decisions. Reports are filled with facts, details, and examples. They contain authors' opinions only if the directions request them.

Report writing is also a common type of academic assignment. Report assignments may ask you to *describe* an experiment, *summarize* work you have completed or material you have read, or *discuss* results of an activity or study. Report writing allows professors to check that you have completed assigned tasks or done assigned reading.

Here are some common types of reports from both academic and work settings:

- article summaries
- laboratory reports
- book reports
- survey findings
- observational memos or reports
- expense reports
- activity or progress memos or reports
- marketing or sales memos or reports

In work settings, short reports often are written in the form of a memo. They have a fixed type of heading as shown in the following example. This format is similar to the format you follow when you send an e-mail message. The benefit of writing memos is that they are short, have a focused subject, and are direct. The information in a memo is usually organized as follows:

Opening paragraph: Background on topic and purpose for writing

Following 1 to 2 paragraphs: Development of ideas on the topic

Final paragraph: Suggestions about how to use the information in the report, or plans for further work

---

MEMORANDUM

To: Dr. Jane E. Doe, Professor of Psychology

From: John Q. Public, Student Research Assistant

Re: Experiments on Memory in Mice

Date: January 1, 1997

After nine months of conducting experiments on whether mice can remember experiences, we have found the following:

Procedures: Fifteen mice were put in a small enclosure that had three doors. Behind one door there was nothing, behind another door was an electric shock device, and behind a third door was a dish with food. The mice were introduced to the enclosure and the doors once, then were removed. After five minutes, the mice were reintroduced to the enclosure five times. We recorded the learning pattern of the mice.

Results: Only 10 of the original 15 mice completed all the trials. Of the 10 mice, 9 did not seem to remember what they had "learned" in previous trips to the enclosure. They repeatedly returned to the door that contained the shock device. Those that had discovered the food door on previous trips were unable to remember this. One mouse, however, was able to remember the door that hid the food between Trips 1, 2, and 3. We examined this mouse to see if there was anything unusual about it and found nothing.

Problems: Two mice died during the course of the experiment—mostly from fright after being shocked by the shocking device. Three others escaped.

Follow-up: We intend to try the same experiment with rats to see if their larger brains give them an increased memory.

LEARNER'S NOTEBOOK

Practicing Memo Writing

From the list in *Warm-up Activity: Writing,* choose one of the types of reports that you have had experience with. Imagine that you have been asked to submit this information in writing. In your learner's notebook, write a memo in which you briefly report this information.

1. Considering What Your Audience Needs to Know

The broad purpose of written reports is to inform readers. The length and focus of reports, as well as the kinds and amounts of information included, will vary because of the audience and the topic.

This sequence of questions and answers is one that a writer of a report might consider before beginning.

Topic: Training Seeing Eye Dogs

Question: What information about my topic is common knowledge?

- Seeing eye dogs are usually German shepherds and Labrador retrievers.
- It is expensive to train these dogs.
- They learn how to cross streets carefully, how to stop at street corners, how to behave calmly in crowded places such as buses, etc.

Question: What questions will readers have about my topic?

- How long does the training take?
- What steps are involved in the training process?
- Who does the training?
- Who pays for the training?
- Do human owners also need some training?

Question: What do I know about this topic that I am fairly sure my readers don't know and would be interested in?

- The price of training a seeing eye dog
- The fact that blind people do not have to pay for a seeing eye dog
- All of the tasks that seeing eye dogs are capable of performing

Question: What information will be most useful to my reader?

- What steps are involved in the training process?

Question: How will the information be used?

- In this case, the report will add to the reader's general knowledge.

Question: What don't I know? Where can I find this information (the World Wide Web, interviews, books, magazine or newspaper articles, writing a letter to get information, etc.)?

- What steps are involved in the training process? (World Wide Web, interview with a trainer, a book, or an article)
- What training do human owners receive? (interview with the owner of a seeing eye dog)

Activity 2-2   Practice Considering Reader's Common Knowledge and Questions

Choose a topic that you have experienced personally. Have a partner or small group tell you what they already know about the topic and create questions that they would want answered in a report on your topic. Here are some suggested topics:

- an activity that you have some expertise in (for instance, if your hobby is skateboarding, you could write a report on various types of skateboards or the types of tricks that expert skateboarders do)
- a project that you completed (here you might report on the procedures you followed to complete the project and/or what you found out by doing the project)
- a research study that you were involved with (here you might report on the procedures you followed and/or the results that you obtained)

LEARNER'S NOTEBOOK

Using Audience Feedback to Plan a Report

Think about the feedback that your partner or group gave you in Activity 2-2. In your learner's notebook, write down the information that will be the most useful to include in your report.

2. Gathering Information

Once you have narrowed the focus of your report, the next task is to gather the appropriate information that you will need to satisfy your readers. Here are some ways to gather information about your topic:

1. *Write down as much as you know about the topic.* This information can be based on your first-hand experience or on knowledge that you already have about the topic.

2. *Consult written materials on your topic.* Some reports will require that you go beyond what you already know. Additional information can be found in newspapers, magazines, books, videotapes, maps, the World Wide Web, or other material.

3. *Interviews.* Although you may often have all the information you need to write a report, you may also want to interview other people who have expertise in or experience with your topic.

4. *Conduct experiments or observations or surveys to gather information about your topic.* Often the audience for the report wants to know your first-hand knowledge about the topic. One invaluable way to gain a lot of information as well as first-hand experience with an issue is to do research yourself.

Activity 2-3   Organizing Your Information

Begin to organize the information for your report on the topic you discussed in Activity 2-2.

1. Consult the notes you made about the *Learner's Notebook: Using Audience Feedback to Plan a Report.* Discard any information that is not relevant to your audience. Add any additional information that you think will interest your audience.

2. Decide whether you need to consult other sources and make a list of these.

3. *If necessary,* make a plan explaining what kind of experiment you will do or what kinds of questions you will ask someone you interview.

    Explain both your background information and your research plan to a partner.

3. Organizing the Whole Report

Another important task for anyone who writes a report is to organize the information into a meaningful and useful form.

The overall shape of reports, regardless of length, remains the same. The audience expects that a report will contain:

- a brief introduction with a thesis statement that reflects the content of the report
- some information that gives background about the topic (in the introduction or in a separate body paragraph)
- several body paragraphs, each with:
    - a general statement (topic sentence) that explains some part of the thesis
    - details, evidence, and examples that support the topic sentence
- a conclusion that summarizes the main ideas of the report (if it is long), makes recommendations, or predicts what will happen in the future

See pages 350–354, Appendix A for more information.

4. Meeting Audience Needs: Deciding What Background Information to Provide

It is crucial to predict the knowledge, interests, and expectations of your readers when providing background information in a report. You may have received this advice: "Assume that your reader knows little or nothing about a topic." This advice is too general. On the other hand, the opposite, "My readers probably already know what I'm saying," is also an oversimplification.

The best piece of advice is: "Treat your readers as partners." Anticipate the experience with or information about the topic that your readers have. If you are unsure, ask several people who might be readers of your report. Also, remember that your task in the background section is not only to inform your audience, but also to arouse their interest. Although some readers may know some or all of the information you give, when you sound interested, the readers will be too.

Activity 2-4 Deciding How Much Background Information to Provide

Below are two background information sections from papers written by student writers. Answer the following questions:

1. How do the background sections differ? Consider such things as length, tone, how focused the writer is on the topic or the audience, the types of information provided.

2. How does the audience's knowledge, interests, and expectations determine both the kind of information included and the way the writer addresses the reader?

Sample

How often do you see young teenagers, especially Asian-American teenagers, driving cars? This is a common scene, I think. If you continue to observe this scene more carefully, you will notice that the cars driven by these youths have been modified: the cars have been lowered, a noisy muffler has been installed, or a powerful stereo has been added. These are the stereotypical cars owned by Asian-American teenagers. Perhaps many people wonder why young people "demolish" their nice new cars, turning them into something that is loud and looks uncomfortable to ride in. In this essay, I want to give you a closer look at how these cars are modified and the advantages of making some of these changes.

Jusak Adidjaja

Sample

Day by day, societies all over the world consume more and more stuff. They follow the example of first world nations, thus making the same mistakes. Garbage is the biggest of them all. It is known that the richer the country, the more waste it produces. The United States alone produces about 209 million tons of municipal waste per year, which is more than four pounds per person per day (*Discover Magazine,* June 1997). This extends from harmless candy wrappings to giant sites where toxic wastes are dumped.

Garbage is our worst enemy. In countries like the U.S., to open a snack package shows one of the infinite reasons why we have so much waste. First there is a regular carton. Then there is the plastic wrapping. And after that, you will still find a plastic or paper tray before you can actually reach your snack. It would be much easier for us and especially for mother nature if that same snack came in only a plastic or paper wrapping or even in a reusable package.

Melissa Castro

5. Organizing the Body Paragraphs of the Report

There are two useful patterns for organizing information in the body paragraphs of the report. An example of each type is given below. The information in the examples is taken from a research report on the hunting habits of domestic cats in Great Britain.

A. Chronological order

When reporting research, writers often report them as a narrative and use time or chronological order. In the following narrative, the writers decide to include themselves as characters—"we." What other features of narrative grammar are included?

GLR   See page 285 in the GLR for more information on narrative grammar.

Chronological Order

We decided to make an intensive study in the small Bedfordshire village. This began with a survey to see how many domestic cats there were in the village and whether their owners would be willing to participate. In the 173 houses in the village there were 78 cats, a slightly higher incidence of cat owning than in Britain as a whole. Only one cat owner refused to take part in the study, which was to take one complete year.

1st Step
details

We gave each cat owner a consecutively numbered supply of polyethylene bags marked with the cat's code letter. We then asked the cat owners to bag the remains of any animals that the cat caught and we collected the bags weekly. In addition, we recorded many catches for which there were no remains. Thus, if a cat was seen to eat the entire specimen, this was recorded as an "unknown." In this category were also any remains that proved impossible to identify. Identification was straightforward for the vast majority of specimens although initially—the study began during the summer months—it was rather smelly.

2nd Step
details

3rd & 4th Steps
examples
details

Source: P. B. Churcher and J. H. Lawton, Beware of well-fed felines, *Natural History*, July 1989, 40–47.

B. Classification or categories

The information in this part of the report is divided according to kinds, factors, classes, or aspects of the larger topic. This particular report combines the researchers' generalizations about the hunting behavior of all cats and statements of fact about the behavior of the cats in this experiment. The writers shift verb tenses to indicate the difference between fact and generalization.

What makes a cat a good hunter? <u>Part of the answer is its age</u>.

Topic Sentence &
Category 1 (age)

Old cats get lazy; the younger the cat, the more animals it catches. Although we looked only at catches of birds and mammals, several owners reported that their kittens practiced their hunting skills on frogs or butterflies, but only a few of them persisted with these types of prey into adulthood. Sex and neutering did not appear to have a marked effect on hunting success.

<u>Where the cats lived</u> did affect both the type and number of prey brought home. Cats in the middle of the village, without easy access to open ground, caught fewer items in total and proportionally fewer small mammals and more birds. This pattern was reversed for cats living at the edge of the village. The density of the cats themselves seemed to have a slight effect on catching success, with cats in areas with more competition for prey catching fewer items.

Category 2 (location)

Source: P. B. Churcher and J. H. Lawton, Beware of well-fed felines, *Natural History*, July 1989, 40–47.

6. Providing Details, Facts, and Examples

Body paragraphs in reports often begin with general statements about some aspect of the topic. These are often called *topic sentences.* The following paragraphs are the introduction and first body paragraph of an essay about animal behavior written by Atsuko Otani, an ESL student from Japan. The second paragraph contains specific information that supports the topic sentence.

Pikas, small high-altitude mammals, are little relatives of rabbits. They live mostly in the taluses, or embankments, below cliffs in the mountains, where the rocks are broken up to provide protection from enemies (Ingles, 1965). <u>Zoologist Andrew Smith's research (1997) has demonstrated that even though pikas are small, their life and behavior is complex, involving many decisions.</u>   Thesis for the Report

    <u>The first decision which pikas have to make before foraging is whether to graze or to hay.</u> This decision seems to determine "the   Topic Sentence
distance the animal travels and the type of vegetation it harvests" (Smith, 1997). When pikas *graze,* they *almost always stay within six feet of their territories.* On the other hand, when pikas *hay, they collect plants as far as sixty feet away from their territories.*   details
<u>These different types of food gathering affect the pikas' safety</u>   Conclusion
when they forage. When they are close to their home, *there are much less possibilities to be captured by natural enemies.*   details
However, there is a reason for pikas not always staying in safe places. This decision is based *on the selection of different kinds of*   details
plants for storage.

Activity 2-5   Organizing Body Paragraph Information for a Report

To help you organize the information that will appear in the body paragraphs of a report about the topic you selected in Activity 2-2, choose one of the following types of organization: chronological order or classification/categories. In the chart on the next page, write in information about your topic and share it with the same partner or small group that you received feedback from in Activity 2-2.

Organizing Body Paragraphs in Your Report	
Type of Organization chronology (procedure/steps)	classification/categories
Chronological Order	**Classification/Categories**
Steps/Procedure followed:	**General categories you will discuss:**
Step 1:	**Category 1:**
details/facts/examples	**details/facts/examples**
Step 2:	**Category 2:**
details/facts/examples	**details/facts/examples**
Step 3:	**Category 3:**
details/facts/examples	**details/facts/examples**
Step 4:	**Category 4:**
details/facts/examples	**details/facts/examples**

7. Presenting and Explaining Non-Text Material

Non-text materials (sometimes called *visual aids*) are often part of a report. Some documents have more non-text materials than paragraphs while some have an equal balance of text paragraphs and graphs. Here is a list of common non-text materials and what they communicate:

a photograph or drawing	*shows*	what something looks like
a drawing or diagram	*shows*	how something works
a bar graph, a line graph	*shows*	how things are related to each other
a flow chart, a decision tree	*shows*	how something is organized
a pie chart, a pictograph	*shows*	how the whole relates to its parts

The most important considerations in choosing and using non-text materials are *audience* and *purpose*. The purpose of all non-text materials is to clarify and demonstrate the information in paragraphs in a way that is visually interesting and memorable.

The following diagram and the accompanying paragraph from a biology textbook found on the next page show how writers combine visual materials and sentences and paragraphs to make an idea clear.

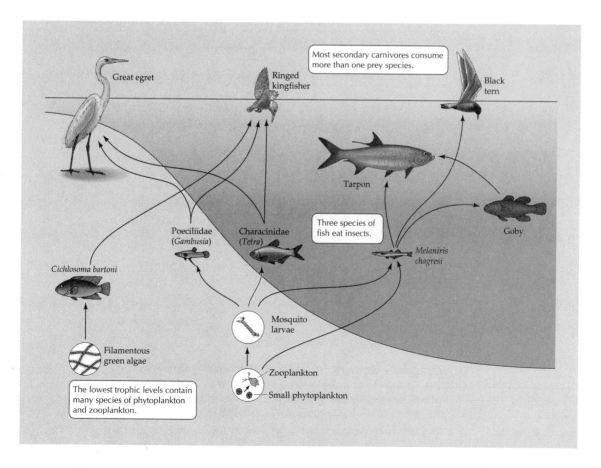

It is useful to group organisms according to their source of energy. The organisms that obtain their energy from a common source constitute a trophic level. For example, organisms that eat plants constitute the trophic level called herbivores. Organisms that eat herbivores are called primary carnivores. A set of linkages in which a plant is eaten by an herbivore, which is in turn eaten by a primary carnivore, and so on, is called a food chain. Food chains are usually interconnected to make a food web. The arrows in representations of food webs show who eats whom. A simplified food web for Gatun Lake, Panama, is shown here. Food webs are a useful summary of predator-prey interactions within a community.

Source: W. K. Purves, et al., *Life: The Science of Biology,*
Fifth Edition. (Sunderland, MA: Sinauer and Associates,
Inc., 1998; NY: W. H. Freeman and Company, 1998).

Activity 2-6   Writing about Non-text Material

Choose one of the following charts, graphs, or diagrams and write an explanation of it. Read your explanation to a small group of classmates.

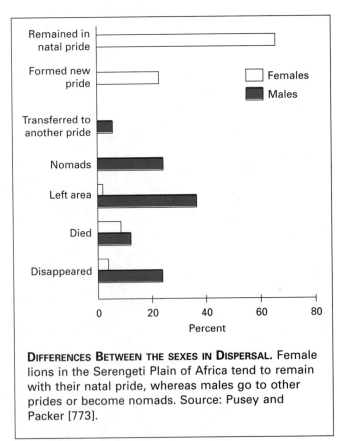

DIFFERENCES BETWEEN THE SEXES IN DISPERSAL. Female lions in the Serengeti Plain of Africa tend to remain with their natal pride, whereas males go to other prides or become nomads. Source: Pusey and Packer [773].

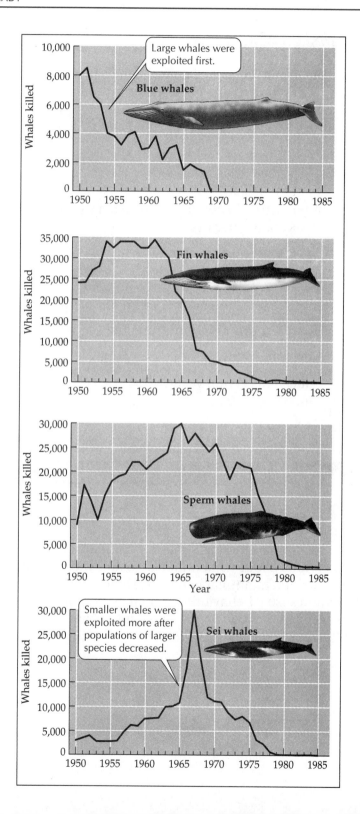

Activity 2-7   Writing a Short Report

For homework, write a short report of no more than two pages on the topic you chose in Activity 2-2. Be sure your report contains an introduction with some background information on the topic, a thesis statement that reflects the content of the report, and at least two well-organized and well-supported body paragraphs.

Activity 2-8   Responding to a Peer's Report

Exchange the report you wrote in Activity 2-7 with a partner who will read it and answer the following questions about your draft:

1. What topic is the writer reporting about?

2. Underline the thesis.

3. How did the writer organize the body paragraphs—chronological or classification?

4. Ask the writer two questions about information that was unclear in the report.

5. What was the most interesting part of this report?

6. Ask journalistic questions (Who? What? When? Why? How?) to help the writer gather more information.

FOCUSING

Introduction to Readings

Animal behavior is a fascinating subject for scientists and non-scientists alike. As humans, we are curious about what animals do and why they do it. Many books have been written that document animal behavior. Their subjects range from animal predator-prey patterns and sexual behavior to animal psychology. The following reports document two aspects of animal behavior: animal intelligence and emotions.

Pre-reading Activity

Activity 2-9   Considering Your Opinion about a Reading Topic

Choose one of the following cartoons and explain what it suggests about animal thinking. In your opinion, are animals capable of thought?

When chickens dream

"Forget these guys."

READING 1: A CAPACITY FOR JOY (EXCERPT FROM A POPULAR BOOK)

When Elephants Weep, published in 1995, met with immediate success because it explored the emotional lives of animals. The book deals with such emotions as sorrow, anger, fear, hope, and compassion. The excerpt below reports on animals' capacity for fun and joy.

Pre-reading Vocabulary

Activity 2-10   Discussing Observations of Animal Play

Have you ever observed an animal at play? Discuss your observations with a partner or in a small group.

A CAPACITY FOR JOY

Play

Joy often expresses itself in play, which many animals may indulge in all their lives. Play is important to animals, and, although it carries risks, since animals can be injured or killed while playing, a variety of evolutionary functions for it have been proposed. Perhaps it is a form of practice, of learning to perform tasks, theorists suggest; or perhaps it exer- 5
cises developing social, neurological, or physical capacities. Cynthia Moss may have spoken for biologists when, watching African elephants play in the rain—running, twirling, flapping ears and trunks, spraying water at each other, flailing branches, uttering loud play trumpets—she wrote in her notes, "How can one do a serious study of animals that behave this way!" 10

Play, which seems to be both a sign and a source of joy, has been increasingly studied in recent years. Elephants, both Indian and African, are particularly playful. A traveling circus once pitched its tents next to a schoolyard with a set of swings. The older elephants were chained, but Norma, a young elephant, was left loose. When Norma saw children swinging she was greatly intrigued. Before long she went over, waved the children away with her 15
trunk, backed up to a swing, and attempted to sit on it. She was notably unsuccessful, even using her tail to hold the swing in place. Finally she flung the swing about irritably and returned to her companions. The children began to swing again, and Norma had to try again. Despite trying periodically for an hour, she was never able to swing.

Alaskan buffalo have been seen playing on ice. One at a time, starting from a ridge 20
above a frozen lake, the buffalo charged down to the shore and plunged onto the ice, bracing their legs so that they spun across the ice, with their tails in the air. As each buffalo skidded to a halt, it let out a loud bellow, "a kind of *gwaaa* sound"—and then awkwardly picked its way back to shore to make another run.

Animals may also play with objects. This can be seen even in some animals that are 25
known to play with other animals. A captive Komodo dragon in a British zoo played with a shovel, pushing it noisily about the enclosure. A meter-long wild alligator in Georgia spent

forty-five minutes playing with the drops of water falling from a pipe into a pond, stalking the pipe, snapping at the drops, letting them fall on his snout and then snapping at them in midair. Captive gorillas and chimpanzees enjoy playing with dolls and spend time in other imaginative play, as when Koko the gorilla pretends to brush her teeth with a toy banana, or when the chimpanzee Loulis, playing alone, puts a board on his head, signing "That's a hat."   30

In other animals, object play becomes social play. A captive dolphin at an oceanarium played with a feather, carrying it to an intake pipe, letting it be swept off by the current, and then chasing it. Another dolphin joined in and they are said to have taken turns. In another game three or four dolphins vied for possession of a feather, and wild dolphins play similar keep-away games with various objects. Beluga whales carry stones or seaweed on their   35 heads and other whales at once try to knock them off. Lions, both adults and cubs, may try to wrest pieces of bark or twigs from each other.

To what extent animals playing games recognize implicit rules is not clear. In a few instances trainers have successfully taught formalized games to animals. A simplified version of cricket was taught to elephants of the Betram Mills' Circus after several months of   40 training. Elephants understand throwing objects, but batting and fielding took time to learn. It is said that after some months the elephants began to "enter into the spirit of the game" and subsequently played with great enthusiasm. At an oceanarium, several dolphins were trained in the skills of water polo. First they learned to put a ball through a goal, each team having a different goal. Then the trainers tried to teach them to compete by keeping the other   45 team from scoring. After three training sessions the dolphins caught on, all too well. Uninterested in strictures against foul play, the dolphins zestfully attacked one another in such an unsporting fashion that the training was discontinued and they were never again given competitive games. There is no indication that the dolphins thereafter tried to play polo on their own.   50

Animals sometimes find playmates across the barrier of species. One family that kept red kangaroos in their backyard with their dogs found the animals quite friendly toward each other, although there were difficulties. The dogs liked to chase and be chased by their friends, barking. The kangaroos preferred to wrestle and box, pastimes the dogs did not care for. Somehow, they managed to play together.   55

Dogs will attempt to play with another animal, cats, for example, but are usually disappointed by their lack of fluency in or indifference to their canid metalanguage, for example, the play bow—when a canid lowers its forelegs to the ground and waves its tail. Dogs do not seem to be unhappy at trying to figure out human rules for the games that people play with them. The concentrated posture a dog assumes over a stick he is waiting for his human   60 friend to move is obviously meant to be slightly humorous: that is part of the game. Playing these games is almost like looking through a window into the dog's mind. We see what he intends. And the dog, too, gets a clear glimpse into our minds and knows what we want. Play, laughter, and friendship burst across the species barrier.

Source: Jeffrey Moussaieff Masson and Susan McCarthy, *When Elephants Weep* (New York: Delta Publishing, 1995, 124–132).

LEARNER'S NOTEBOOK

Writing About an Interesting Animal Behavior

Think of a type of behavior exhibited by an animal or animals that you know about. Consider such behaviors as the predator-prey relationship between certain animals, the emotions of a given animal, an animal's mating behavior, or social organization in a certain animal group. Write a description of this behavior and give specific examples of it. Explain why it fascinates you. Share your learner's notebook entry with two other classmates.

Active Reading

Activity 2-11   Finding Key Information in a Reading

Reread "A Capacity for Joy." Fill in the key information, that is, thesis, the paragraph where it is located, and the background information included.

> **Thesis:**
>
> **Paragraph in which background information appears:** _____
>
> **Information included:** _____
>
> _____
>
> _____

Activity 2-12   Examining the Organization of Body Paragraphs

A "A Capacity for Joy"organizes the information in its body paragraphs by categories related to animal play. Find two topic sentences that introduce a category related to animal play. Then list facts, details, or examples that the writers give to support their topic sentence. Not all paragraphs contain sentences that introduce a category related to animal play. An example is provided.

Body Paragraphs Organized by Categories

Topic Sentence 1:
Play, which seems to be both a sign and a source of joy, has been

increasingly studied in recent years.

facts/details/examples: When Alaskan buffalo play on ice, they charge down a hill and

onto the ice, spinning around on their legs and making a sound.

Norma, a baby elephant, attempted to play with swings.

Topic Sentence:

_____

facts/details/examples: _____

_____

Topic Sentence:

_____

facts/details/examples:

_____

READING 2   ANIMAL THINKING (JOURNAL ARTICLE)

The following article appeared in *American Scientist,* a journal for scientists. This article reports on a general issue related to the behavior of all animals: the capacity for conscious thinking.

Pre-reading Vocabulary: The Grammar of New Vocabulary

Learning vocabulary helps readers understand what they read better. But if you want to use the new words you encounter, you must also learn <u>how</u>, and this means you have to understand a bit about grammar. Verbs usually have certain types of grammatical structures that can follow them. It is important to learn this information when you learn the new word. The verbs in Activity 2-13 appear in reports about research studies and observations. You will find them in italics in "Animal Thinking." The verbs below can be followed by a noun or a clause.

noun/noun phrase

Some biologists <u>interpret</u> *the meaning of animal behavior.*

clause

Most pet owners <u>have determined</u> *that their animals have emotions.*

 See pages 258 and 342–343 in the GLR for an explanation of phrases and clauses and pages 362–363, Appendix B.

Activity 2-13   Learning the Grammar of New Vocabulary

Look at the following sentences from "Animal Thinking." Do the following:

1. To make sure you understand the meaning, look up the *italicized* verb in a dictionary and find a synonym.

2. Underline and label the grammar structure that follows each verb as a *noun/noun phrases,* or a *clause.*

3. Use the verb to write your own sentence. If the example shows the verb followed by a noun phrase, try to use a noun phrase in your own sentence. Similarly, if the verb is followed by a *that* clause, use a *that* clause in your sentence.

   An example is done for you.

   that clause

   a. While biologists do not deny their existence, they *emphasize* <u>that it is extremely difficult to learn anything about the subjective experiences of another species.</u>

Synonym: stress

that clause

New Sentence: Animal psychologists emphasize <u>that emotions are important in the life of animals.</u>

   b. Heinrich also *observed* a further indication of real understanding by the ravens that had learned this specialized form of food gathering.

Synonym: _____

New Sentence: _____

_____

c. We *make inferences about* people's feelings and thoughts, especially those of very young children, from many kinds of communication, verbal and nonverbal; we should similarly use all available evidence in exploring the possibility of thoughts or feelings in other species.

Synonym: _____

New Sentence: _____

_____

d. Communication may either inform or misinform, but in either case it can *reveal* something about the conscious thinking of the communicator.

Synonym: _____

New Sentence: _____

_____

Vocabulary in Fixed Expressions and Phrases

Another effective way to deal with vocabulary is to learn the phrases or expressions that the new word often appears in. You can understand, memorize, and use vocabulary more effectively if you know how expressions are structured. One common type of expression combines a verb + noun + prepositional phrase.

verb
Non-verbal communication of mood or intentions *plays* a large and increasingly
noun   prepositional phrase
recognized role **in human affairs.**

Learning vocabulary in this way has another benefit. It helps you to learn prepositions.

Activity 2-14   Discovering Expressions in which New Vocabulary Appear

To learn more about these expressions, do the following:

a. Combine a verb, a noun, and the appropriate preposition to create an expression that is useful in writing. (*Hint:* You may already know some of these expressions, but if you don't, look through "Animal Thinking" to find the verb or noun and discover the expression it is used in.)

b. Write the sentence from "Animal Thinking" that the expression appears in.

c. Write your own sentence using the expression in a new way.

You will use some prepositions more than once. An example is provided.

Verb	Noun or Noun Phrase	Preposition
explore	*a role*	for
judge	the same degree	*in*
require	the criteria	of
play	the intentions	
refine	the possibility	

Expression: _____ *play a role in* _____

Published Sentence:

Non-verbal communication of mood or intentions plays a (large

and increasingly recognized) role in human affairs.

New Sentence: _____ *People's outlook on life plays an important role in how happy they are.*

1. **Expression:** _____

   Published Sentence: _____.

   New Sentence: _____.

2. **Expression:** _____

   Published Sentence: _____.

   New Sentence: _____.

3. **Expression:** _____

   Published Sentence: _____.

   New Sentence: _____.

4. **Expression:** _____

   Published Sentence: _____.

   New Sentence: _____.

ANIMAL THINKING

    What is it like to be an animal? What do monkeys, dolphins, crows, sunfishes, bees, and ants think about? Or do nonhuman animals experience any thoughts and subjective feelings at all? Very few biologists or psychologists have discussed animal thoughts and feelings. While they do not deny their existence, they *emphasize* that it is extremely difficult, perhaps impossible, to learn anything at all about the subjective experiences of another species. But 5 the difficulties do not justify a refusal to face up to the issue. As Savory (1959) put the matter, "Of course to interpret the thoughts, or their equivalent, which determine an animal's behavior is difficult, but this is no reason for not making the attempt to do so. If it were not difficult, there would be very little interest in the study of animal behavior, and very few books about it" (p. 78). Just what is it about some kinds of behavior that leads us to feel that it is accompanied by conscious thinking? 10

Adaptations to Novelty

Considering how humans learn new things can help us refine the criteria for determining whether or not conscious thought exists. As humans, we can easily change back and forth between thinking consciously about our own behavior and not doing so. When we are 15 learning some new task such as swimming, riding a bicycle, driving an automobile, flying an airplane, operating a vacuum cleaner, caring for our teeth by some new technique recommended by a dentist, or any of a large number of actions we did not formerly know how to do, we think about it in considerable detail. But once the behavior is thoroughly mastered, we give no conscious thought to the details that once required close attention. 20

The fact that our own consciousness can be turned on and off with respect to particular activities tells us that in at least one species certain behavior patterns, which require a great deal of attention when they are first being learned, eventually become so automatic that they no longer require conscious thought. It is reasonable to guess that this is true also for other species. Well-learned behavior patterns may not require the same degree of conscious atten- 25 tion as those the animal is learning how to perform. This in turn means that conscious awareness is more likely when the activity is novel and challenging; striking and unexpected events are more likely to produce conscious awareness.

Heinrich (1995) has recently studied a specialized form of tool used by ravens that suggests insight into novel and somewhat complex relationships. Five ravens were captured as 30 nestlings and held in large outdoor cages until they were well grown. The cage was equipped with two horizontal poles well above the ground. The ravens had been fed for many months with road-killed animals and other pieces of meat placed on the ground within the cage. During the experiments, Heinrich provided the hungry ravens with only a small piece of meat suspended from one of the horizontal poles by a piece of string. At first the 35 ravens flew to the suspended food but were unable to detach anything edible from it; they also seized the string while perched on the horizontal pole, and pulled at it from time to time. But the string was too long to allow a single pull to lift the meat within reach. After six hours one raven suddenly carried out a complex series of actions that did bring the suspended meat within reach. This entailed reaching down, grasping the string in the bill, 40 pulling it up, holding the string with one foot, releasing it from the bill, reaching down again to grasp the string below the pole, and repeating the sequence four or five times.

For a few days only this raven obtained suspended meat in this way, but in time all but one of its companions began to pull up the string, hold it with one foot and repeat those actions until the food could be reached directly. They performed this procedure in slightly 45 different ways; two birds moved sideways during stages of holding the string with the foot so that the string was held at different points along the horizontal pole. The other two piled the string in loops, standing in roughly the same spot while holding the string. All but the first raven to perform this string-pulling action could have learned it by observing the

successful bird, but Heinrich's impression was that each bird solved the problem for itself, 50
using slightly different maneuvers. The efforts of each bird, however, may have been
encouraged by watching its companion obtain food in this unusual way.

Heinrich also observed a further indication of real understanding by the ravens that had
learned this specialized form of food gathering. When a raven is startled while holding a
small piece of meat in its bill, it typically flies off without dropping the food. But all four 55
of Heinrich's ravens that had obtained their food by the string-pulling procedure always (in
more than one hundred trials) dropped the meat before flying to another part of the cage.
They apparently realized that the string would prevent the meat from being carried away.
One raven never did learn to obtain food by string pulling, although it had obtained food
from its string-pulling companions. When this less talented bird was startled while holding 60
a piece of meat still attached to a string, it did fly off without releasing the meat—which
was jerked from its bill when the string became taut.

Another consideration regarding conscious thinking is whether an animal can anticipate
and intentionally plan an action, knowing its possible results. An impressive example is the
use of small stones by sea otters to detach and open shellfish (Kenyon 1969). These intelli- 65
gent aquatic carnivores feed mostly on sea urchins and mollusks. The sea otter must dive to
the bottom and pry the mollusk loose with claws or teeth, but some shells, especially
abalone, are tightly attached to the rocks and have shells that are too tough to be loosened
in this fashion. The otter will search for a suitable stone, which it carries while diving, then
uses the stone to hammer the shellfish loose, holding its breath all the while.   70

The otter usually eats while floating on its back. If it cannot get at the fleshy animal
inside the shell, it will hold the shell against its chest with one paw and pound the shellfish
against the stone, which it uses as an "anvil." The otter often tucks a good stone under an
armpit as it swims or dives. Although otters do not change the shapes of the stones, they do
select ones of suitable size and weight and often keep them for a long time. The otters use 75
tools only in areas where sufficient food cannot be obtained by other methods. In some areas
only the young and very old sea otters use stones; vigorous adults can dislodge the shellfish
by simply using their claws or teeth.

Animal Communication

Human communication is hardly limited to formal language; nonverbal communication 80
of mood or intentions also plays a large and increasingly recognized role in human affairs.
We make inferences about people's feelings and thoughts, especially those of very young
children, from many kinds of communication, verbal and nonverbal; we should similarly
use all available evidence in exploring the possibility of thoughts or feelings in other
species. When animals live in a group and depend on each other for food, shelter, warning 85
of dangers, or help in raising the young, they need to be able to judge correctly the moods
and intentions of their companions. This extends to animals of other species as well, especially predators or prey. It is important for the animal to know whether a predator is likely
to attack or whether the prey is so alert and likely to escape that a chase is not worth the
effort. Communication may either inform or misinform, but in either case it can reveal 90
something about the conscious thinking of the communicator.

Vervet monkeys, for example, have at least three different categories of alarm calls,
which were described by Struhsaker (1967) after extensive periods of observation. He found

that when a leopard or other large meat-eating animal approached, the monkeys gave one type of alarm call; quite a different call was used at the sight of a martial eagle, one of the few flying predators that captures vervet monkeys. A third type of alarm call was given when a large snake approached the group. This degree of variety in alarm calls is not unique, although it has been described in only a few kinds of animals. For example, squirrels of western North America use different types of calls when frightened by a ground predator or by a predatory bird such as a hawk (Owings and Leger 1980). 100

The question is whether the vervet monkey's three types of alarm calls convey to other monkeys information about the type of predator. Such information is important because the animals' defense tactics, or strategies, are different in the three cases. When a leopard or other large carnivore approaches, the monkeys climb into trees. But leopards are good climbers, so the monkeys can escape them only by climbing out onto the smallest branches, 105 which are too weak to support a leopard. When the monkeys see a martial eagle, they move into thick vegetation close to a tree trunk or at ground level. Thus the tactics that help them escape from a leopard make them highly vulnerable to a martial eagle, and vice versa. In response to the threat of a large snake they stand on their hind legs and look around to locate the snake, then simply move away from it, either along the ground or by climbing into a 110 tree.

To answer this question, Seyfarth, Cheney, and Marler (1980a, b) conducted some carefully controlled experiments under natural conditions in East Africa. From a hidden loudspeaker, they played tape recordings of vervet alarm calls and found that the playbacks of the three calls did indeed produce the appropriate responses. The monkeys responded to the 115 leopard alarm call by climbing into the nearest tree; the martial eagle alarm caused them to dive into thick vegetation; and the python alarm produced the typical behavior of standing on the hind legs and looking all around for the nonexistent snake.

References

Heinrich, B. 1995. An experimental investigation of insight in common ravens. (Corvus corax). *The Auk 112*: 994–1003.

Janes, S.W. 1976. The apparent use of rocks by a raven in nest defense. *Condor 78*: 409.

Kenyon, K.W. 1969. *The Sea Otter in the Eastern Pacific Ocean*. North American Fauna, no. 68. US Bureau of Sport Fisheries and Wildlife.

Owings, D.H., and D.W. Leger. 1980. Chatter vocalizations of California ground squirrels: Predator- and social-role specificity. *Z. Tiperspychol. 54*: 163–184.

Savory, T.H. 1959. *Instinctive Living, a Study of Invertebrate Behaviour*. London: Pergamon.

Seyfarth, R.M., D.L. Cheney, and P. Marler. 1980a. Monkey responses to three different alarm calls: Evidence for predator classification and semantic communication. *Science 210*: 801–03.

Seyfarth, R.M., D.L. Cheney, and P. Marler. 1980b. Vervet monkey alarm calls: Semantic communication in a free-ranging primates. *Animal Behavior 28*: 1070–94.

Struhsaker, T.T. 1967. *The Red Colobus Monkey*. Chicago: University of Chicago Press.

Source: Paul W. Sherman and John Alcock, *Exploring Animal Behavior: Readings from American Scientist* (Sunderland, MA: Sinauer Associates Inc., Publishers, 1993). Donald R. Griffin, *Animal Minds* (Chicago: University of Chicago Press, 104–105, 1992).

Active Reading

Activity 2-15   Identifying Key Information in a Reading

From the reading, "Animal Thinking," fill in the key information; that is, thesis, paragraph where it is located, and the background information included.

Thesis: (not directly stated)

Paragraph in which background information appears: _____

Information included: _____

_____

_____

Activity 2-16   Examining the Organization of Body Paragraphs

"Animal Thinking" organizes the information in its body paragraphs by categories related to animal thought. Beginning with paragraph 3, list topic sentences that introduce a category related to animal thinking. Then list facts, details, or examples that the writer gives to support his topic sentence. Note that not all paragraphs contain sentences that introduce a category and topic sentences are not always the first sentence in the paragraph. An example has been done for you.

Body Paragraphs Organized by Categories

Topic Sentence 1:
Conscious awareness is more likely when an activity is novel and challenging: striking and unexpected events are more likely to produce conscious awareness, and thus, adaptation to novelty.

facts/details/examples:
Heinrich put five ravens in an experimental situation to see if they could learn how to get food suspended from a string. After six hours, one bird developed a series of complex actions to get the food. Several days later, three other ravens came up with their own series of actions to get the food. Only one raven never learned to get the food.

In contrast to wild ravens, who usually fly away without dropping food when they are frightened, the birds in Heinrich's study dropped their food when startled (because

---

Body Paragraphs Organized by Categories

they seemed to know that it was attached to a string and they could come back

and get it later).

Topic Sentence 2: _____

_____

facts/details/examples:

_____

_____

_____

Topic Sentence 3: _____

_____

facts/details/examples:

_____

_____

_____

Analysis of Language: Using Informational Grammar to Write Reports

A. Passive and Active Voice

Passive sentences are a characteristic feature of reports, especially reports of how research was conducted. The passive voice allows the report writer to put the focus on the processes being studied rather than on the actions of the scientists. Compare the two sentences below. One contains active verbs; the other contains passive verbs, and would most likely appear in a research report.

Active Voice: If the owners <u>saw</u> a cat eat the entire specimen, they <u>recorded</u> it as an "unknown."

Passive Voice: If a cat <u>was seen</u> to eat the entire specimen, this <u>was recorded</u> as an "unknown."

Many books on style and computer grammar checkers caution against using the passive voice. In reality, however, writers can choose to use either active or passive verbs. Among several reasons that writers choose to use the passive voice in academic writing, three of the most common are:

Functions of the Passive Voice	**Examples**
A. To achieve cohesion. In this example, the entire idea in the first sentence becomes the subject of the second sentence.	Animals may also play with objects. ***This** can be seen* even in some animals that *are known* to play with other animals.
B. To emphasize something other than the subject or "doer" of the action either because it is not known or not important. In this sentence, it is not necessary or possible to identify the "doer" of the verb "define."	Most ethical problems arise from the transnational corporation, or TNC, which *is* generally *defined* as a firm that has a direct investment in two or more companies.
C. To avoid a "weak" subject in active (e.g., everyone). The understood subject or "doer" is people.	Although prescription and over-the-counter drugs have done much to alleviate suffering and increase the well-being of people around the globe, the major drug companies *are* also *faulted* for many of their practices.

> **GLR**   See pages 304–305 of the GLR for more information.

Activity 2-17   Using the Passive Voice to Write a Research Report

The following paragraph is accurate but not in an appropriate style for the intended audience of scientific readers. Create a new paragraph by changing the underlined verbs from active voice to passive voice. Make sure to choose a new subject for the passive verbs. Delete the subject of the active sentence in the new passive sentences if you think it sounds better. Your new paragraph has been started for you.

Verbs in Active Voice

(1) We <u>undertook</u> an intensive study in the small Bedfordshire village. (2) We <u>surveyed</u> many villagers to see how many domestic cats lived in the village and whether their owners would be willing to participate. In the 173 houses in the village there were 78 cats, a slightly higher incidence of cat owning than in Britain as a whole. (3) We <u>gave</u> each cat owner a consecutively numbered supply of polyethylene bags marked with the cat's code letter. (4) We then <u>asked</u> the cat owners to bag the remains of any animals that the cat caught and we collected the bags weekly. (5) In addition, we <u>recorded</u> many catches for which there were no remains.

Verbs in Passive Voice

(1) An intensive study of the prey and hunting habits of cats was undertaken in the small Bedfordshire village.

(2)

(3) A supply of consecutively numbered polyethylene bags marked with the cat's code letter was given to each cat owner.

(4)

(5)

Activity 2-18   Identifying the Functions of the Passive Voice

Learning to use passive sentences effectively is an important task for university students. The following activity is designed to help you think about good reasons for selecting the passive version of a sentence rather than the active version. Read the following passages to determine the function of the underlined verbs in the passive voice. Write the function of the passive voice in the blank provided. Discuss your explanation with other members of your class. An example is provided.

Passage	**Function of the Passive Voice**
Passage 1 When we are learning some new task such as swimming or riding a bicycle, we think about it in considerable detail. But once the behavior *is* thoroughly *mastered*, we give no conscious thought to the details that once required close attention.	to achieve cohesion
Passage 2 Elephants understand throwing objects, but batting and fielding took time to learn. It *is said* that after some months the elephants began to "enter into the spirit of the game" and subsequently played with great enthusiasm.	_____ _____

Passage	Function of the Passive Voice
Passage 3 The fact that our own consciousness <u>*can be turned on*</u> and <u>*off*</u> with respect to particular activities tells us that in at least one species certain behavior patterns, which require a great deal of attention when they are first being learned, eventually become so automatic that they no longer require conscious thought.	_____ _____
Passage 4 A simplified version of cricket <u>*was taught*</u> to elephants of the Betram Mills' Circus after several months of training.	_____ _____

Activity 2-19   Examining Passive vs. Active Versions of a Sentence in Context

To learn more about the difference between active and passive sentences, write the active version of the passive sentence in Passages 1 and 4 in Activity 2-18 to see how it changes the passage. Find the original sentence in the reading. See how the active version works with the other sentences around it. Do you agree with the writer's decision to use the passive version of the sentence? Explain your analysis. An example is provided.

EXAMPLE

Passive Version	**Active Version**
It is said that after some months the elephants began to "enter into the spirit of the game" and subsequently played with great enthusiasm.	People say that after some months the elephants began to "enter into the spirit of the game" and subsequently played with great enthusiasm.

Original Context: A simplified version of cricket was taught to elephants of the Betram Mills' Circus after several months of training. Elephants understand throwing objects, but batting and fielding took time to learn. ~~It is said~~ [people say] that after some months the elephants began to "enter into the spirit of the game" and subsequently played with great enthusiasm.

My Analysis: The writer's decision to use passive voice was a good one because putting "people" in the sentence seems to distract the reader's attention from the main focus, elephants' learning to play a game, and interrupts the flow.

B. Writing Generalizations: Indicating General Reference with Articles and Nouns

Reports often contain generalizations about the topic, and therefore, use nouns that refer to a whole group of people, things, or ideas. These are called **generic reference nouns**. When writing nouns with generic reference meaning, it is important to remember two things: 1) plural and noncount nouns do not have articles or determiners, indicated as ø in the examples, and 2) singular count nouns use the articles *a* or *an*. Look at the noun phrases in the following sentences to see the form of the noun phrase and the article.

Plural Count Nouns with General Meaning

What do ø *monkeys,* ø *dolphins,* ø *crows,* and ø *ants* think about? Or do ø *nonhuman animals* experience any ø *thoughts* or ø *subjective feelings?*

Noncount Nouns with General Meaning

One consideration can help us understand the presence of ø *conscious thought.*

A/An + Singular Noun with General Meaning

A/An + a singular noun can also indicate that the noun is a representative of a class or group. *A/An* + a singular noun often occurs in definitions, descriptions, and generalizations to indicate that the noun is a generalized instance.

A *thermometer* is an instrument used to measure temperature.

When you write a report, you will use generalizations:

to describe group behavior or activities

to define terms

to introduce the general topic

to generalize about what a particular behavior means

To write these generalizations, you will often need to use noncount nouns, but you will need to pay attention to the meaning of the nouns in your sentence to decide whether they are count or noncount. Many nouns can be either count or noncount depending on the meaning the writer gives them. Compare:

Wine (as a substance) is believed to have health benefits.
The wines of France (instances of a substance) are expensive.

Hair (a substance) can be a problem; some people have too little, others too much.
Waiter! There's *a hair* (an instance of a substance) in my soup.

> **GLR** See pages 277–281 in the GLR for more information on generic reference and noun phrases, articles, and determiners.

| Activity 2-20   Identifying Count and Noncount Nouns |

Like many scientific reports, the passage below combines statements of theory with an example to illustrate how the theory works. Examine it to complete these tasks. An example is provided.

1. How is this paragraph organized? In which sentences is the writer stating a theory? Which sentences give examples/facts?

2. In the examples/facts, the writer uses plural nouns and noun phrases to refer to groups. Write them in the appropriate place in the table below.

3. The writer uses both noncount nouns and plural noun phrases in the statements of theory. Find them in the passage and write them in the appropriate places in the table below.

> Another criterion of conscious thinking is whether animals display versatile behavior when completing a sequence of actions. Effective and versatile behavior often entails many steps, each one modified according to the results of previous steps. An example of this is how chimpanzees use probes to gather termites from termite mounds. Chimpanzees undertake the process by selecting a suitable branch, pulling off the leaves, and then breaking the stick to the right length. These sticks are used to force termites out of their holes, thereby allowing the chimps to secure a tasty and easy meal. Young chimps have been observed making crude attempts to prepare probes. This termite "fishing" provides evidence of learned behavior.
>
> Source: Donald R. Griffin, "Animal Thinking" in Paul W. Sherman & John Alcock,
> *Exploring Animal Behavior: Readings from American Scientist*
> (Sunderland, MA: Sinauer Associates Inc., Publishers, 1992).

Generic plural nouns and noun phrases in the example/facts	chimpanzees termites
Generic noncount nouns and noun phrases in the statements of theory	conscious thinking versatile behavior
Generic plural nouns and noun phrases in the generalizations	

Activity 2-21   Practicing Writing Generalizations with Count and Noncount Nouns

Using the information about chimpanzees and the noun phrases in Activity 2-20, write your answer to the following questions:

1. What does chimpanzees' use of probes demonstrate about animal behavior?

2. Give an example of your own (from your experience with animals or reading you have done) that illustrates the theory stated in this passage.

Activity 2-22   Writing a Summary Using Generic Nouns for Generalizations

To practice using generic nouns (and count and noncount forms), use the nouns in the list below to write a paragraph summarizing everything you have learned about sea otters from reading "Animal Thinking." Before you write, work with a partner or in a small group to:

1. Find the nouns from the list below that can be both count or noncount.

2. Discuss the differences in meaning between the count and noncount versions of those nouns.

3. Look back at the reading to see which versions and which meanings are used by the author.

In your paragraph, be sure to use the correct form to convey both the meaning of the noun and to signal whether or not it is generic.

conscious thought	awareness	sea otter	tool
food	planning	behavior	behavior
shell	shellfish	stone	attention

B. Subject-Verb Agreement in Generalizations

Academic writers discuss complex ideas and generalizations. Instead of having people or objects as their subjects, these sentences contain abstract subjects. Writers must pay particular attention to subject-verb agreement with two types of subjects:

Noun phrases (noun + *of* + noun): Noun phrases often consist of a noun + *of*-phrase. When these noun phrases are the subjects of a sentence, they make subject-verb agreement difficult because there are two nouns that the verb might agree with. In fact, the verb only agrees with the *first* noun and *not* the noun in the *of*-phrase. To find the first noun, cross out the *of*-phrase and you will be left with the noun that the verb should agree with. If the first noun is singular, add *s* to the verb.

Richard Friedman, a professor of psychiatry at the State University of New York at Stoney Brook, said these studies and others leave little doubt that **episodes [of anger]** <u>*are*</u> dangerous.

Casual observation [of our own cats] <u>suggests</u>, not surprisingly, that they spend little time out of doors on wet and windy days.

Gerunds: These look like verbs, but they are nouns. When they are the subject of the sentence, they are singular (like *it*) and therefore the verb adds *s*.

***Considering* how humans learn new things** <u>helps</u> us refine the definition of conscious thought.

GLR See pages 303 and 347 in the GLR for more information on gerunds and subject-verb agreement with gerunds.

Activity 2-23   Practice Subject-Verb Agreement in Generalizations

Underline the subject in each sentence and then determine if the subject is a singular subject and if you must add *s* to the verb or not. Circle the form of the verb that agrees with the subject. An example is done for you.

1. <u>The subjective experiences of animals</u> *is/(are)* often difficult, perhaps impossible for us to learn about.

2. Learning a new task ***require/requires*** conscious attention at first, but eventually the task becomes automatic.

3. Nonverbal communication of mood or intentions ***play/plays*** a large role in human affairs.

4. The conscious thoughts of an animal ***are/is*** often communicated by the types of calls it gives.

5. Playing recordings of three different alarm calls ***allow/allows*** scientists to test how monkeys respond to each type of call.

Activity 2-24   Writing a Reporting Paragraph and Editing for Grammar

With a partner or in a small group, create a paragraph describing the steps in a research study or experiment that you did or a project involving a series of activities. Edit your paragraph for passive vs. active voice, the form of count and noncount nouns with general reference meaning, and subject-verb agreement. An example is provided.

To determine how pigeons find their way back to their lofts, scientists studied a group of pigeons. As soon as young pigeons were able to fly, the pigeon handlers allowed them to fly freely around their loft. The young pigeons were then released in groups at increasing distances from the loft. This was done to get them used to flying home. When they were able to return home from 50 miles away, each bird was released alone at shorter distances. This was done to build up their enthusiasm for flying alone.

Source: Charles Walcott, "Show Me the Way You Go Home,"
Natural History, November 1989, 43–46.

PUTTING IT ALL TOGETHER

FINAL WRITING ASSIGNMENT

Choose one of the following topics and write a report of no more than three pages. Consult *The Basics of Writing a Report* on pages 41–52. Use non-text material to help explain your information if it will make your explanations clearer to your audience.

1. Choose an activity or special interest that you have first-hand experience with. Write a report in which you give the reader useful and interesting information on the topic.

2. Choose an animal whose behavior interests you and write a report on some aspect of its behavior. This topic will involve library research or research on the World Wide Web. If you use information from other sources, you must give them credit. See pages 90–91 in Chapter 3 for information about how to do this. *Possible* topics include:

   • What is imprinting?
   • What are the social responsibilities of female lions?
   • How do bees communicate?
   • How do wild animals that are raised in captivity behave?

3. Conduct observational research on a topic that interests you and write a report on both your procedure and your findings. Here are some *possible* topics:

    - waste of electricity in your place of residence or at your work
    - methods used by street musicians or panhandlers to get money from strangers
    - how strangers engage others in conversation
    - how people serve themselves in self-serve restaurants (cafeterias, salad or dessert bars, or buffets)

Audience and Purpose

Explore the audience for your report by answering these questions.

Topic:

Audience:

Key Questions:

- What information is my reader expecting?
  * What information about my topic is common knowledge?
  * What questions will readers have about my topic?
  * What do I know about this topic that I am fairly sure my readers don't know and would be interested in?
- What information will be most useful to my readers?
- How will the information be used?

Exploring Your Research Needs:

- Write down as much as you know about your topic.
- Decide whether you need to consult other sources and make a list of these including library research, interviews, the World Wide Web, and/or observations.
- If necessary, make a plan explaining what kind of experiment you will do or what kinds of questions you will ask.

Preparing to Write

The following diagram will help you gather all of your information together and think strategically about what and how to write your report. Fill it in as completely as possible.

Thesis:

Background Information:

Organizing Body Paragraphs in Your Report
(Choose one type of organization and fill in only one side of the chart)

Chronological Order	Classification/Categories
Steps/Procedure followed	**General categories you will discuss**
Step 1:	Category 1:
facts/details/examples	facts/details/examples
Step 2:	Category 2:
facts/details/examples	facts/details/examples
Step 3:	Category 3:
facts/details/examples	facts/details/examples
Step 4:	Category 4:
facts/details/examples	facts/details/examples
Non-text material to clearly present your ideas	**Non-text material to clearly present your ideas**

Self-editing Activity

1. Before giving your draft to a peer, read it again to make sure that it says what you intended and is organized in the best way for this particular writing task. Make any changes needed to improve meaning and organization.

2. Choose and edit your draft for two of the language features reviewed in this chapter. Where indicated, turn to the GLR ⬤ and use the recommended self-editing strategies.

   ❏ use of the passive vs. the active voice to achieve your intended meaning. Also check that passive verbs appear in the correct form

   ❏ correct form of count and noncount nouns when expressing generalizations

   ❏ subject-verb agreement with complex noun phrases

   > **GLR** See page 305, Section 3, for more information on editing passive vs. active voice, page 303 in Section 3 for information on editing for subject-verb agreement, and pages 280–281 in Section 1 for information on editing nouns and articles.

3. Edit your draft for one of the language features reviewed in Chapter 1 that you think may need more careful attention in your writing. Consult the self-editing activity in the previous chapter.

Peer Response Activity

Exchange papers with a partner. Answer the following questions about your partner's paper. Give your peer advice about how to improve the paper:

1. What topic is the writer reporting about?

2. How did the writer organize the information in the body paragraphs of the report? By categories? In chronological order?

3. What did you learn from reading this report? How did the writer make this interesting to you?

4. List sources the writer used. Which source did you find the most informative? Why?

5. Ask the writer two questions about ideas that were unclear in the paper.

6. Make one suggestion to help the writer revise the draft.

LEARNER'S NOTEBOOK

Reflecting on Your Learning about Report Writing

Report what you have learned about writing an effective report. Consider the way you wrote your report as well as the strategies your peers used.

Revise

At the end of your report, write a memo to your teacher explaining two changes you made to your report so that it would be more effective.

• •

This section gives you a chance to apply what you have learned in the chapter to authentic academic assignments. The point here is <u>not</u> to write the assignment, but to <u>analyze</u> how you might deal with the assignment using the skills that you have learned in the chapter.

Human Resources Management

Job Analysis Project: Pick an entry level job in your area. For example, marketing majors should choose jobs in sales, promotions, distribution, etc. MIS majors should choose jobs such as computer programmer, system analyst, etc.

Contact a person who currently holds this type of job (or the person's supervisor) and schedule an appointment. Observe the job incumbent at his/her workplace. Conduct an informal interview with the job incumbent and his/her supervisor in order to collect job-related information. Make sure to take extensive notes. Generate a list of activities and duties from your observation and interviews. Categorize the activities on the list and present these as a questionnaire to the job incumbent. Ask the incumbent to complete the questionnaire. Have the person's supervisor check the questionnaire for accuracy. Based on all the information that you have gathered, write a job description and job specification of the entry-level position that you have observed.

DISCUSSION

With a partner or in a small group, analyze the assignment. Use the following questions for your discussion.

1. In what ways will this report differ from what you have learned about reports? Describe specific differences that you notice.

2. What can you learn about the professor and his/her expectations by reading the assignment? Be specific in this audience analysis.

3. What problems do you anticipate for the writer of this report? What solutions can you offer?

Chapter 3

*I*nvestigating

Aging

GOALS

WRITING
- formulate and investigate a focused research question
- find appropriate sources to answer a research question

GRAMMAR
- practice the grammar of past time narratives to provide evidence
    - use of past tense verbs
    - shifting tenses from present to past tense
    - use of chronological organizers
- practice the difference between colloquial and formal vocabulary
- practice structures used to introduce other people's ideas, words, or research
- practice controlling the strength of generalizations with adverbs

CONTENT
- learn about the secrets of people who live to be over one-hundred years old
- learn about changes in mandatory retirement policies

ACADEMIC FIELDS
Sociology
Economics
Gerontology

Sample Authentic College/University Writing Assignments

The investigating skills you will learn in this chapter can be used to complete college/university assignments like this:

Atmospheric Sciences

In 1986 scientists discovered a large hole in the Earth's ozone layer over Antarctica. Go to the library and **investigate** the current status of this ominous feature. Is the situation getting worse or better?

Sociology of Everyday Life

Investigate what it means to be unoccupied or unemployed. Go to a public place—off campus—with other people around and "do nothing" for ten minutes. That is, stand still and be unoccupied, unemployed. Do not pretend you are "waiting," "sight-seeing," or "doing" anything else. Write a paper that analyzes your experience and why "doing nothing" puts people in such an awkward position.

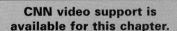

GETTING READY

Warm-up Activity: Writing

In our daily lives we often have questions to answer or problems to solve. For example, you might want to buy a used car, transfer your checking account to a bank that offers smaller service charges, rectify a mistaken charge on your credit card bill, or find the best school to attend.

If you've moved to a new city, you might notice differences between your former community and the new one. What makes the public bus system so convenient? Why don't people recycle their cans and bottles? Why are older buildings torn down and replaced with new ones? Why are there so many ethnic groups living in your neighborhood?

To answer these questions, you could consult a variety of sources: ask a friend or long-time resident for information; make inquiries over the phone or via e-mail; read ads in a newspaper; go to the library; contact a government or private agency; or consult the Internet home pages for various schools.

Activity 3-1   Using Research Skills for Personal Purposes

Imagine you have just won a trip around the world. When you read the fine print at the bottom of the letter that announced your prize, you realize that you have been awarded only $6,000 and that you will have to make at least one stop on all seven continents. In a small group or with a partner, brainstorm the sources you will consult to plan your trip. What sources would you use to obtain the following information?

1. costs and availability of airfare and other transportation

   1. _____
      _____
      _____

2. the exchange rates in various countries

   2. _____
      _____
      _____

3. costs and location of hotels

   3. _____
      _____
      _____

4. interesting sites   4. _____

                                                    _____

                                                    _____

5. weather patterns   5. _____

                                                    _____

                                                    _____

6. special events such as festivals or   6. _____
    religious ceremonies
                                                    _____

                                                    _____

The Basics of Writing a Short Investigative Report

In daily life, you are free to investigate any topic that you need to or that captures your imagination. In college courses, on the other hand, your choice of topics is usually determined by the course syllabus, the topics covered in the course, or the professor's expectations. College courses often present you with problems to solve through investigative research. Here are some examples:

- In a biology class, for example, the professor might ask students to investigate why frogs in a local lake exhibit many physical deformities.
- In a sociology class, students might have to interview women who hold what have traditionally been male jobs to discover what motivated them to choose these professions.
- Engineering students might be asked to consult local building contractors about the challenges of constructing walls capable of withstanding a large earthquake.

LEARNER'S NOTEBOOK

Recalling an Experience Doing Research

In your learner's notebook, write about a problem or question, either academic or personal, that required you to use your investigative skills. What did you investigate? What sources of information did you find most helpful? What was the most interesting information that you found during your search? Compare your experience with that of another classmate.

1. Analyzing Audience and Requirements of Investigating Assignments

In college, each assignment you receive will suggest or specify an audience and purpose. It will shape what kind of information you have to find, what information you will be able to use, and where you will look for it. You can use information about audience and purpose to help you focus your research process.

When professors give a *research* assignment, they often expect that:

in some part or all of your assignment, you will *display* knowledge or research skills that the professor already knows;

in some part or all of the assignment, you will *inform* the professor and your classmates of information that they may not have known before (for example, the most recent research, a new perspective, or interesting organization of facts).

Asking yourself the following questions will help you decide how much to *display* and how much to *inform*.

- Who is my audience? Is it anyone besides the professor? What does the professor already know about the topic? What do other readers already know?
- What information does the professor want me to include?
- What aspect of the topic can I investigate that will provide my audience with new information or new insight about the topic?
- What sources does the professor expect me to use to obtain the information? Are these stated in the assignment or syllabus?
- What sources of information do I have access to? Which do I feel comfortable using? Which don't I feel comfortable using? How can I become more comfortable using these sources?
- Does the professor want me to relate the information I find to course readings and lectures? How should I do this?
- Is there a format to follow when writing the results of my investigation?

Activity 3-2   Analyzing Writing Assignments to Determine When to *Display* and When to *Inform*

With a partner, use the questions listed in *Analyzing Audience and Requirements of Investigating Assignments* to analyze the professor's expectations for each of the following two investigating assignments. Discuss your answers with the rest of the class.

Introduction to Economics
What were the economic effects of the 1992 Los Angeles riots on small businesses in south central Los Angeles?

Introduction to Political Science
Interview several people who have served on a jury within the last year to ascertain their opinions about the experience and the effectiveness of the jury system.

2. Making a Question "Researchable"

Not all questions about a topic will lead to good investigative papers. *Most* questions are too broad, requiring entire books to answer them. Others are too narrow; they can be answered in a paragraph or less. Questions that will result in a fruitful investigation for a paper of about three pages will:

- Require more than a yes/no or a single numerical answer. (What percent of U.S. citizens over 80 experience no major health problems? Answer: 3%.)
- Require more than one-word or one-paragraph answers.
- Lead you on a search for many types of information (reading books, talking with experts, interviewing people who have experience with the topic, viewing documentaries, or searching the World Wide Web).
- Lead to a deeper understanding of the topic. After your investigation, you should know more than when you started, and your knowledge should go beyond everyday knowledge about the topic.

Questions that are too broad can be narrowed so that they can be answered in three to five pages.

EXAMPLE

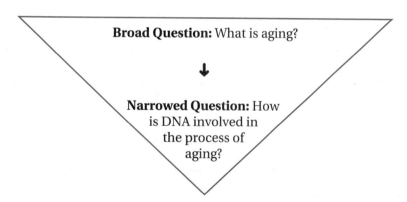

Broad Question: What is aging?

↓

Narrowed Question: How is DNA involved in the process of aging?

When questions are too narrow, you can make them broader. Here is an example of how to make a narrow question broader:

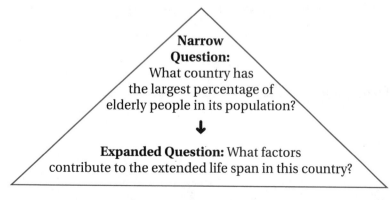

Narrow Question: What country has the largest percentage of elderly people in its population?

↓

Expanded Question: What factors contribute to the extended life span in this country?

Activity 3-3   Brainstorming Questions about Aging and the Elderly

One way to make a question "researchable" is to decide what you already know about the topic and, based on this knowledge, develop a set of questions that you might like to research. To practice this, explore what you know about the topic of this chapter: aging. On a separate piece of paper, make a chart consisting of two columns: *What I Know or Have Observed about Aging and the Elderly*, and *Questions I Have about Aging and the Elderly*. With a partner or in a small group, fill in the chart with any information that you currently know about aging and the elderly. Then generate a list of questions that you would like to find the answers to.

Activity 3-4   Categorizing Questions about Aging and the Elderly

With the whole class, categorize the questions about aging that you developed in Activity 3–3. If you have questions that don't fit the categories below, create new categories.

Aging and Lifestyle _____

_____

_____

Aging and Income _____

_____

_____

The Biology of Aging _____

_____

_____

The Psychology of Aging _____

_____

_____

Aging and Demographics _____

_____

_____

3. Consulting Outside Sources

Some people think that research consists only of reading books or conducting studies in laboratories. Interviews with experts and ordinary people, observations, and consulting the Internet are also considered to be research.

Methods of research

- interviewing experts or people who have experienced the problem
- observing people, places, and events
- reading books, popular magazines, and newspapers
- reading academic journals and research summaries
- obtaining information from the Internet, especially World Wide Web sites
- obtaining brochures and information from private organizations
- consulting government documents
- consulting maps
- viewing television programs, videotapes, or listening to audiotapes

Rich sources of evidence for investigative papers

- personal experience from an interview
- case studies (detailed research on a particular person, group, or situation over a period of time)
- facts
- statistics
- laws and regulations related to the topic
- research findings
- descriptions of places or events
- examples
- quotations from experts

Your goal in researching is to give readers new information or to bring a different perspective to the topic. Make sure that you take notes on all your reading and try to tape record interviews.

Activity 3-5   Discussing the Use of Sources

In a small group, choose and discuss one of the questions about the elderly from Activity 3-4. On the next page, list the question, the audience for whom you will write, and your purpose. Brainstorm a list of sources you might use to investigate your question.

INVESTIGATION PROCESS

Research Question: _____

_____

_____

⬇

Audience: _____

Purpose: _____

⬇

Sources to Consult:

- _____
- _____
- _____
- _____
- _____

Types of Evidence:

- _____
- _____
- _____

---

4. Drafting an Investigative Report

An investigative report should contain:

- A general introduction containing background on the topic you have investigated and a thesis statement that summarizes your "researchable" question.
- Paragraphs to support and explain your thesis statement, each with:
    a general statement (topic sentence) that explains some aspect of the topic;
    details, quotations, and examples that support the topic sentence.
- A conclusion that summarizes the main information in the investigative report.

For further information, consult *Appendix A: Basics Features of Academic Writing.*

The following investigative report was written by Trang Bui, a community college student. Her researchable question was *"What factors contribute to longevity or long life?"* To research this, she read several articles.

"The 120 Year Man," an article that was written in September 1991 by Dava Sobel, shows how people could have a long life. The term "longevity," for most people, was thought to be an impossible thing to achieve not very long ago. Scientists all over the world have been trying to do research in order to help peoples' dreams come true. Fortunately, scientists' endeavors have not been wasted because finally they discovered <u>several factors that contribute to extending the life of elderly people.</u>

Background on the topic

Thesis statement

<u>First</u>, according to James Mold, director of the Oklahoma Geriatric Education Center, <u>"Genetic background is the key factor in determining how long a person can be expected to live"</u> (Sobel, p. 18). He believes that hereditary factors can frequently allow people to get away with harmful behaviors and still lead a long life. Someone could live a longer life than others if their families have a good genetic background generation to generation. In Russia, while researchers were working on their process, they found a village where most of the people were 70 and older. After scientists had investigated, they concluded that those people there had a high age genetic background (Reid, p. 352).

Paragraph Topic sentence

Supporting information from sources

Example from research

<u>Second, although the first factor is very important, eating habits or eating the right way is a good method to prolong our lives too.</u> Roy Walford, an authority on gerontology and longevity, and a professor of pathology at UCLA, hopes and believes that if we follow a carefully devised calorie-restricted diet, we could have a longer life. In his experiments with many laboratory animals, he found that animals lived longer than their normal life span and kept healthy on a restricted diet (Walford, pp. 48–51). As a result, Professor Walford thinks he can do as much for humans as he tested on the animals.

Paragraph Topic Sentence

Supporting information from sources

Paraphrase and details

In conclusion, one of the fantastic dreams of the humanity has become true. People who used to think that life span cannot be extended are now changing their "big mental block." Elderly people can still enjoy healthy lives. Although the explorations of Professor Roy Walford and some other scientists do not get to the final answer yet, those factors bring happiness to a lot of people.

Conclusion

References

Sobel, Dava. (1991). The 120 Year Old Man. *American Health, 10:* 8–19.

Reid, D. P. (1989). *The Tao of Health, Sex, and Longevity: A Modern Practical Guide to the Ancient Way.* New York: Simon and Schuster.

Walford, R. L. (1988). *The 120 Year Diet: How to Double Your Vital Years.* New York: Simon and Schuster.

5. Incorporating Sources

Writers of investigative reports incorporate information from other sources into their writing in the form of direct quotations and paraphrases.

Paraphrase

Paraphrasing means taking a short passage from a source (usually between one and three sentences) and rephrasing it so that it is in your voice and fits into your piece of writing. A paraphrase contains all the information from the original passage, but puts that information largely in your own words. Paraphrases are usually the same length as the source text. We write paraphrases because:

- the words are not memorable enough to quote, and
- the ideas in the source need to be changed in some way to fit the ideas in your paper.

Writing a paraphrase involves the following:

- Select a passage (of 1–3 sentences) that you think makes an important point or supports an idea in your paper.
- Put the passage into your own words and grammar. The best way to do this is to cover up the original passage and rewrite the main ideas.
- Then, reread the original passage again and add to or revise your paraphrase.

Original

One recent study suggests that the numbers of those afflicted with Alzheimer's disease are much higher than previously thought. For the eighty-five and over age group, nearly half may be suffering from this irreversible disease, which strikes most often in later years.

Paraphrase

According to a research study on Alzheimer's disease, more people suffer from this disease than was thought before. About 50% of people over the age of 85 suffer from Alzheimer's.

Quotation

The writing you do represents your ideas and, therefore, should be done in your "voice." In academic writing, however, you are usually balancing your voice with the ideas, research, and theories of other people. You will incorporate quotations from these experts into your writing. Writers are careful about how and what they quote. Here are some guidelines.

- Keep exceptionally memorable quotations.
- Strengthen arguments by referring to acknowledged authorities on the topic.
- Capture the original flavor of the speech used by the person who said the words originally. (This use of quotations is prominent in investigative reports based on interviews.)

Citing Sources

Whether using quotations or paraphrases, academic writers *always identify their sources of information.* This serves to: (1) give their ideas more credibility in the eyes of readers (especially their professors') and (2) allow the reader to consult the same sources as the writer. Academic writers identify sources in three ways, often using all three in the same paper:

1. Identifying people or research they quote or paraphrase:

   "It appears that marked physical and mental decline is typical of the majority of cente- narians," states *Erdmore Palmer, Ph.D.,* in *The Encyclopedia of Aging* (1987).

   A World Health Organization (WHO) study of older people's working capacity recently gathered together the biological facts and concluded that "the definition of an aging worker could be considered to apply from 45 years." Physical performance, at a peak in the early 20s, declines gradually thereafter.

2. Noting the author's last name, year and page number of the source where they found the information:

   As Savory (1959) put the matter, "Of course to interpret the thoughts, or their equiva- lent, which determine an animal's behavior is difficult, but this is no reason for not mak- ing the attempt to do so. If it were not difficult, there would be very little interest in the study of animal behavior, and very few books about it" *(p. 78).*

3. Giving the reader the last name and initials of the author, year, full title of the article or book, journal, or magazine that the article appeared in, page numbers, place of publication, and publisher's name in a *reference page* at the end of their paper. The sources appear in alphabetical order according to the author's last name. An entry appears in the reference page for every source that a writer cites, including all para- phrases, all quotations, and summaries of information from sources.

References

Sobel, Dava. 1991. The 120 Year Old Man. *American Health, 10:* 18–19.
Reid, D. P. (1989). *The Tao of Health, Sex, and Longevity: A Modern Practical Guide to the Ancient Way.* New York: Simon and Schuster.
Walford, R. L. 1988. *The 120 Year Diet: How to Double Your Vital Years.* New York: Simon and Schuster.

GLR   See pages 310–313 in the GLR for more information.

Activity 3-6   Writing Entries for a Reference Page

Turn to pages 310–313 in the GLR and read about the two formats for references. Choose one of the formats and create entries in a reference page for each source below. An example is provided in each format.

1. **Author:** Lynn Peters Adler

   Title: Centenarians: The Bonus Years

   Type of Source: Chapter in a book

   Publisher: Health Press

   Year/Date of Publication: 1995

   Place of Publication: Santa Fe, New Mexico

   Reference Page Entry in APA Format: Adler, L.P. (1995). Centenarians: The Bonus Years. Santa Fe, N.M.: Health Press.

   Reference Page Entry in MLA Format: Adler, Lynn P. Centenarians: The Bonus Years. Santa Fe, N.M.: Health Press, 1995.

2. **Author:** Carol Tavris

   Title: Anger: The Misunderstood Emotion

   Type of Source: Book

   Publisher: Simon Schuster

   Year/Date of Publication: 1982

   Place of Publication: New York

   Reference Page Entry in _____ **Format:**

3. **Author:** Peter B. Churcher and John H. Lawton

   Title: Beware of Well-fed Felines

   Type of Source: Article in a magazine

   Published in: Natural History

   Year/Date of Publication: July 1989

   Page Numbers: pp. 40–47

   Reference Page Entry in _____ **Format:**

FOCUSING

Introduction to Readings

Getting old is inevitable, even though we may not want to think about it when we are younger. Each author in this chapter investigates a different aspect of aging and presents a variety of sources to explore the topic.

Pre-reading Activity

Activity 3-7   Aging Tic-Tac-Toe

Divide the class into two teams, one team X, the other team O. Team X will begin by choosing a question to answer. If team X answers correctly, they put an X in the box. If not, team O gets a chance to provide the correct response or choose a different question and put an O in the box. To win, a team must get three Xs or Os in a row. The correct answers are on the last page of this chapter.

EXAMPLE

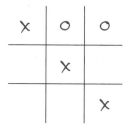

1. In what country do people live the longest? a. Japan b. Russia c. Iceland	2. What is the fountain of youth? a. a mineral bath in southern France b. a mythical source of youth c. a decorative pool in Rome	3. Why do women live longer than men? a. their superior endocrine system and their ability to have children b. their ability to cope with stress better than men c. their genes
4. By how many years is your life shortened if you live in a polluted environment? a. 20 years b. 5 years c. 1 year	5. What factor has no influence on longevity? a. a person's eye color b. diet and nutrition c. the environment they live in	6. What is the best type of physical exercise to do to increase longevity? a. exercise that loosens and stretches b. exercise that is intense and works the body c. exercises that increase your muscles
7. How many people over 100 years old will there be in the U.S. population by the year 2050? a. 25,000 b. 2 million c. 1 million	8. Which socio-economic class lives longer? a. the poor b. the middle class c. the wealthy	9. What is the relationship between alcohol consumption and aging? a. consumption of even small amounts of alcohol shortens one's life b. moderate consumption increases life c. heavy consumption increases longevity

> ### Activity 3-8   Discussing Factors Leading to a Long Life

Think of someone you know who is very old (a relative, friend, acquaintance, or a well-known figure). Explain why you think they have lived such a long life. Would you like to live to be that old? Why or why not? List the advantages and disadvantages of living to be very old. Compare your ideas with a partner's.

READING 1   CENTENARIANS: THE BONUS YEARS (CHAPTER FROM A BOOK)

The following reading is an excerpt from the first chapter in a book about people who live to be 100 years or older. This is not an academic book, but it does contain some references—although not the same as they would be in academic writing. The author who wrote this book interviewed many people who had reached the age of 100 in order to investigate a central question.

Pre-reading Vocabulary: Participial Adjectives and Adjective Compounds

Writers of reports and other types of informational writing often use descriptive adjectives to create nouns that convey more information. These adjectives describe a quality of the noun they modify.

Living to 100 was considered a *rare* phenomenon.

Writers also use other types of adjectives that are created from verbs. These are called participial adjectives and adjective compounds with participles.

Participial adjectives

Centenarians are a *growing* age group in the U.S. population.

Billy enjoys good general health but has one of the common physical impairments of *advanced* age, near blindness.

Adjective Compounds with Participles

Lifesaving drugs and *life-prolonging* devices such as organ transplants and heart pacemakers have also helped people live longer lives.

A good way to increase the adjectives in your vocabulary is to notice single-word adjectives, participial adjectives, and adjective compounds as you read and make a list of new ones that you encounter.

GLR   See page 342 and page 334–335 in the GLR for more information.

Activity 3-9   Using Descriptive Adjectives

Adjectives allow writers to add more information to nouns, but it is sometimes difficult to think of adjectives other than those with general meanings like *many, important, different,* or *various.* To practice using adjectives that have a more precise meaning, rewrite the following sentences by replacing the bolded adjective with an adjective that fits the meaning of the sentence. Choose from the list of participial adjectives and adjective compounds below. An example is provided.

debilitating	life-affirming
diminished	lifesaving
fastest-growing	long-held
increasing	marked

1. **Many** drugs have enhanced the possibility of longevity.

    Lifesaving drugs have enhanced the possibility of longevity.

2. **Large** numbers of people have realized that they can control their lifestyle and live longer.

3. The numbers of centenarians have doubled, making them a **big** segment of the U.S. population.

4. The **common** stereotype of advanced age as a period of decrepitude and disinterest in life is breaking down.

5. Some centenarians are active and alert; others suffer from **harmful** physical impairments and mental diseases.

6. According to some experts, a majority of centenarians experience **obvious** physical and mental decline.

7. Interviews with centenarians show that they exhibit **important** attributes.

CENTENARIANS: THE BONUS YEARS

Americans have been fascinated by longevity ever since learning of Ponce de Leon's search in Florida, five centuries ago, for the fountain of youth. In this century, the search for longevity, and the good health that makes it possible, has been enhanced by discoveries such as antibiotics and other lifesaving drugs, heroic medical interventions, which include organ transplants, heart pacemakers and other life-prolonging devices, the emergence of preven- 5 tive medicine, and a new focus on wellness. On an individual level, people are realizing that, to an ever-increasing extent, they are able to influence life-style factors that can lead to a healthier and longer life—perhaps even a life of 100 years or more.

Until recently, living to 100 was considered a rare phenomenon. Within the past few years, however, with several hundred people reaching the century mark every month, sci- 10 entists and laypeople alike are beginning to look upon these oldest of the old as beacons guiding us to a new, longer lived age—possibly the Age of Centenarians.

We laud those now at the pinnacle of old age—centenarians—who have lived to cele- brate 100 years or more. Today's centenarians are the survivors of a generation born in the 1880s and 1890s. The 1990 census counted 37,306 centenarians, 29,405 of them women. 15 Over the past ten years, their numbers have doubled making centenarians the most rapidly growing age group within the fastest-growing segment of the United States population— those eighty-five and over. Some estimates place the number of centenarians today at 45,000, a number predicted to continue to increase dramatically in the near future, to 108,000 centenarians by the turn of the century and to 400,000 by the year 2025. 20 Worldwide, by the year 2000, it is anticipated that there will be more than one million cen- tenarians.

This is just the tip of the aging iceberg. The number of people living into their eighties and nineties is expected to increase dramatically as well. In fact, there are such great numbers of Americans living beyond what was once considered old age (sixty-five) that 25 some sociologists have begun to delineate three tiers of aging: the young, the middle, and the old of "old age."

To be sure, the long-held stereotype of advanced age as a period of decrepitude and dis- interest in life is breaking down. This stereotype is as obsolete as is the arbitrary age of sixty-five for the time in life when people become, or are considered, old. Centenarians are 30 playing an important part in bringing about this change in attitude about the aging process and about what life can be like in old age: They are the vanguard of aging and highlight its future. As many centenarians demonstrate, not only are people living longer, but they also are remaining physically active and mentally alert while retaining an interest in life into very great ages. 35

By their examples, centenarians are showing us what is possible, and what can be real- ized, if one not only lives long but ages well. Interestingly, many centenarians say they don't feel old—that age is, in large part, a state of mind. Underscoring this thought is the Reverend Roy Miller of Glendale, Arizona, who at 101 often remarked that he did not feel his age. The phrase "young at heart" readily comes to mind in the company of centenarians 40 such as Roy, who was fond of saying "when someone says 'Go,' I'm ready."

Like his peers, Roy did not look his age. This sounds humorous when speaking of a person who has lived so long, yet it is startling to see how good one can look after 100 years of living. "Keeping active definitely improves the way you look and feel," Roy advised, "and makes life merry." 45

Mrs. Lynn Billy Earley of Florence, Arizona has as her motto, "105 and still alive!" Born in New York City on December 10, 1888, Billy says, "There may be old men and women out there, but I'm not one of them." As a friend observed, "Billy takes care of her health. She goes to the doctor whenever necessary and to the dentist regularly; she takes care of her skin and everything!" 50

Anyone who meets her remembers her indomitable spirit, lively sense of humor, and *joie de vivre*. "I refuse to let anything be a problem," she says affably. Yet, like many centenarians, Billy enjoys good general health but has one of the common physical impairments of advanced age, near blindness. Nevertheless, she relishes life and stays active, both at home and on her frequent travels—most notably traveling to Hawaii in 1992 55 to attend the Pearl Harbor anniversary ceremonies and to Washington DC in 1993 to attend the presidential inauguration, including several of the receptions. In the spring of 1994, she visited Graceland and is headed next to New York City "because I want to see Greenwich Village again. I love Arizona, but I miss New York." Sharing her recollections of Greenwich Village eight decades ago, Billy adds "I'm a Greenwich Village 60 person."

Unfortunately, not everyone ages well or ages evenly. For some, physical energy and mobility are diminished and impaired while they remain mentally sound. As 100-year-old Elizabeth Paukert of Faribault, Minnesota tells: "I admire the other centenarians I read about in the newspaper and see on television who can get out to events and do things—I 65 would like to very much. But I try to stay as active as I can, even with my [mobility] limitations. I belong to a volunteer network of other shut-ins through my church and I call people each day. I watch a lot of television and read the newspapers so I can keep track of what's going on in the world. Mentally, I'm very alert and I enjoy being with people; I would love it if I could get around." Aware of the importance of keeping their minds active, 70 many others read newspapers, watch television news and programs, and do crossword puzzles. Some, such as Helen Gibson Cope, who remains both physically and mentally active, enjoy playing word games, especially Scrabble. "She still beats me," Helen's son-in-law and frequent opponent reports.

Then there are thousands of centenarians and others of advanced age who are in good 75 physical health while suffering from debilitating mental diseases, such as Alzheimer's. One recent study suggests that the numbers of those afflicted with Alzheimer's disease are much higher than previously thought. For the eighty-five and over age group, nearly half may be suffering from this irreversible disease, which strikes most often in later years. Some centenarians suffer from other forms of memory loss and dementia, as well as from physical 80 decline. "It appears that marked physical and mental decline is typical of the majority of centenarians," states Erdmore Palmore, Ph.D., in *The Encyclopedia of Aging* (1987), "but there are many exceptions, and many manage to remain alert and positive toward life, despite their [physical] declines."

Active centenarians are inspirations for all who wish to live life to the fullest extent. They are our role models. The knowledge they possess is a tremendous resource. 85 Centenarians know things others do not. No one else knows what it is like to live so long; they are the true experts. Others can speculate, researchers can study, but a centenarian knows for sure, from experience. In order to discover this knowledge, which they are most willing to share, we need to look at what they are doing now and how they have lived in the past. Centenarians can be consulted about the aging process and how to cope with it suc- 90 cessfully.

Certainly, heredity plays a significant role. Most centenarians, but not all, say either one or both of their parents lived to a "ripe old age" for their generation. But then, they wonder, "Why me?" Of several siblings in a typical centenarian's family, often there is only one to survive to the century mark.   95

Longevity studies, by a number of scientific researchers and medical doctors, list factors that appear to contribute to long life, such as a favorable genetic makeup, simple diets with little animal fat, moderation in the use of tobacco and alcohol, physical activity, and a positive mental attitude. However, some centenarians have smoked for decades and some have been overweight. Yet most share the basic advice given by Eli Finn, 102, of Norwalk, 100 Connecticut for anyone wanting to live long: "Eat the right food, exercise, and remain mentally curious."

In general, no particular ethnic group or nationality appears to have a monopoly on reaching 100. There have been reports over the years of so-called "pockets of centenarians" in certain parts of the world, such as Soviet Georgia and Tibet. There, it has been said, the 105 clean air and low-fat diet promote longevity and result in greater numbers living to 100. However, this claim is controversial. Centenarians in America live in all kinds of environments. Some live in the clean air of the Rocky Mountains. Others have survived 100 years in New York City.

By looking at centenarians both individually and as a group, questions about the qual- 110 ity of advanced age are explored. Here, in this piece, the centenarians themselves speak. Their comments dispel some of the myths about the very old. To begin, contrary to one popular perception of old people, most centenarians neither yearn for the past nor live in the past. Most are oriented in the present, and while they appreciate aspects of life that they believe were better years ago, such as more time for socializing, neighborliness, compan- 115 ionship, and the absence of pervasive crime, violence, and drugs, these are the same conditions that people of every age would like to see changed about life.

"In the old days you had time, neighbors and family who cared for each other, and a greater sense of community," explains Mary Ogburn, 105. "Some things were better. But all in all, I like the new days best." Adds the Reverend Joseph Penn, 103, "Every day is a good 120 day." This contemporaneity of today's eldest citizens is amazing. For instance, Lu Lu Doran, 105, who recalls the many years of cooking on the family's wood stove in Nebraska as she was growing up, comments on how much she enjoys the convenience of her microwave oven. Billy Earley's favorite gift on her 100th birthday was a cordless phone: "I can take it around the house with me," she says. "Everybody should have one of these."   125

Another surprising fact is the number of centenarians who are living independently; it is estimated that approximately one-quarter live alone, dispelling the view that nearly everyone of advanced age is institutionalized in a nursing home. As Agnes McDonald, 102, of Bridgeport, Connecticut, says, "I live alone and like it." More often than not, though, they live with family members. Also surprising was the number of men who had remarried in 130 their mid-eighties, usually to "younger women," fifteen to twenty years their junior.

Most of the centenarians had a common denominator among them: a history of hard work. Most believe that "hard work never hurt anybody" and report that they have done plenty of it. Another common denominator seems to be their individualism and a strong sense of self. This self-determination, they say, has helped them get through hard times and 135 heartbreak, the losses of family and friends, and even illnesses that threatened to shorten their lives. Looking at it from their perspective, the ability to cope with losses, to remain optimistic and determined, and to renegotiate life at every turn, is a powerful life force.

Perhaps most surprising of all is the love of life, interest in living, and sense of fun so many express, even at the pinnacle of old age. These life-affirming attributes reverberate 140 through the collective centenarian voice in this survey: "I enjoyed answering these questions and the memories they called forth." "I enjoy everyday of my life." "I get up in the morning happy." "I'm never bored." "I love to laugh." "This was fun."

Source: L. P. Adler, *Centenarians: The Bonus Years* (Santa Fe, NM: Health Press, 1995, 9–18).

Active Reading

Activity 3-10   Identifying the Researchable Question from a Reading Passage

Write the central question that you think led the author to write this investigative report. Share your question with your classmates.

Central Investigative Question: _____

_____

Activity 3-11   Examining Sources

Below is a list of different sources that a writer can consult when investigating a topic. In the first column, put a check (✓) next to the types of sources used by the writer of *Centenarians: The Bonus Years*. Find one example of each type of source you have checked. Then explain the information about aging that each source contributes to the investigative report. An example is provided.

Types of Sources	Information
____ **1.** interviews with experts on the topic	
____ **2.** interviews with people who have experience with the topic	
____ **3.** surveys	
____ **4.** observations of people, places, and events	
____ **5.** books about the topic	
____ **6.** popular magazines and newspapers	
✓ **7.** academic journals and research summaries	Longevity studies, by a number of scientific researchers and medical doctors, list factors that appear to contribute to long life . . .

_____ **8.** information from the
            Internet

_____

_____

_____

_____ **9.** information from private
            organizations

_____

_____

_____

_____ **10.** government documents

_____

_____

_____

LEARNER'S NOTEBOOK

Practicing Paraphrasing Skills

Find one or two sentences that generalize about the attitudes and lifestyle of centenarians from *Centenarians: The Bonus Years.* Try to choose generalizations that will relate to the topic that you chose in Activity 3-5. Paraphrase this idea to use in an investigative report. An example is provided.

Original: As many centenarians demonstrate, not only are people living longer, but they also are remaining physically active and mentally alert while retaining an interest in life into very great ages.

Paraphrase: Many people who have lived to be 100 years prove that people can reach advanced ages and still be physically and mentally active.

READING 2   A GRADUAL GOODBYE (JOURNAL ARTICLE)

The fact that people are living longer not only has consequences for individuals; it also poses political and economic challenges. The authors of the following article investigate the economic problem that will be created as more and more people reach retirement age after the year 2000. Again, because this article was published in a popular journal, it does not contain formal references.

Pre-reading Vocabulary: The Function of Adverbs in Academic Writing

You have probably learned that writers use adverbs to add richness, clarity, and precision to sentences—to give information about *how, when, where*, and *why* things happen. More importantly, academic writers use adverbs to soften or modify the strengths of the general statements they make.

Centenarians *probably* represent the most resilient genetic strain within each generation.

The prediction that there will be more than 1 million centenarians is based *partly* on larger number of people who have been able to reach 100.

GLR   Consult pages 321–324 in the GLR for more information.

Activity 3-12   Controlling the Strength of Generalizations with Adverbs

Compare the following pairs of sentences from "A Gradual Goodbye." How does adding the adverb change the tone and meaning of the sentence? If necessary, look up the adverb in the dictionary. An example is provided.

1. Offering older employees an attractive way to take early retirement minimized the fuss and upheaval. And employees **for the most part** accepted eagerly.

    Offering older employees an attractive way out minimized the fuss and upheaval. And employees eagerly accepted.

    Change in Tone/Meaning: The adverb "for the most part" leaves the possibility that

    there were some employees who didn't want to take early retirement.

2. If people even at the official retirement age can now **typically** expect to live another 15 or 20 years, an early exit might award them half an adult lifetime of economic inactivity.

    If people even at the official retirement age can now expect to live another 15 or 20 years, an early exit might award them half an adult lifetime of economic inactivity.

    Change in Tone/Meaning: _____

    _____

3. Depressingly, the World Health Organization also found that "the speed at which information is processed **usually** slows down **substantially** in older individuals."

Depressingly, the World Health Organization also found that "the speed at which information is processed slows down in older individuals."

Change in Tone/Meaning: _____

_____

4. **To some extent**, older workers can compensate for their slower reactions by experience.

Older workers can compensate for their slower reactions by experience.

Change in Tone/Meaning: _____

_____

5. One solution, used **widely** in Japan and the United States, is for older workers to turn self-employed.

One solution, used in Japan and the United States, is for older workers to turn self-employed.

Change in Tone/Meaning: _____

_____

Activity 3-13   Using Adverbs to Control the Strength of Generalizations in Your Writing

Write three generalizations about retirement. Use adverbs from Activity 3-12 or those **bolded** in "A Gradual Goodbye" to help you control the strength of the generalization you write. Consult a dictionary as well as *Adverbs in Academic Writing* on pages 321–324 of the GLR ⬤. Have a partner or small group check your sentences.

Sentence from "A Gradual Goodbye": Only a generation ago, retirement in rich countries went by the book. The book *generally* said that men were entitled to a pension at age 65, women sometimes earlier.

New Sentence: Society *generally* thinks that once a person reaches the age of 65, he or she can no longer work productively or efficiently.

A GRADUAL GOODBYE

Only a generation ago, retirement in rich countries went by the book. The book **generally** said that men were entitled to a pension at age 65, women sometimes earlier. Until then, most people diligently worked on. In 1970, in most countries 70–80% of men aged 60–64 were still at work.

Twenty years later that proportion had halved. The other half had quietly taken early retirement, often at their employers' suggestion. The arrangement suited both sides. Employers may have wanted to rejuvenate or reduce their workforce, or perhaps even had to close down. Offering older employees an attractive way out minimized the fuss and upheaval. And employees **for the most part** accepted eagerly.

Today's workers have begun to think that it will be their turn to retire next. In France, for example, new rules introduced in the 1970s allowed many people to retire at 60. In 1982 the pension age itself was reduced to 60. "Solidarity contracts" in the 1980s allowed many to go at 55. In Europe and America an early-retirement culture has taken root.

Yet over the past few years many governments have had to rethink. If people even at the official retirement age can now **typically** expect to live another 15 or 20 years, an early exit might award them half an adult lifetime of economic inactivity. Since their numbers are growing fast, this will soon become unaffordable. So some countries are now raising their official retirement age, though they are doing it gradually. America, for example, is increasing the age at which it pays a full social security pension from 65 to 67, but in such tiny steps that it will take until 2022. Other countries, including Germany, Italy, Britain, and Japan are moving in the same way.

On the face of it, raising the retirement age seems an ideal way of dealing with the problem of too many old people. If people are living longer, they should also be fit for work longer, and so can contribute to the cost of their own good fortune. However, paying pensions later will not necessarily keep people in work. The old are often the first to be made obsolete. Once out of a job, they often find it hard to get another one.

Prejudice against older people at work is universal. In an opinion poll taken throughout the European Union, 80% of respondents—of all ages—believed that older workers were discriminated against in job recruitment.

The main reason that employers do not hire older workers is that they suspect them of not being up to the job. Again there may be a grain of truth in this. A World Health Organization (WHO) study of older people's working capacity recently gathered together the biological facts and concluded that "the definition of an aging worker could be considered to apply from 45 years." Physical performance, at a peak in the early 20s, declines gradually thereafter. Eyesight deteriorates and hearing gets worse. This may matter less as fewer jobs rely on physical strength, but depressingly the WHO also found that "the speed at which information is processed **usually** slows down **substantially** in older individuals." On the other hand, "while older managers take more time to reach decisions, they . . . appear to be as competent as younger managers in overall decision-making."

In praise of older workers

According to many employers, older workers—say those over 50—are more reliable, conscientious and loyal than younger ones. They tend to be good at dealing with people and happy to work in teams, though less likely to turn in a sparkling, rather than merely competent, performance. **To some extent**, older workers can compensate for their slower reactions by experience. In one much-quoted American study of typists aged between 19 45 and 72, the older women managed to work as fast as the younger ones, despite slower responses, simply by processing longer chunks of text at one time.

Some employers are taking the hint. In Britain, B&Q, a do-it-yourself chain, has tried staffing some of its stores with over-50s, who are more experienced and better at dealing with customers than younger workers. In France, Aérospatiale has introduced incentives for 50 its experienced staff to stay on until 60, and at Société Générale Sucrière employees between 55 and 60 in part-time retirement come to work during the beet harvest. There are other examples, but not many.

Gently does it

Changing entrenched attitudes will take time. "The age of retirement will have to go 55 up," says Winfried Schmähl, an expert on work for older people at Bremen University. "People understand what needs to be done—they are just not doing it yet." Another German academic, Gerd Naegele of the Institute of Gerontology at Dortmund University, agrees that the lead time must be long: "It takes 10–15 years for the business culture to adjust."

With retirement ages going up, many more older people are likely to run out of formal, 60 conventional employment some time before they are able to draw their pensions. They will need "bridge" jobs, which are likely to be less prestigious, less well-paid, and less skilled than the jobs they had in their main careers. They can also be hard to find. One solution, used **widely** in Japan and the United States, is for older workers to turn self-employed, **usually** in the same broad area that they worked in before. This can offer a dignified, flexible 65 way to keep going.

The idea of making retirement less categorical and more gradual is catching on. In a recent report Geneviève Reday-Mulvey, of the International Association for the Study of Insurance Economics, and Lei Delsen of Nijmegen University argue strongly against what they call "guillotine retirement." Instead, they advocate a flexible transition period between 70 a full-time career and full retirement, typically lasting about five years, which can both spread the pensions burden and give individuals more choice. The spread of part-time employment in a number of countries may offer opportunities along these lines.

Of all the rich countries, Japan keeps its people (or at least its men) at work longest. Although at present the mandatory pension age is only 60, more than a third of Japanese 75 men over 65 are still at work. Since life expectancies in Japan are now the highest in the world—76 at birth for a man, 82 for a woman—that may be a good thing. In a country which by 2030 will have some 32 million over-65s, well over a quarter of the population, it would be unwise to encourage expectations of early retirement. To reinforce the message, Japan has reformed its pension system so that by early next century the basic state pension 80 starts at 65, and early retirement becomes less attractive. The government also offers various subsidies for firms employing people over 60.

Making this work has required flexibility all around. For example, the regular pay raises that in Japan go with increasing seniority now mostly stop at 50. Workers who retire at the mandatory retirement age of 60 are often re-employed either by their firms or by a sub- 85 sidiary, but this always involves a big cut in pay and sometimes a move to part-time work.

Many retirees become self-employed. In a survey of Japanese employees, some 60% said they wanted to go on working even after 65, possibly part-time—not so much for financial reasons, but because they thought it would help them maintain good health and remain active in society. Perhaps these long-lived people know something the West does not. But 90 perhaps the size of their prospective pension has something to do with it after all.

References

Delsen, Lei & Reday-Mulvey. 1996. *Gradual Retirement in the OECD Countries*. Dartmouth Publishing Company.
McManus, Susan A. 1996. *Young vs. Old*. Westview Press.
World Bank. 1994. *Averting the Old Age Crisis*. Oxford University Press.

Source: A Gradual Goodbye in "All Our Tomorrows: A Survey of the Economics of Aging," *The Economist*, January 27, 1996, 5–8.

Active Reading

Activity 3-14   Reading Comprehension: Answering Journalistic Questions

"A Gradual Goodbye" investigates how countries, companies, and individuals are dealing with an increase in the number of elderly in the overall population. After reading, answer the following journalistic questions about new approaches to work and retirement among the elderly.

Journalistic questions about the investigation	Responses from "A Gradual Goodbye"
Who?	
When?	
What?	
Where?	
How?	
Why?	
So what?	

LEARNER'S NOTEBOOK

Practicing Paraphrasing Skills

Choose a one-to-three sentence passage from "A Gradual Goodbye" that interests you or relates to the topic about the elderly that you chose in Activity 3-5.
Paraphrase this idea to use in an investigative report.

Analysis of Language: Using the Grammar of Past Time Narrative to Write an Investigative Report

A. Past Time Verbs and Chronological Organizers

To explain or illustrate a general statement, writers often include narratives. These narratives feature a variety of past tense verbs including *simple past, past perfect,* and *past progressive.* Writers often include chronological organizers to help them organize their story and to help the readers follow the order of events.

In the following example, the authors have used several chronological organizers (marked in *italics*) to indicate when events occurred and that they are changing the time reference. The writers use more verbs in the *simple past* than any other tense. The writers change from *simple past* to *past perfect* to indicate that they are shifting from one time reference to another in the past. In this case, the second paragraph occurs 20 years after the time reference of the first paragraph. The *past progressive* allows the writers to emphasize the ongoing or co-occurring nature of the past event.

Only a generation ago, retirement in rich countries **followed** a pattern. The pattern generally **was** that men were entitled to a pension at age 65, sometimes earlier. *Until then,* most people diligently **worked** on. *In 1970,* in most countries 70–80% of men aged 60–64 **were working.**	simple past simple past simple past past progressive
Twenty years later that proportion **had halved**. The other half **had** quietly **taken** early retirement, often at their employers' suggestion. The arrangement **suited** both sides. Employers **wanted** to rejuvenate or reduce their workforce. Offering older employees an attractive way out **minimized** the fuss and upheaval. And employees for the most part **accepted** eagerly.	past perfect past perfect simple past simple past simple past

GLR   See pages 275–277 and pages 285–286 in the GLR for more information.

Activity 3-15   Identifying Past Tense Verbs

The following paragraph comes from *Centenarians: The Bonus Years*. It contains various past time verbs. Complete the following tasks:

1. Identify the past tenses of the underlined verbs. An example has been provided.
2. Explain why the writer switches from one tense in (2) to another in (3).
3. Explain why the writer switches from one tense in (11) to another in (12).
4. Circle chronological organizers that the writer has used.

Personal Narrative

Louis Kelly, 103, of Scottsdale, Arizona, (1) recalls a memory that (2) <u>imparts</u> a vivid image of one way people (3) <u>lived</u> and <u>traveled</u> long ago: "I can recall it as clearly as if it were yesterday," he says, "And I can see it in my mind's eye. I (4) <u>was standing</u> in a covered wagon looking out the back; my younger sister (5) <u>was sleeping</u> on the bedding on the floor beside me. I (6) <u>realized</u> that my father (7) <u>was driving</u> the team of horses and that this wagon (8) <u>belonged to</u> us—that this <u>was</u> our home. My mother (9) <u>was holding</u> my four-month-old brother in her arms."

In 1890, the Kelly family (10) <u>was traveling</u> from Saunders County in eastern Nebraska, near Omaha, where the children were born, northwest to the Black Hills of South Dakota. Louis's father (11) <u>had heard</u> there (12) <u>was</u> work on the railroad then under construction near what is now Custer National Park.

Verb Tenses

1. _____
2. _____
3. _____
4. _past progressive_
5. _____
6. _____
7. _____
8. _____
9. _____
10. _____
11. _____
12. _____

Activity 3-16   Writing a Past Time Narrative

Interview an elderly person about his or her most memorable experience. Write a short past time narrative (between two and four paragraphs) of this experience, using a variety of past time verbs and chronological organizers. Underline the past time verbs and circle the chronological organizers you have used.

B. Shifting Between Present and Past Tense Verbs in a Paragraph

Since academic writers usually use past time narratives to support general statements, they shift from general statements in the present or present perfect tenses to supporting examples or research studies written in the past tense.

By talking with centenarians, we **begin** to realize just how long 100 years actually **is**, and we **begin** to develop an appreciation for the tremendous changes that have occurred in America during their life times. Take for example, Louis Kelly, 103, of Scottsdale Arizona, whose earliest memory **imparts** a vivid image of the way people lived and traveled long ago. "I can recall it as clearly as if it were yesterday," he says, "And I can see it in my mind's eye. I **was standing** in a covered wagon looking out the back; my younger sister **was asleep** on the bedding on the floor beside me. I **realized** that my father **was driving** the team of horses and that this wagon **belonged** to us—that this **was** our home. My mother **was** on the seat beside him holding my four-month-old brother in her arms."

general statements—
simple present

supporting past time
narratives—past tense
verbs

GLR See pages 178–180 and 298–299 in the GLR for more information.

Activity 3-17 Practice Shifting Between Past and Present Tenses

Fill in the blanks with one of the verbs from the list below to complete the meaning of the sentence. Put the verb in the appropriate tense. If the statement is a generalization, put the verb in present or present perfect tense. If the sentence contains supporting information from past examples or research, put the verb in past tense. An example is provided.

- allow
- begin
- introduce
- make
- reduce
- take

1. Today's workers (a) ___have begun___ to think that it will be their turn to retire next. In France, for example, new rules (b) ___introduced___ in the 1970s (c) _____ many people to retire at 60. In 1982 the pension age itself (e) _____ (*Hint:* passive voice) to 60. "Solidarity contracts" in the 1980s (e) _____ it possible for many to go at 55. In Europe and America an early-retirement culture (f) ___has taken___ root.

• be   • believe   • discriminate

2. Prejudice against older people at work (a) _____ universal. In an opinion poll taken throughout the European Union, 80% of respondents—of all ages—(b) _____ that older workers (c)_____ (*Hint:* passive voice) against in job recruitment.

• be   • manage   • tend

3. According to many employers, older workers—say those over 50—(a) _____ more reliable, conscientious and loyal than younger ones. They (b) _____ to be good at dealing with people and happy to work in teams, though less likely to turn in a sparkling, rather than merely competent, performance. To some extent, older workers can compensate for their slower reactions by experience. In one much-quoted American study of typists aged between 19 and 72, the older women (c) _____ to work as fast as the younger ones, despite slower responses, simply by processing longer chunks of text at one time.

Analysis of Language: Using Informational Grammar to Report Other People's Ideas, Research, or Words

A. Using Adjectives, Nouns, and Pronouns to Identify People

Academic writing often contains quotations from experts or from ordinary people with experience with the topic. When reporting their words, writers identify who these experts are and give their qualifications. They use adjectives, nouns, and pronouns to do this. Quotations from experts and authorities are an important way that writers support their arguments or explanations.

First Reference to an Expert

The first time an expert is quoted, the writer uses the person's full name, occupation or title, and where the person works.

Molecular biologist *Gerard D. Schellenberg* of the Seattle VA Medical Center has reported on a newly discovered gene associated with aging.

Subsequent Reference to Experts

When writers refer to an expert a second time in the paper, they will use the expert's last, or family, name.

If the third reference comes within the same sentence as the second reference or in the following sentence, the writer will use a pronoun.

According to *Schellenberg,* the gene is an exciting discovery and will advance aging research. *He* acknowledges that the gene will not reverse the aging process, but will help people live healthier lives.

First Reference to Non-Experts

When ordinary people are quoted, usually writers give their name and some distinguishing feature such as their age, their occupation, or where they live. The writer uses the person's full name.

Mrs. Lynn Billy Earley of Florence, Arizona has as her motto, "105 and still alive!"

Subsequent Reference to Non-Experts

When writers refer to a non-expert a second time in the paper, they will usually use the person's last, or family name. This gives a more distanced, formal tone to the writing.

Earley says, "There may be old men and women out there, but I'm not one of them." Anyone who meets *her* remembers her indomitable spirit and sense of humor.

Writers sometimes refer to a non-expert by their first names. This gives a more informal or familiar tone to the writing. As with the reference to experts, the third reference to a person within the same sentence or in the following sentence will use a pronoun.

Billy says, "There may be old men and women out there, but I'm not one of them." Anyone who meets *her* remembers her indomitable spirit and sense of humor.

Activity 3-18   Practice Using Adjectives and Pronouns to Identify Experts and Non-Experts

Use the information in the table about experts and nonexperts who have opinions about aging and centenarians to fill in the blanks in the sentences below. Keep in mind whether the reference is the first mention or a subsequent mention.

Full Name	Title	Institutional Affiliation	Gender
Carolyn Bowden	spokeswoman	DC Office on Aging	female
Geneviève Reday-Mulvey		International Association for the Study of Economics	female
Roy Miller	Reverend		male

First Mention

1. Carolyn Bowden, _____ at the _____ , said improvements in health and health care have contributed to people's longevity.

2. In a recent report Geneviève Reday-Mulvey, of _____ , argues strongly against the "guillotine approach" to retirement.

Subsequent Mention

3. In addition, Bowden said that people are eating better and keeping fit. _____ predicts that these habits will continue and more people will reach the age of 100.

4. Instead of a "guillotine approach" to retirement, _____ advocates a flexible transition period between a full-time career and full retirement, typically lasting about five years.

5. Reverend Roy Miller often remarked that he did not feel his age. "Keeping active definitely improves the way you look and feel," _____ advised, "and makes life merry."

B. Reporting Verbs

Academic writers often refer to other people's research and ideas. They signal this to the audience by using verbs such as *show, report, suggest, find, propose,* and *say.* These verbs are usually followed by a *that* clause consisting of *that* + a complete sentence.

> A study by Dr. Murray Mittleman and his colleagues at Harvard Medical School *suggests that* an angry outburst can more than double the risk of a heart attack in some people.

The verb that a writer chooses often gives a signal to the audience about how they should interpret the reported information. Here are some of the possible meanings that these verbs indicate.

1. Some verbs indicate that the writer *agrees* with or is presenting the information in a *neutral* manner, letting the reader judge the information. The writer uses these reporting verbs to signal that the reader can accept the reported information as true.

> The World Health Organization also *found that* "the speed at which information is processed usually slows down substantially in older individuals."

2. Some verbs introduce an element of *doubt, opinion,* or *evaluation* about the reported information. The writer may *doubt* the reported information or may wish the reader to know that not everyone has the same opinion about it.

> Critics *claimed that* the company's decision to close its factory was unjust toward the community because it was violating a contract made 31 years ago when it began operations there.

3. Writers use some reporting verbs to *weaken a general statement.* They use these verbs when they are *not 100% sure* that what they are reporting is true.

> A study by Dr. Murray Mittleman and his colleagues at Harvard Medical School *suggests that* an angry outburst can more than double the risk of a heart attack in some people.

> **GLR** See pages 308–309 in the GLR for more information.

Activity 3-19   Getting the Meaning Right: Reporting Verbs

Writers are very careful when they choose reporting verbs to choose the one that will convey to readers how to interpret the reported information. To become more familiar with the meanings of common reporting verbs, complete the table below. Provide a dictionary definition, as well as an example from the readings in this chapter, the dictionary, or other readings that you are doing. Then make any notes on the meaning that will help you remember how writers use this verb.

Verb	Dictionary Definition	Example	Notes on the Meaning
agree			
argue	to state the reasons for or against	Geneviève Reday-Mulvey, of the International Association for the study of Insurance Economics, argues strongly that people should not be forced to retire.	"argue" signals that the reported information is an opinion and controversial. Notice the contrast with "says" or "states"

Verb	Dictionary Definition	Example	Notes on the Meaning
claim			
conclude			
find			
note			
predict			
report			
show			

Verb	Dictionary Definition	Example	Notes on the Meaning
suggest			
think			

Activity 3-20   Working with the Meaning of Reporting Verbs

Writers are usually very careful about the reporting verbs they choose so that they convey just the right meaning about the information they are quoting or paraphrasing. With a partner or in a small group, eliminate one reporting verb that could not be used in each sentence below. Explain why the two remaining verbs convey the appropriate meaning. Use the meanings from the chart in Activity 3-19 to help you. An example is provided.

1. A recent World Heath Organization study of older people's working capacity *has shown/has suggested/has argued* that physical ability declines slowly after the age of 20.

   "To show" means to find or to clearly demonstrate. "To suggest" implies that a conclusion from research is less certain. "To argue" is not appropriate because studies provide conclusions and studies cannot argue; people argue.

2. Scientists working on the WHO study *have also found/have also claimed/have also observed* that older workers are as good at making decisions as younger ones.

3. Geneviève Reday-Mulvey and Lei Delsen, experts on aging, *argue/think/predict* that governments should not use the "guillotine approach" to retirement, but allow people to keep working even after they pass the official retirement age, if they are able and want to.

4. Many demographic experts *think/predict/conclude* that there will be one million Americans over the age of 100 by the year 2050.

PUTTING IT ALL TOGETHER

FINAL WRITING ASSIGNMENT

Write a three-page investigative report on some aspect of aging that interests you. Either choose one of the topics below or go back to the topic you chose in Activity 3-5. If you choose your own topic, be sure to consult your instructor to determine whether your question is "researchable."

- What treatment is available for elderly people with Alzheimer's disease?
- How do elderly people view the aging process? What do they lose? What do they gain?
- Does your city have an agency responsible for protecting the rights of the elderly? What role does it play?
- What problems with health insurance do the elderly encounter?
- How do families make a decision to put an elderly relative in a nursing home?

Follow the guidelines in *The Basics of Writing a Short Investigative Report* on pages 83–91.

Audience and Purpose

Choose readers who you can inform about the topic you select; in other words, choose a reader or readers outside your class that would find this information useful in some way. The purpose is to *inform* your readers (not to *display* your learning, as you would for a professor).

LEARNER'S NOTEBOOK

Describing Your Audience

In a learner's notebook entry, answer the following questions as fully as you can in order to determine what your audience will need to know about the topic.

1. Who is my audience?
2. What does my audience already know about this topic?
3. What might they want to know or need to know about the topic?
4. What will interest them?
5. What aspect of the topic can I investigate that will provide my audience the information they will need about the topic?
6. If my audience is my professor, what information does the professor want me to include?

LEARNER'S NOTEBOOK

Describing Your Audience (continued)

7. What sources does the professor expect me to use to obtain the information? Are these stated in the assignment or syllabus?
8. Does the professor want me to relate the information I find to course readings and lectures? How should I do this?

Preparing to Write

Use the information from your learner's notebook entry above and what you know about formulating "researchable" questions to revise the question that you will investigate so that it is narrow and focused enough to research.

Original Question: _____?

Revised Question: _____?

Decide which sources you will consult to write this short investigative report:

Sources to Consult

- _____
- _____
- _____
- _____

Types of Evidence

- _____
- _____
- _____
- _____
- _____

Self-editing Activity

1. Before giving your draft to a peer, read it again to make sure that it says what you intended and is organized in the best way for this particular writing task. Make any changes needed to improve meaning and organization.

2. Choose and edit your draft for two of the language features reviewed in this chapter. Where indicated, turn to the GLR 🔘 and use the recommended self-editing strategies.

    ☐ use of past verb tenses, time expressions, and pronouns to give examples from the past

    ☐ clear shifts between the past tense and present tense that are appropriate and clearly signaled to your reader.

    ☐ use of adjectives and nouns and pronouns to identify experts and other people you quote in your draft

    ☐ use of reporting verbs when quoting or paraphrasing the ideas, research, or words of another person.

    ☐ use of adverbs to control the strength of generalizations in your writing

    > **GLR** See page 300, Section 3, for more information on editing for verb tense shift, page 309 in Section 4 for information on editing reporting verbs, and pages 321–324 in Section 5 for information on correct placement of adverbs.

3. Edit your draft for one of the language features reviewed in the previous chapters that you think may need more careful attention in your writing. Consult the self-editing activity in the previous chapters.

Peer Response Activity

Exchange papers with a partner. Answer the following questions about your partner's paper:

1. What investigative question is this writer discussing?

2. What is the most interesting thing you learned about the topic from reading this paper? Why did you find it interesting?

3. What sources did the writer use? Which source did you find the most convincing? Why?

4. Ask the writer two journalistic questions about ideas that were unclear in the paper.

5. Make one suggestion to help the writer revise the draft.

LEARNER'S NOTEBOOK

Reflecting on Your Learning

Report what you have learned about investigating a topic and writing a researchable question. Consider the approach you took to the paper as well as that taken by your peers.

Revise

On your draft, list one part of your paper that needs more support from your sources. Rewrite your paper, including additional information from sources.

* * *

L O O K I N G   A H E A D

With a partner or in a small group, analyze the sample college assignment below using the discussion questions that follow.

Anthropology 9
Life History Assignment

Each person's experience is like a window on his or her culture. Your task is to have a minimum of two interview sessions with a person of your choosing. Select and describe data from your interviews that reflect that person's life history. Analyze how such traditional categories as work, child rearing, social relationships, and belief systems have shaped this person's life.

DISCUSSION

1. What is the purpose of this assignment? To demonstrate knowledge to the professor or to inform the professor and classmates?

2. In what ways will this investigative report differ from what you have learned about investigating? Describe specific differences that you notice.

3. What questions might you need to ask the professor to complete this assignment successfully? Formulate one specific question.

4. What problems do you anticipate for the person doing this investigation? What solutions can you offer?

Chapter 4

Evaluating
Reality in Film and TV

GOALS

WRITING
- create a concise and balanced summary of the subject you will evaluate
- develop criteria on which to base a written evaluation and support your evaluation with examples

GRAMMAR
- practice structures writers use in evaluations to show the logical relationship between ideas and sentences in a text including:

    transition words and expressions
    coordination and subordination

- practice how writers use nouns in writing:

    complex noun phrases or noun + prepositional phrases
    possessive adjectives with complex nouns
    subject-verb agreement when the subject is a complex noun

- practice the use of adjectives and adverbs to convey positive, negative, or neutral tone

CONTENT
- learn how some writers evaluate films based on historical accuracy and realistic portrayal of minority groups
- learn about underlying bias in some films, television programs, and advertisements

ACADEMIC FIELDS
Film and Television
Communication Studies

Sample Authentic College/University Writing Assignments

The evaluating skills you will learn in this chapter can be used to complete college/university assignments like the ones below.

Environmental Geography

Evaluate land use and land-use planning by your college or university.

Political Science

Write a three-page book review of any book that treats a historical topic about the government and politics of the former USSR (pre-Gorbachev). The review should note the main lines of argument in the book and then state your opinion on the quality of the argument, with explicit reasons for your **evaluation.** Note that if you only describe the book and do not evaluate it, the review will be considered incomplete.

 CNN video support is available for this chapter. *Turner* Le@rning
A Time Warner Company

GETTING READY

Warm-up Activity: Writing

Many choices you make are a result of evaluating several options using various *criteria*. When you buy a car or a CD player, a camera or even a pair of jeans, you choose the product on the basis of one or more *criteria*. For example, deciding which car to buy might depend on your *financial situation* (the down payment, monthly payments, and insurance costs), your preference in *color and style*, the *reliability* of the model, etc.

LEARNER'S NOTEBOOK

Identifying Criteria

When you chose the college or school that you now attend, you probably chose among several alternatives and decided which one best met your criteria. Write a letter to a friend who is considering attending your college. Explain the schools you considered and explain the criteria you used to make your choice.

Activity 4-1   Discussing Criteria

Compare your learner's notebook entry with other students in a small group. Make a list of the criteria that all groups members had in common.

LEARNER'S NOTEBOOK

Using Criteria to Make a Decision

In your learner's notebook, write about another decision you have made that required you to make an evaluation. For example, you might discuss such decisions as buying a car, taking a job, choosing a place to take a vacation, choosing which course to take, etc. Explain your decision-making process and list the criteria you used to arrive at your final decision. Compare your experience with that of another classmate.

The Basics of Writing an Evaluation

The questions and problems posed in the warm-up writing activity were of a more personal nature and reflect kinds of evaluating we do on a daily basis. These evaluations, however, are usually done informally, not in writing. You may not have had much experience writing formal evaluations, but you certainly have had exposure to the skills and strategies associated with evaluating.

Evaluation is important in most academic work. Perhaps the most common questions in any academic class are:

- Do you think this is true?
- Do you agree with this?

In your course reading and writing, particularly in social science and humanities courses, you are asked to think critically about what you have read before you accept it. In order to do this, you might ask yourself questions such as "Is this true according to my experience? Is it useful?"

1. Summarizing the Subject

Previous chapters have discussed study summaries and paraphrasing. These are both related to summary writing. Summaries are required everywhere in academic work, on essay exams as well as in term papers. They are especially important in writing an evaluation because your summary provides essential background about the concrete or abstract items/ideas you will evaluate. To create a good summary:

1. Find the key information, ideas, or arguments of whatever you will evaluate. This can be a theory, a law or policy, the plot of a film, book or story, a program or project you participated in. Identify what you consider to be the most important information that <u>your reader</u> will need to know to understand the subject. This will include the *topic*, the *purpose, key information, ideas,* or *arguments.*

2. Write this information as concisely as possible. A summary is always shorter than the original reading.

3. If you are summarizing something you have read, be sure to use your own sentences and words as much as possible to express the author's ideas. There may be cases where you have to use technical or specialized words from the original text.

4. Do <u>not</u> include <u>your own</u> opinion (negative or positive) in the summary.

In the following, Etsuko Nozawa, a university student, summarizes the film *Black Rain* for readers who may not have seen it. A summary of the film is followed by an evaluation of its accuracy in portraying life in Japan and the life of *yakuza* (the Japanese mafia).

Black Rain was released in the early 1990s. Two police officers, Nick and Charlie, in New York City, witness a murder and catch the murderer who is Japanese. Since the murderer, Sato, is a member of the Japanese mafia, *yakuza,* Nick and Charlie are ordered by their boss to transport Sato back to Osaka, Japan. Nick and Charlie, however, are tricked by "pretend" detectives who are really *yakuza* and thus let Sato escape. Nick and Charlie with Masa, who is a Japanese and an assistant detective of Osaka prefecture, start to pursue Sato in Osaka. Because most of the scenes take place in Japan, it also portrays Japanese ordinary people and their customs as well as Japanese *yakuza* and their customs.

Summary of the film's story

It seems that it does not matter to the American moviemakers whether the portrait of Japan is correct or not because their intention is only to give viewers the impression that the story takes place in Japan. *Thus, the movie emphasizes its visual effect more than accuracy. The depictions of Japan and Japanese life in Black Rain are unnatural and emphasize stereotypes.*

Writer's judgment of the film

2. Formulating the Criteria You Will Use to Evaluate Your Subject

Most of the time when we evaluate informally, we merely express our opinion, without necessarily telling our audience our criteria for reaching that opinion. For example, we may say "Nice haircut." We have judged the haircut as "nice" based on certain criteria, but we may not verbalize the criteria. In certain cases we may follow our stated opinion with a reason for it, such as "Nice haircut. *It's very stylish and looks good on you."* Here we have articulated our criteria; it is a nice haircut because it is (1) stylish and (2) looks attractive.

In academic writing, it is important to make your criteria clear to your readers because they will want to see the reasoning or thinking behind your opinion. In the following example of an opinion, the criterion (singular of *criteria*) for evaluating drama programs, *accuracy,* is italicized.

Drama programs on TV are not *accurate* in their portrayal of society because these shows contain too many characters who are professionals while under-representing characters from the working class.

When evaluating more abstract items or ideas like television programs, movies, laws, or policies, the criteria you use might vary widely depending on what you as a writer find important. For example, the writer of the preceding statement used the criterion "accuracy" or "true to reality" to evaluate TV dramas. You could also evaluate TV dramas based on how entertaining the story is or how well the actors performed.

Notice that the smaller and more concrete the item is, the easier criteria are to develop and the more people evaluating will tend to use the same criteria. The more abstract and complex the item or idea is (e.g., laws, policies, issues), the more complicated criteria development is and the less people will agree on what criteria to use when evaluating.

Activity 4-2   Practice Developing Appropriate Criteria for an Evaluation

Working with a partner or in a small group, choose two items from each list that you might evaluate. On a separate piece of paper, list the criteria that you would use if you were to evaluate each one. An example is provided.

Concrete Items to Evaluate	**More Abstract Items or Policies**	**Abstract Ideas, Issues, or Policies**
(Criteria are easy to develop and agree on)	*(Criteria are fairly easy to develop and agree on)*	*(Criteria are difficult to develop and agree on)*
• chocolate chip cookies	• college grading and transfer credit policies	• changes in laws (e.g., a new traffic law, a new law on immigration)
• athletic shoes	• performance of a particular sports team or player	• the issue of whether doctor-assisted suicide should be legalized
• a computer	• a teacher or course	
• a CD player		
• an apartment/place to live		
• a long distance phone company		
• a restaurant		

EXAMPLE

Concrete Item	*Abstract Item*
laundry soap	no-smoking laws (laws passed by cities that prohibit smoking in restaurants and inside public buildings such as schools and administrative offices)
Criteria	*Criteria*
price	fairness to the smoker
effective cleaning power	fairness to the non-smoker
the scent it leaves in clothes	government's responsibility to promote and maintain health
the texture it leaves	protection of smoker's constitutional rights
availability (where you can buy it)	protection of non-smoker's constitutional rights
environmental impact	

3. Stating Your Judgment of the Subject

When you evaluate, the easiest step is to state your judgment (opinion) about the topic. For example, "The movie *Gone With the Wind* is excellent/interesting in places, but mostly boring." The judgment can be negative, positive, or contain elements of both, but it must be clear for the reader. Usually, academic writers include both their judgment and their overall criteria in their thesis statement.

EXAMPLES OF NEGATIVE JUDGMENTS

The movie *Black Rain does not transmit correct information about the Japanese,* but rather *emphasizes stereotypes.* It seems that *it does not matter to* the American movie-makers *whether the portrait of Japan is correct* or not because their intention is only to give viewers the impression that the story takes place in Japan.

Islam and Islamic characters have been a subject of *too many negative images.* Both are portrayed as sexist, abusive, and violent. *This false ethnic character* has been promoted by Hollywood and the media. The film, *Not Without My Daughter,* is one such Hollywood film. It is *without any understanding* of the people, the country, and the religion it condemns.

EXAMPLES OF POSITIVE JUDGMENTS

Gone with the Wind accurately portrays the life of white plantation owners in Georgia before the Civil War.

The movie *Black Rain portrays* Japanese *yakuza* and their customs *well.* The *yakuza's* practices *are shown accurately* in the movie by introducing the relation between a boss and his followers.

See page 349, Appendix A for more information.

4. Supporting Your Judgment with Examples

Writers help readers understand and accept their evaluation by further developing their evaluations with examples. Here is how the student who evaluated the film *Black Rain* supported her evaluation.

In order to **give the impression of typical Japan**, certain scenes in the movie *Black Rain* are shown based on **stereotypes with some exaggeration**. In all eating scenes (which happen five times), for example, Japanese people and even Nick only eat noodles. Surely, noodles are Japanese traditional food, but it does not mean Japanese people eat noodles at every meal every day. Just like Americans, Japanese also eat other foods such as Italian, French, Chinese, other	Statement of Evaluation and Criteria ⇨ *not accurate; not typical* Example 1: Japanese food

kinds of Japanese food. Another example is the way Japanese men are portrayed in the movie. A man in the police station is shown according to a stereotype; that is, wearing glasses and often making bows. Particularly the Japanese custom of greeting is exaggerated comically. Most Japanese men in the movie make bows unnecessarily, saying "*Hai, Hai.*" The movie confirms the stereotypes that Americans are familiar with.

Example 2: men's greeting and appearance

5. Audience and Tone

Because people often hold opposing opinions about the same subject, it is important to adopt a tone in your evaluation that will not offend. We can think of tone in evaluation as being on a continuum from strongly positive to strongly negative. In newspaper editorials or letters to the editor, a tone that conveys the writer's emotions, even strong emotions, is often acceptable. On the other hand, academic writers often adopt a more neutral tone while at the same time giving a clear positive or negative evaluation.

Here are some examples. Notice how the writer's choice of verbs, adjectives, and adverbs affect the tone.

Tone	Example	Reader's Impression of the Content or the Writer
overly positive	This *powerful and moving* film is *the most excellent* depiction of plantation life in pre-War Georgia *ever made.*	Readers might be somewhat doubtful about the accuracy of the content. The writer may seem superficial or insincere.
strongly positive	The film is an *excellent* depiction of the historical reality of plantation life in pre-War Georgia.	The content seems clearly positive. The writer seems enthusiastic and sure of the positive judgment.
somewhat positive	The film is a *fairly accurate* depiction of the historical reality of plantation life in pre-War Georgia.	The content seem balanced, and is not too positive. The writer seems credible, and not overly enthusiastic.

Tone	Example	Reader's Impression of the Content or the Writer
neutral	The film *is* a depiction of plantation life in pre-War Georgia.	Notice the absence of adjectives or adverbs and the use of a neutral verb. The content seems informative, and lacks any kind of judgment. The writer seems to have no opinion.
somewhat negative	The film *attempts* to present a *fairly accurate* depiction of the historical reality of plantation life in pre-War Georgia.	The content seems somewhat critical. The writer seems credible, but negative.
strongly negative	The film *fails* to *accurately* depict the historical reality of plantation life in pre-War Georgia.	The content is categorically critical. The writer seems sure of the negative judgment.
overly negative	The film *fails miserably* in its attempt to depict plantation life in pre-War Georgia. In fact, it *completely distorts* the historical reality of what it was trying to portray.	The content is potentially offensive. The writer seems angry and unable to be sensitive to readers.

Activity 4-3   Developing the Components of an Evaluation

In a group or with a partner, choose a television commercial or a popular magazine advertisement to evaluate. Work together to develop the components of a formal evaluation. Choose your criteria from the list in Column 2 below. In the form of a class presentation, explain the components of your evaluation.

Summarize the commercial	Choose the criteria for your evaluation
	Realism • How does the commercial portray a certain group? • How accurately does it capture everyday life? Is it realistic? **Truth/Accuracy of Claim** • Can the product do what the commercial promises? • Is there inaccuracy in the commercial? **Effectiveness** • Does it convey its intended message successfully?
State your evaluation	**Provide one example to support your evaluation**

FOCUSING

Introduction to Readings

Television, films, and newspapers not only entertain, but also give us messages about our lives and our world. The media are so powerful that they often subtly (or not so subtly) teach us about history and society. Because of their widespread influence, it is important to critically examine the images of history and society that the media communicate. Each author in this chapter evaluates the way in which the media depict an aspect of society or history, basing this evaluation on the criterion of *accuracy*.

Pre-reading Activities

Activity 4-4   Making and Supporting a Judgment

Think of a film that deals with a historical event, an important period of history, or the life of a particular ethnic group. What was your judgment of this film? Why? Develop criteria to evaluate the film, and give examples from the film to support your judgment. Share your judgment and criteria with a partner.

Pre-reading Vocabulary

Activity 4-5   Working with Word Forms

The words below are found in this chapter's readings, *Gone with the Wind* and *Luigi, Tony, and the Family*. Consult a dictionary to find the other forms of the word. Keep in mind that the meanings may change slightly as the word form changes. An example has been done for you.

Verb	Noun	Adjective	Adverb
	authenticity	authentic	authentically
XXXXXXXX	accuracy		
	exploitation		XXXXXXXXX
XXXXXXXXX	reality/realism		
XXXXXXXXX	flaw		XXXXXXXXX
		idealized	XXXXXXXXX
	stereotype		
		reflective	XXXXXXXXX
		distorted	XXXXXXXXX
	misinterpretation		XXXXXXXXX
misrepresent			XXXXXXXXX
XXXXXXXXX	intelligence		

Activity 4-6   Expanding Vocabulary for Writing

Past Imperfect: History According to the Movies was written for a general audience. It contains words and expressions that are colloquial. Academic writers tend to use different words than those they would use when speaking. These more formal words often allow them to create sentences with more precise meaning. Rewrite the following sentences for an academic audience by replacing the italicized verbs with appropriate synonyms in the list. Make sure that the verb replacement agrees with the subject and is in the correct tense. In some cases, more than one synonym is possible. An example has been done for you.

- symbolize
- attempt
- encourage
- recognize
- focus on

- overlook
- sacrifice
- witness
- address
- opt

1. Most films that feature African American characters do not *deal with* the contemporary concerns about their treatment in society.

   Most films that feature African American characters *do not address/focus* on the contemporary concerns about their treatment in society.

2. The movie never *tries* to highlight the racial struggles of the day.

3. The media's treatment of ethnic groups *asks* all of us to accept pre-fabricated images of other groups.

4. The film's story *looks at* how two brothers resolve their differences.

5. Because many women couldn't handle the demands of managing a large plantation, they *chose* instead to pretend they were ill.

6. If we say that the media accurately reflects ethnic experiences, this *leaves out* the distorted dimension of "reality" in films and TV.

7. At the beginning of the Civil War, Rhett Butler *understands* that the North is militarily superior to the South.

8. David O. Selznick *gave up* accuracy to suit the goal of making a popular film.

9. Butler's decision to enlist in a nearly defeated Southern army *stands for* what thousands of other Southern men did at the time.

10. Rhett Butler *sees* the heartbreak that Southern defeat is causing.

LEARNER'S NOTEBOOK

Using Academic Expressions

In your learner's notebook, use four of the academic words or expressions from Activity 4-6 to write a sentence about a film you have seen.

READING 1   *GONE WITH THE WIND* (CHAPTER FROM A POPULAR BOOK)

Gone with the Wind is probably one of the most popular films ever made in the United States. Made in the 1930s, the film portrayed the effects of the Civil War on a plantation-owning family, particularly the daughter, Scarlett O'Hara. The movie is also a love story between Scarlett and Rhett Butler. In the following chapter from a book, the writer evaluates the historical accuracy of how the film depicts life in the Civil War South for two groups: white plantation owners and African Americans.

GONE WITH THE WIND

Gone with the Wind is the most popular American historical film ever made. The single most influential interpretation of the Civil War in twentieth-century popular culture, the film has defined that war 5 for a mass audience. Boldly claiming to be true to history, *Gone with the Wind* inserts dates and other historical material before key scenes, using such "history" to legitimize its Hollywood version of the planta- 10 tion past.

The filmmakers may have proclaimed their commitment to authenticity, but their commitment to accuracy was limited. In the film's opening scenes, blacks pick cot- 15 ton despite the fact that plantations never harvested cotton in spring. (We know it's spring because the drama opens with news of the April 1861 attack on Fort Sumter.) In this case, as in many others, producer 20 David O. Selznick sacrificed accuracy to suit his larger goals.

Gone with the Wind was designed to succeed simultaneously as a war film and as a "woman's picture." In telling the story of 25 Rhett Butler's heroic role in the Civil War and Scarlett O'Hara's emotional saga, Selznick combined two winning formulas of Hollywood's Golden Age. All else is merely backdrop for the characters' 30 struggles.

The film's most controversial aspect remains its portrayal of race relations. *Gone with the Wind* may have been the first plantation film to feature African-American characters who *don't* sponta- 35 neously burst into song, but the picture still reflects historians' inaccurate view of the African-American experience, portraying happy-go-lucky "darkies" loyal to benevolent masters. This view dominated 40 the study of U.S. history during the first half of this century. Although Selznick consulted with the NAACP (National Association for the Advancement of Colored People), he nevertheless concen- 45 trated on his white audience, not the black protesters, and the film reflects his attitude.

The film contains stereotypical images—slave children fanning sleeping 50 belles, a loyal slave being rewarded with his late master's watch, and a grinning black carpetbagger riding in a fine carriage beside an unscrupulous white man. The movie never attempts to highlight the 55 racial struggles of the day. Nor does it take any effort to address the very articulate and eloquent challenges made by African Americans seeking their own autonomy.

Gone with the Wind does not address 60 contemporary concerns about the treatment of African Americans. Hattie McDaniel's portrait of Mammy may have won her an Academy Award in 1939 (the first black performer to win such an honor), but because of Georgia's segregation laws she didn't attend the film's Atlanta premiere.

Not surprisingly, the film more accurately depicts the white South. Its glimpses of the O'Hara household reflect the historical reality of an up-country plantation in prewar Georgia. Gerald O'Hara's humble foreign origins mirror the experiences of a large percentage of ante-bellum planters. Jonas Wilkerson reports to Ellen O'Hara on his daily planting, demonstrating the plantation mistress's authority on the estate—a fact rarely reflected in historiography, although frequently underscored in historical fiction.

Ellen O'Hara's brief appearances demonstrate the mistress's competent and crucial role in managing her husband's property—as well as in caring for the sick, delegating responsibility, ministering to neighbors, and enforcing moral standards. Mrs. O'Hara is the very soul and engine for not only her family but also her husband's slaves and employees. In fact, the job of mistress of the house was so rigorous and demanding that many women checked out of the process altogether, opting instead to feign illness.

Scheming southern women have long been a popular focus of fiction (Lillian Hellman's *The Little Foxes*, for example). Thus Scarlett O'Hara's famed conniving and fierce independence are often seen as just another instance of literary fantasy.

However, Scarlett's transformation in the face of calamity from southern belle to matriarch was not unusual during Reconstruction. Like most women of her time, Scarlett found herself forced by economic necessity into a male domain.

Scarlett's desire to protect her home, Tara, and her family (indeed, even to commit murder); her mercenary marriage and disreputable business deals; her exploitation of convict labor; and her flaunting of gender conventions create a heroine both unforgettable and quite faithful to the historical record.

Rhett Butler's character is even more accurately grounded. At the outset, he recognizes, as did many southern moderates, that "the Yankees are better equipped than we. They've got factories, shipyards, coal mines, and a fleet to bottle up our harbors and starve us to death." However, once Butler witnesses the heartbreak of impending defeat ("Take a good look, my dear. It's a historic moment. You can tell your grandchildren how you watched the Old South disappear"), the former cynic, in a noble and honorable gesture, heroically enlists in the Confederate army. Butler's conversion experience—to sacrifice for a higher cause—symbolized that of thousands of volunteers whose decision to go to war redefined mid-century America. Butler's soul is the soul of every soldier. Thus, despite flawed historical interpretation, the movie still flourishes and entertains. Its Technicolor historical pageantry is every bit as seductive now as when the film premiered in 1939.

Catherine Clinton, "Gone with the Wind," in Mark C. Carnes, Ed., *Past Imperfect: History According to the Movies* (Henry Holt & Company, Inc., 1995).

Active Reading

Activity 4-7 Annotating Key Information in a Reading Passage

Reread and annotate the article *Gone with the Wind* in the following way:

- Underline sentences in which the author evaluates (praises or criticizes) the historical accuracy of the movie.
- Circle words that state the criteria used by the writer.
- Bracket several examples that the writer gives to support her evaluation.

Activity 4-8 Writing a Summary

Based on the parts you have annotated, write a summary of the article *Gone with the Wind* for someone who has not read the original. See pages 17 and 123–124 for information about how to write an effective summary.

Activity 4-9 Identifying Judgments and Tone

In the following sentences, circle the adjectives and adverbs that express the writer's judgment and convey her tone. Some sentences will contain both an adjective and an adverb that modify the tone. An example has been done for you.

1. The filmmakers may have been committed to authenticity, but this commitment was (limited.)

2. *Gone with the Wind* may have been the first plantation film to feature African-American characters who *don't* spontaneously burst into song, but the picture still gives an inaccurate view of the African-American experience at that time.

3. The film more accurately depicts life among white southern plantation owners.

4. As hundreds of diaries and letters from the era testify, Scarlett's hardships are all factual.

5. Scarlett's actions during the war—her desire to protect her home and her family, her marriage for money—create a heroine both unforgettable and quite faithful to the historical record.

Activity 4-10 Using Adjectives and Adverbs to Convey Tone

Write four sentences that evaluate a film you have seen. Use adverbs and adjectives from the list below to control the tone of these evaluative statements. Nouns and verbs that might be useful are also listed.

EXAMPLES

Black Rain is an <u>inaccurate portrayal</u> of daily life in Japan.

Black Rain <u>quite accurately depicts</u> the rules that exist among members of the *yakuza* or the Japanese mafia.

Adverbs	Adjectives	Nouns	Verbs
quite	accurate	commitment to accuracy	reflect
more	inaccurate	view of	portray
all	excellent	portrayal of	depict
fairly	limited	image of	present
accurately	factual	depiction of	
inaccurately	faithful to reality		
in a limited way	true to life		
excellently	stereotypical		

READING 2   LUIGI, TONY, AND THE FAMILY (CHAPTER FROM A BOOK)

This chapter, taken from the 1992 book *Make-Believe Media: The Politics of Entertainment*, evaluates the way in which Italian-Americans have been portrayed in films and television. Read to discover the author's evaluation of how this group has been viewed.

LUIGI, TONY, AND THE FAMILY

By the 1970s, ethnicity had become a subject of popular interest, enough so to attract the attention of the mass media. Ethnic characters and explicit ethnic references soon became common fare in television situation comedies, cop and crime shows, commercials, and Hollywood films. 5

To illustrate how the media handle or mishandle the ethnic experience, I will concentrate on Italian-Americans. The screen treatment of this group provides one of the many unfortunate examples of what the make-believe media are capable of doing. In the late 1970s, the Italians were "discovered" by Hollywood. With 10

stars like Al Pacino, Robert De Niro, Sylvester Stallone, and John Travolta shouting, shooting, punching, or dancing their way across the screen, the Italians had become one of Hollywood's favorite ethnic groups. But at what price? 20

The Stages of Stereotype

How have Italian-Americans been represented in the media? In ways not unlike other ethnic groups: 25

The Invisible Man. For a long time the Italian, like every other ethnic, was invisible, nonexistent. Be it radio, movies, television dramas, or popular literature, the world was inhabited by middle- and upper- 30 middle-class whites, creamy-faced suburban youngsters with executive-looking fathers and trim American-beauty mothers, visions of Anglo-Protestant affluence and gentility.

The Grateful Immigrant. One of the typical characters of the late 1940s and early 1950s became a featured personality in a radio series and subsequently a television series called *Life with Luigi.* Played by an Irish-American actor, J. Carroll Naish, Luigi was the sweet immigrant who spent his time gratefully exclaiming, "Mama mia, I'm-a-love-a dees-a bootifull-a country, Amerrreca!" Naish's understanding of an Italian immigrant's looks, accent, and mannerisms bore little resemblance to the real thing. In Luigi and characters like him, we had evidence that the immigrant was not a victim but a joyful, appreciative beneficiary of his adopted country.

The Mafia Gangster. In the fearful imagination of nativistic America, crime was always associated with the big city and the swarthy foreigner. In the 1930s and 1940s, the Italian mobster had to share the Hollywood screen with his Irish and Jewish counterparts. In later years, with television series like "The Untouchables" and movies like *The Godfather,* the Italian was fashioned into the archetypal gangster, so that eventually the association of Italian-Americans with crime was instantaneous and international.

With the help of the media, a few thousand hoodlums in the organized rackets who are of Italian origin, representing a tiny fraction of the Italian-American population, became representative of an entire ethnic group. The Mafia association became one of those respectable forms of bigotry.

There have been Irish, Jewish, Black, Latino, Italian, and even Anglo-Protestant mobsters in our history. None of these gangsters is representative of the larger ethnic groups from which they happened to originate. Needless to say, none of the movies dealing with such characters has ever provided an authentic rendition of the rich cultural heritages and working-class histories of these groups.

The Jivy Proletarian. In the 1970s, the media discovered commercial success in a new working-class, streetwise Italian such as characters like Henry Winkler's "the Fonz" or John Travolta's Vinnie Barbarino (unschooled even when going to school), and sometimes a Cinderella as in *Rocky* (I, II, III, IV, V) or in *Saturday Night Fever* (1978). The frequent appearance of this Italian working-class type, action-prone, nonintellectual, at home with sex and violence, was a flashy variation of an older stereotype—nonintellectual, acting on their emotions, living a life worth escaping. The media's ethnic bigotry is also class bigotry.

Sempre Mafia

Of the various Italian stereotypes in the media, the Mafia image is the most enduring. Almost forty years after television first featured the Italian mobster in "The Untouchables," Mafia characters continued in abundant supply in films and TV series. As if to demonstrate that nothing changes, in 1990 alone Hollywood gave us *The Freshman, My Blue Heaven, King of New York, Miller's Crossing, Godfather III,* and *Good Fellas.* In all of them, Italian mobsters either are the central characters or play important supporting roles.

After being fed enough of this fare, we need to remind ourselves that not all Italians are gangsters and not all gangsters are Italian. As with other ethnic groups, in the last several decades Italians have moved in noticeable numbers into government service, political life, the professions, and the arts. And the introduction of ethnic themes into story lines other than those occupied by Hollywood stereotypes might represent a refreshing and appealing departure from the usual fare.

A film featuring Italian-Americans that is done with more intelligence and realism is *Dominic and Eugene* (1988), which tells the story of fraternal twins who plan on sharing a house together. One brother is being helped through medical school by the other, who is a sanitation worker. The story focuses on how they resolve the contradictions that face them while managing to remain close. *Dominic and Eugene* is touching, but not oversentimentalized or overdone. The Italian-American identities of the brothers and some neighbors are established early and easily and do not figure into the plot in any prominent way, except to leave us with an impression that Italian working-class people are human and decent, capable of living lives that are worthy of narrative treatment—without the assistance of a single gangster.

Spaghetti Benders for Madison Avenue

Once ethnicity became an acceptable media topic, it was not long before ethnic types were worked into television ads. The TV commercial is the quintessential propaganda message: single-minded, brief, simple, slick, and repetitive. Ethnic stereotypes offer their own instant recognition: elegant and snobbish French recommend the best wines, perfumes, and mustards; sweaty, robust Irishmen endorse the right deodorant soap; Germans offer up the best beer; while Japanese prove their love for the extra light beer in the way they supposedly know best—by smashing a table in half with a karate blow.

In the world of commercials, Italians tend to be simple-minded creatures who like to eat. They taste, sip, eat, chew, and offer exclamations such as "Mama mia! Datza spicy meatball!" The stereotypic linking of Italians with food so predominates as to preclude this ethnic group's association with other areas of life (except crime, of course).

Their days taken up with trips to and from the kitchen, Italians, no doubt, would be a poor choice when it comes to chairing a board meeting, offering medical advice, or conducting a scientific experiment, notes Marco Ciolli. "Certainly, no commercial has ever shown an Italian-American involved in any professional activity." A leader of the National Italian-American Foundation complained that "commercials are outdated and subconsciously give a negative image to people who have never had any personal contact with Italians."

To say that the media merely reflect reality is to overlook the distorted dimension of the "reality" presented. The media's tactic is to move *with* (rather than against) the stereotypical notions about one group or another, rather than against them. If there are misconceptions that can easily be made plausible, amusing, or sensational, then the media will use them. Madison Avenue's goal is to manipulate rather than educate. So the media merchandisers promote the crudest impression of ethnics held by the public, encouraging each group to accept the prefabricated images of other groups.

Source: Michael Parenti, *The Make-Believe Media* (St. Martin's Press, Inc., 1992).

Active Reading

Activity 4-11   Finding Key Information in Reading Excerpts

Read the following excerpts from *Luigi, Tony, and the Family* and, in the box provided:

1. Circle the type of judgment (positive or negative) contained in each excerpt.

2. Write down the key words or phrases that indicate the writer's judgment.

An example is provided.

1. There have been Irish, Jewish, Black, Latino, Italian, and Anglo-Protestant mobsters in our history. None of these hoodlums is representative of the larger ethnic groups from which they happened to originate. Needless to say, none of the movies dealing with such characters has ever provided an authentic rendition of the rich cultural heritages and working-class histories of these groups.

Writer's judgment
positive   negative

Support from paragraph

none of these hoodlums is
representative

none of the movies provide an
authentic rendition

Writer's criterion
realistic or accurate portrayal of the
actual lives of the ethnic group

---

2. In the 1970s, the media discovered commercial success in a new working-class, streetwise Italian who was neither a cop or a crook, but sometimes a comedy character like Henry Winkler's "the Fonz," and sometimes a Cinderella as in *Rocky* or in *Saturday Night Fever* (1978). The frequent appearance of this Italian working-class type, action-prone, at home with sex and violence, was a flashy variation of an older stereotype—nonintellectual, acting on their emotions, living a life worth escaping. The media's ethnic bigotry is also class bigotry.

Writer's judgment
positive   negative

Support from paragraph

Writer's criterion
realistic or accurate portrayal of the
actual lives of the ethnic group

---

3. A film done with intelligence and realism is *Dominic and Eugene* (1988), which tells the story of fraternal twins who plan on sharing a house together. The story focuses on how they resolve the contradictions that face them while managing to remain close and stay committed to each other. The Italian-American identities of the brothers and some neighbors are established easily and do not figure in the plot in any prominent way, except to leave us with an impression that Italian working-class people are human and decent.

Writer's judgment positive negative **Support from paragraph**	**Writer's criterion** realistic or accurate portrayal of the actual lives of the ethnic group

4. In the world of commercials, Italians tend to be simple-minded, oral creatures. They taste, sip, eat, chew, and offer exclamations such as "Mama mia! Datza spicy meatball!" The stereotypic linking of Italians with food so predominates as to preclude this ethnic group's association with other realms (except crime, of course).

Writer's judgment positive negative **Support from paragraph**	**Writer's criterion** realistic or accurate portrayal of the actual lives of the ethnic group

Activity 4-12   Summarizing a Reading Passage

Reread and annotate the key information, ideas, and arguments in *Luigi, Tony, and the Family*. Then write a summary for someone who has not read the original article. See pages 17 and 123–124 for effective summary writing strategies.

Activity 4-13   Identifying Tone

Read the following sentences from *Luigi, Tony, and the Family*. Write the tone of each sentence in the blank and underline the words that contribute to its tone. An example is provided.

- strongly positive   • somewhat positive   • neutral
- somewhat negative   • strongly negative

strongly negative   **1.** <u>Needless to say</u>, <u>none</u> of the movies dealing with such characters has <u>ever</u> provided an authentic rendition of the rich cultural heritages and working class histories of these groups.

_____   **2.** The screen treatment of this group provides one of the many unfortunate examples of what the make-believe media are capable of doing.

_____   **3.** To say that the media merely reflect reality is to overlook the distorted dimension of the reality presented.

_____   **4.** A film done with more intelligence and realism is *Dominic and Eugene* (1988).

_____   **5.** The media's tactic is to portray cheap, simplistic notions about one group or another.

_____   **6.** The media merchandisers appeal to the crudest impressions of ethnic groups held by the public.

LEARNER'S NOTEBOOK

Considering How the Media Portrays Ethnic Groups

Imagine that the author of *Luigi, Tony, and the Family* asked you to write an article evaluating how the media portray your ethnic group. What evaluation would you make of this portrayal? What examples could you use to support your evaluation? Share your evaluation with the class.

Analysis of Language: Using Informational Grammar to Write an Evaluation

A. Creating Logical Connections Within and Among Sentences

In academic writing, writers are expected to use language that helps readers understand the logical relationships between sentences and ideas in the readings. Writers include words such as *however, thus, in fact,* and *for example* to be sure that their readers understand the logic of the piece of writing.

for example—signals that the sentence contains details or information that show what the writer means.

> This in turn means that conscious awareness is more likely when the activity is novel and challenging; striking and unexpected events are more likely to produce conscious awareness. *For example,* Janes (1976) observed nesting ravens make an enterprising use of rocks.

thus—signals that the idea in the sentence is the result or logical conclusion of something that has been previously mentioned.

> When a leopard or other large carnivore approaches, the monkeys climb into trees. But leopards are good climbers, so the monkeys can escape them only by climbing out onto the smallest branches, which are too weak to support a leopard. When the monkeys see a martial eagle, they move into thick vegetation close to a tree trunk or at ground level. *Thus* the tactics that help them escape from a leopard make them highly vulnerable to a martial eagle, and vice versa.

nevertheless—signals an unexpected piece of information or result from what readers would expect based on the information in the previous sentence.

> Selznick consulted with the NAACP (National Association for the Advancement of Colored People) about how to portray the African Americans in his film. *Nevertheless,* he concentrated on his white audience, not the black protesters.

however—signals that the idea or information in the sentence is different or contrasts with the information in the previous sentence.

> One treatment for diarrhea is Lomotil, marked by G.D. Searle. This drug does not treat the underlying causes of diarrhea, *however,* but merely relieves the symptoms.

in fact—signals that the writer wants to both add and emphasize information. This word is used especially if the information is surprising.

> All of the negative effects of downsizing hurt a company over the long run because they undermine the whole notion of employee empowerment and the crucial process of idea sharing. *In fact,* many companies that have engaged in

layoffs have discovered that their productivity was worse off afterward, even though they continued more rounds of downsizing.

> GLR   See pages 261–270 in GLR for more information on logical relationships.

Activity 4-14   Identifying Transition Words and Logical Relationships Between Sentences

To see how another writer uses transition words, read the following sentences. Fill in the blank with the transition word from above that you think best connects the two sentences. Go back to the reading *Gone with the Wind* and locate the paragraph in which these sentences are found. Write the transition word that the author used and indicate the logical relationship that each word signals.

1. Selznick consulted with the NAACP (National Association for the Advancement of Colored People) about how to portray the African Americans in his film. ___Nevertheless,___ he concentrated on his white audience, not the black protesters. (Paragraph 4)

   Author's Transition Word: ____nevertheless____

   Logical Relationship: "Nevertheless" indicates that the second sentence contains information that is unexpected given the information in the first sentence. Since Selznick talked to African American leaders before making Gone with the Wind, we expect him to sensitively portray them in the film. But, the second sentence indicates that he did not do this — an unexpected result.

2. Ellen O'Hara's brief appearances demonstrate the plantation mistress's competence and crucial role in managing her husband's property. Mrs. O'Hara is the very soul and engine for not only her family but also her husband's slaves and employees. _____, the job of mistress of the house was so rigorous and demanding that many women checked out of the process altogether, opting instead to feign illness. (Paragraph 8)

   Author's Transition Word: _____

   Logical Relationship: _____

   _____

   _____

   _____

   _____

3. Scheming southern women have long been a popular focus of fiction (Lillian Hellman's *The Little Foxes*, for example). _____ Scarlett O'Hara's famed conniving and fierce independence are often seen as just another instance of literary fantasy. _____, Scarlett's transformation in the face of calamity from southern belle to matriarch was not unusual during Reconstruction. (Paragraph 9)

Author's Transition Word 1: _____

Logical Relationship: _____

_____

_____

_____

_____

Author's Transition Word 2: _____

Logical Relationship: _____

_____

_____

_____

_____

4. Rhett Butler's character is even more accurately grounded. At the outset, he recognizes, as did many southern moderates, that "the Yankees are better equipped than we. They've got factories, shipyards, coal mines, and a fleet to bottle up our harbors and starve us to death." _____, once Butler witnesses the heartbreak of the South's impending defeat, he heroically enlists in the Confederate army. (Paragraph 11)

Author's Transition Word: _____

Logical Relationship: _____

_____

_____

_____

_____

B. Using Subordination and Coordination to Show Logical Relationships Between Sentences

Academic writers use a variety of sentence types—simple, compound, complex, and compound-complex. They use two important techniques to make logical connections between and within sentences. See pages 28–29 in Chapter 1.

Combining Sentences

1. dependent clauses with a subordinator

   Although Selznick consulted with the NAACP (National Association for the Advancement of Colored People), he nevertheless concentrated on his white audience, not the black protesters, and the film reflects his attitude.

2. combining two independent clauses with a conjunction

   Dominic and Eugene is touching, *but* it is not oversentimentalized or overdone.

Linking Sentences with Transition Words or Expressions

3. using a transition word or expression

   At the outset, he recognizes, as did many southern moderates, that "the Yankees are better equipped than we. *However,* once Butler witnesses the heartbreak of impending defeat, the former cynic, in a noble and honorable gesture, heroically enlists in the Confederate army.

> **GLR** See pages 258–270 in the GLR for more information on basic sentence structure and logical relationships.

Activity 4-15   Identifying Ways of Signaling Logical Relationships

Underline the clause that expresses the writer's evaluation or opinion. In the blank next to each sentence, label the word that signals the logical relationship between the two clauses as follows:

1. Write "transition word" if a transition word or phrase is used.

2. Write "subordinator" if the word begins a dependent clause.

3. Write "coordinator" if a coordinating conjunction is used.

An example is provided.

Type of Signal	Sentence

coordinator   **1.** The filmmakers may have proclaimed their commitment to authenticity, <u>but their commitment to accuracy was limited.</u>

2. *Gone with the Wind* may have been the first plantation film to feature African American characters who don't spontaneously burst into song, but the picture still reflects an inaccurate view of the African-American experience.

3. Despite its flawed historical interpretation, the movie still flourishes and entertains.

4. Hattie McDaniel's portrait of Mammy may have won her an Academy Award in 1939, but because of Georgia's segregation laws, she didn't attend the film's Atlanta premier.

5. Scheming southern women have long been a popular focus of fiction. However, Scarlett's transformation in the face of calamity from southern belle to powerful matriarch was not unusual during Reconstruction.

Activity 4-16   Combining Sentences to Show Logical Relationships

Combine the two sentences in Column I and Column II below to express a complete evaluation of the portrayal of Italian-Americans in film and TV. Create two different sentences. Use dependent clauses, coordinating conjunctions, or transition words to express the contrasts of information. Three possible ways of combining the three sentences are shown below.

EXAMPLE

The media may contend that they reflect reality in the types of Italian-American characters presented.

In actuality, the media present a distorted dimension of life among ethnic groups.

1. <u>While</u> the media may contend that they reflect reality in the types of Italian-American characters presented, in actuality, the media present a distorted dimension of life among ethnic groups.

2. The media may contend that they reflect reality in the types of Italian-American characters presented, <u>but,</u> in actuality, the media present a distorted dimension of life among ethnic groups.

3. The media may contend that they reflect reality in the types of Italian-American characters presented. <u>However,</u> in actuality, the media present a distorted dimension of life among ethnic groups.

Column I	Column II
1. The film industry made a few thousand Italian-American gangsters representative of the entire ethnic community.	**1.** The film industry only represented a tiny fraction of the entire Italian-American population.
2. All forms of media feature Italian-Americans.	**2.** The media mishandles the ethnic experience of this group.
3. Gangster movies have been made which focus on other ethnic groups.	**3.** These movies end up being offensive to each group they attempt to portray.
4. The media has the opportunity to dispel misconceptions about ethnic groups.	**4.** The media chooses to manipulate rather than educate.
5. Ordinary Italian-Americans do less sensational and horrifying things than mobsters.	**5.** Their real lives are deserving of attention by films and TV.
6. Italian-Americans today are represented in all types of professions.	**6.** The media fail to reflect their professional involvement accurately.

Activity 4-17   Writing Evaluative Statements

Write several sentences expressing your evaluation of the film you chose in Activity 4-4. Use either dependent clauses, coordinating conjunctions, or transition words to express the contrasts of information.

EXAMPLE

1. Although many films about World War II portray people who collaborated with Germany as ruthless and unfeeling, the character of Rolf in *The Sound of Music* attempts to accurately reflect the moral struggles many of these people experienced during that war.
2. *Out of Africa,* a film about colonial life in Kenya, contains many scenes of life among the various ethnic groups in Kenya. However, the film fails to focus on or develop any of these characters.

C. Choosing Between Noun + *of*-Phrases and *'s* Possessive Noun Phrases

Complex noun phrases consist of one central noun with information added to it. In addition to relative clauses, another way to add information to the central noun is to attach prepositional phrases. One of the most common types of prepositional phrases to add to a noun is a phrase beginning with *of.* These noun + *of*-phrases appear frequently in informational writing. In fact, *of* is one of the most frequently used words in

English and is by far the most frequently used preposition. It is an important word to learn to use well.

> The film's most controversial aspect remains <u>its portrayal **of** race relations</u>. *Gone with the Wind* may have been the first plantation film to feature African-American characters who don't spontaneously burst into song, but the picture still reflects <u>historians' inaccurate view **of** the African-American experience</u>. This view dominated <u>the study **of** U.S. history during the first half **of** this century</u>. Although Selznick consulted with the NAACP (National Association for the Advancement of Colored People), he nevertheless concentrated on his white audience, not the black protesters, and the film reflects his attitude.

There are two problems that you must consider when using noun + *of*-phrases. One problem is a grammatical problem. The other is a problem of meaning.

Problem 1: Subject-Verb Agreement

When a complex noun phrase is in the subject position, deciding on the correct subject-verb agreement can be difficult.

Its glimpses [of the O'Hara household] <u>reflect</u>/~~reflects~~ the historical reality of an up-country plantation in prewar Georgia.

To solve this problem, find the first core noun in the noun phrase and then make the verb agree with that noun.

The screen treatment [of this group] <u>provides</u>/~~provide~~ one of the many unfortunate examples of what the make-believe media are capable of doing.

Problem 2: Deciding between the *'s* possessive and the noun + *of*-phrase

Sometimes a writer has only one grammatical choice in a statement of possessive meaning. The writer will choose either the *'s* possessive or the noun + *of*-phrase.

women's work

an inaccurate view of plantation life

Sometimes a possessive adjective + a noun has the same meaning as a noun + *of*-phrase and a writer can choose between the two.

the opening scenes of the film   the <u>film's</u> opening scenes

the struggles of the characters   the <u>characters'</u> struggles

Here are some guidelines for choosing between the two forms:

Four Guidelines When Choosing between 's Possessive and of Possessive

1. **The meaning of the *of*-phrase.** *Of* in these phrases has different meanings. It can mean ownership or measurement or can be a substitute for *about*. When it means ownership/possession, the 's possessive can often replace the noun + *of*-phrase. When it means about, the 's possessive cannot be used. See the chart below for more information.

   ownership
   Jennifer**'s** passport

   time measurement
   the first **of** the month

2. **The type of noun that will be made possessive.** If the noun refers to a human, to a collective noun (*government, the nation, society*), to a geographical name (*earth, the mountain*), or to anything that is considered able to possess something (*a pet, a car*, etc.), and the meaning is "belonging to" or possession, the 's possessive can be used. The 's possessive is generally preferred in this situation.

   society**'s** problems
   the earth**'s** rotation

3. **Phrases that generally require *of*.**

   the top **of** the morning
   the issue **of** racism

4. **Phrases where the writer chooses which noun to emphasize or focus on.** The noun that the reader will focus on is usually the last noun in a sequence. The information focus is indicated in bold in the two noun phrases below. As a writer, you will choose the 's possessive or the noun + *of*-phrase depending on which information you want your reader to focus on.

   the opening scenes of ***the film***
   OR
   the film's ***opening scenes***

Meaning	Noun + *of*-Phrases (* indicates that noun + *of*- phrase is preferred)	's Possessive Equivalent (* indicates that 's is preferred)
belonging to (possession)	• ~~the passport of Jennifer~~ • the gravity of the earth • the opening scenes of the film	⇨ Jennifer's passport* ⇨ the earth's gravity* ⇨ the film's opening scenes

Meaning	Noun + *of*-Phrases (* indicates that noun + *of*- phrase is preferred)	*'s* Possessive Equivalent (* indicates that *'s* is preferred)
done, made, or given or produced by	• the consent of parents • the conversion experience of Rhett Butler	⇨ the parent's consent ⇨ Butler's conversion experience
given to or received by	• the treatment of African Americans*	⇨ African-Americans' treatment [at the hands of white slave owners]
	• the exploitation of convict labor*	⇨ convict labor's exploitation [at the hands of desperate former slave owners]
about	• the issue of student financial aid	can't be made into a possessive adjective + a noun
	• the story of Rhett Butler's heroic role in the Civil War	
appositive—the *of*-phrase defines the first noun or makes it more specific	• the hope of winning a prize • the city of Los Angeles	can't be made into a possessive adjective + a noun
measure/time	• the height of the tower • the length of the film • the end of the year*	⇨ the tower's height ⇨ the film's length ⇨ [at] year's end

---

Activity 4-18   Examining the Meaning of *'s* Possessive and *of* Noun Phrases

Look at the following *'s* possessive and *of* noun phrases and write the meaning of each in the blank next to the phrase. Refer to the chart above for the possible meanings of these phrases. An example is provided.

1. the ethnic bigotry of the media   a. _____ *belonging/possession* _____

2. the film's opening scenes   b. _____

3. the news of the attack on Fort Sumter   c. _____

4. Gerald O'Hara's foreign origins   d. _____

5. an inaccurate view of the African-American experience   e. _____

6. the exploitation of prisoners   f. _____

Activity 4-19   Determining When to Use *'s* Possessive or *of* Noun Phrases

To practice making decisions between noun + *of*-phrases and *'s* possessive noun phrases, look at the noun + *of*-phrases in the paragraph below. Do the following:

- Decide the meaning of *of* in each noun phrase and write it in the blank provided.
- Decide whether you can change the noun + *of*-phrase to an *'s* possessive noun phrase. If you can't change it, write "can't change." If you can change the phrase, write the *'s* possessive form in the blank provided. Also explain if you would prefer the *'s* possessive form or the noun + *of*-phrase and why.

Two examples are done for you.

Gone with the Wind is [1]**the most influential interpretation of the Civil War** ever made. This Hollywood version of the plantation past has influenced [2]**many people's views of life** in both the modern and antebellum South. But the film puts forth many stereotypes and contains much inaccurate information—especially about the lives of black slaves.

1) Meaning: *about* _____
   Change: *can't change* _____
   _____

2) Meaning: _____
   Change: _____
   _____
   _____
   _____
   _____
   _____

³**The opening scenes of the film** show black slaves picking cotton in the spring, something they never did. ⁴**The film's portrayal of slave attitudes** was also false. *Gone with the Wind* shows happy, loyal slaves who were sad to see slavery end. The director never addressed ⁵**the racial struggles of the period**. The film was more accurate in its glimpses at ⁶**the life of white southern women**.

3) Meaning: belonging to/possession

Change: the film's opening scenes. I could choose either one. If I choose the films opening scenes, "opening scenes" is empha-sized. If I choose the opening scenes of the film, "film" is emphasized.

4) Meaning: _____

Change: _____

_____

_____

_____

_____

5) Meaning: _____

Change: _____

_____

_____

_____

_____

6) Meaning: _____

Change: _____

_____

_____

_____

_____

Activity 4-20   Practice with Subject-Verb Agreement

The subjects of the following sentences contain a noun + prepositional phrase, (many of them are noun + *of*-phrases). Identify the subject of each sentence. Determine whether the subject is singular (*it*) or plural (*they*). Then circle the correct form of the verb that agrees with the subject. (*Hint:* To find the subject that the verb agrees with, it is helpful to cross out prepositional phrases.)

EXAMPLE

1. [Two winning formulas ~~for Hollywood films~~] accounts/ (account for)the success of *Gone with the Wind.*

2. The frequent appearance of stereotyped Italian-American characters **offends/ offend** many in the Italian-American community.

3. Concerns about the treatment of African-Americans still **troubles/trouble** film-makers.

4. The most enduring of the media's Italian-American stereotypes **is/are** that of Italian-Americans as Mafia gangsters.

5. Scarlett's exploitation of convict labor and her flaunting of gender conventions **creates/create** a heroine both unforgettable and quite faithful to the historical record.

PUTTING IT ALL TOGETHER

FINAL WRITING ASSIGNMENT

Your writing task is to evaluate one of the following:

- a film's portrayal of an historical event or period
- the American media's portrayal (in film, television, or advertisements) of a particular ethnic group
- how the media in another country portray a particular ethnic group
- the differences in how men and women are portrayed in films (e.g., science fiction films, westerns, action films, romance films, etc.)
- the media's portrayal of women (in film, television, or advertisements)

You might consider watching a film more than once or watching more than one film to help you get a clear understanding of your subject and to develop the criteria on which you will base your evaluation. Consult *The Basics of Writing an Evaluation* on pages 123–128.

Audience and Purpose

Write for readers in an academic course who will respect you if your evaluation seems reasonable and not too emotional.

Preparing to Write

With your group members or alone, make an action plan that outlines how you will gather the information for your evaluation paper to submit to your instructor. Consider including such things as: the topic you will write about, titles of films you will view, other sources (magazines, television advertisements) you will consult, the criteria you will use to evaluate your topic, and how you will divide the work among group members.

The following diagram will help you to think strategically about the steps you will take to complete the assignment.

Summary of the subject or film you will evaluate: _____

_____

_____

⇓

Audience: Readers in an academic environment

⇓

Listing of Criteria: _____

⇓

Statement of Your Evaluation: _____

_____

_____

⇓

Sources to Consult: opinion surveys
 books
 popular magazines and newspapers
 information from the World Wide Web

⇓

Types of Evidence: facts
 statistics
 examples and descriptions from one or several films, TV shows, or
 advertisements
 quotations from experts

⇓

Written Draft

Presenting Your Ideas

Make a class presentation in which you explain the basic elements of the evaluation you or your group will write. (Do not read your draft.) Include an explanation of the criteria you used, a statement of your evaluation, and several examples to make your opinion clear to your audience.

Self-editing Activity

1. Before giving your draft to a peer, read it again to make sure that it says what you intended and is organized in the best way for this particular writing task. Make any changes needed to improve meaning and organization.

2. Choose and edit your draft for two of the language features reviewed in this chapter. Where indicated, turn to the GLR ⬭ and use the recommended self-editing strategies.

   ☐ use and formation of complex noun phrases including noun + *of*-phrases and possessive adjectives + noun

   ☐ use of transition words that clearly and appropriately signal to your audience the relationship between sentences and ideas

   ☐ use of subordination and coordination to clearly and appropriately signal logical relationships between ideas

   GLR See pages 270–271, Section 1, for more information on editing transition words, subordination, and coordination.

3. Edit your draft for one of the language features reviewed in the previous chapters that you think may need more careful attention in your writing. Consult the self-editing activities in the previous chapters.

Peer Response

Exchange papers with a partner or someone from another group. Answer the following questions about your partner's paper:

1. What is being evaluated?

2. What criteria has the writer based the evaluation on?

3. What is the opinion expressed in the paper? Do you agree or disagree with this evaluation? Why or why not?

4. What is the most convincing reason(s) or example(s) the writer gives to support the judgment expressed? Why?

5. Ask the writer two questions about ideas that were unclear in the paper.

6. What is the tone of the paper: strongly positive; somewhat positive; neutral; somewhat negative, or strongly negative? Is the tone appropriate? Why or why not? Copy down several sentences where you find the tone is appropriate.

7. Make one suggestion to help the writer(s) revise the draft.

LEARNER'S NOTEBOOK

Reflecting on Your Learning

Report what you have learned about writing an effective evaluation. Consider the way you wrote your evaluation as well as the way your peers wrote their evaluations.

Revising

At the end of your draft, list two changes that you will make to your evaluation. Rewrite your paper, including these changes.

• •

L O O K I N G   A H E A D

With a partner or in a small group, analyze the college assignment below using the discussion questions that follow.

Communication Studies 101

The Limits of Freedom—The First Amendment

Recently, there has been an increase in racial and ethnic tension across American college and university campuses. Sometimes these tensions have resulted in acts of violence, such as at the University of Mississippi, where the first African-American fraternity house was burned down. Other tensions manifest themselves in "hate speech." At Rutgers University, for example, walls were defaced with swastikas and slogans saying "Die Jew."

Assume that the following regulation will be voted on by the student body: *Offensive speech is a kind of harassment (and can therefore be punished and censored) when it is intended to insult or stigmatize an individual because of sex, race, color, or religion and employs "fighting words" or non-verbal symbols that are commonly understood to convey direct hatred. Anyone caught using such speech will be severely disciplined or expelled.*

How will you vote and why? Evaluate this proposal in light of what you have learned about the first amendment and free speech in course readings and lectures.

DISCUSSION

1. What criteria might be used to evaluate this proposal? What kinds of support could the writer use to support the judgment?

2. In what ways will this evaluation differ from what you have learned about evaluating? Describe specific differences that you notice.

3. What questions might you need to ask the professor to complete this assignment successfully? Formulate one specific question.

4. What problems do you anticipate for the person doing this evaluation? What solutions can you offer?

Chapter 5

*A*nalyzing Causes,

Reasons, and Factors

Causes and Unexpected Consequences of Climate Change

GOALS

WRITING
◆ write an analytical thesis state-ment
◆ learn strategies for organizing information about causes and con-sequences in an analytical paper

GRAMMAR
◆ practice the grammar of past time narrative including time expressions for chronological organization
◆ practice structures writers use when presenting information
◆ practice writing *-ing* participle phrases

CONTENT
◆ learn how climate change affects and has affected not only geogra-phy but economic and cultural development
◆ learn that the current problem with global warming is not the only major climate change that has influenced human civilization

ACADEMIC FIELDS

Geography
Atmospheric Science
History

Sample Authentic College/University Writing Assignments

The analyzing skills you will learn in this chapter can be used to complete college and university assignments like the ones below.

Philosophy

"The induction problem forever haunts us," according to some philosophers. What is "the induction problem" and **why** might it so haunt us?

Political Science

Discuss recent changes or reforms in at least three Eastern European countries. **Explain** the causes of the events that you described.

 CNN video support is available for this chapter.

GETTING READY

Warm-up Activity: Writing

Analyze means to examine something carefully in order to understand it better or to see what it consists of. In academic writing, assignments often ask writers to analyze causes, reasons, or factors that contribute to something. Such writing tasks ask you to discover *why* something happened.

In real life, you probably analyze all the time. When students receive an unexpectedly low grade on an exam or assignment, they may analyze how their study habits or use of time contributed to their failure. When a couple decides to stop dating, each one might analyze why the relationship did not work successfully. Whenever we encounter something difficult to understand or something mysterious, we naturally want to figure it out, and we use our analytical skills to do so.

LEARNER'S NOTEBOOK

Looking Back at a Family Decision

List the reasons why you or your family decided to come to the United States. Try to remember the decisions that led you to where you are now. Don't simply say, "I came here to study," or "My family came to escape a horrible political situation."

Activity 5-1   Discussing Common Reasons for Coming to the United States

Compare your learner's notebook with other students in a small group. List the common reasons that led your classmates or their families to come to the United States.

LEARNER'S NOTEBOOK

Giving Reasons to Support a Job Application

Find an interesting job announcement in the classified section of your local newspaper. In your learner's notebook, write a letter to your future employer, giving reasons why you would be a qualified candidate for this position. Think about both personal and professional factors that qualify you. Share your letter with a partner.

The Basics of Writing an Analysis

One reason that companies hire college graduates is that educated employees can analyze problems or issues. In other words, they have acquired the ability to break the larger problem down into parts or aspects, much like a mechanic does when trying to repair a car. Instead of looking at parts of an engine, a person with good analytical skills might look at certain key aspects of the problem: the causes, the consequences, the component parts of the problem, or how the problem came about in the first place.

Analyzing is one of the most common and important tasks in all academic work. It is also the most complex. Students are asked to analyze a problem or issue so that they can thoroughly understand it *before* offering an opinion or offering a solution. Analysis is the key to developing an *informed* opinion or devising an appropriate solution.

You've already had practice analyzing in previous chapters. When you read for academic purposes, you analyze the reading (examine it carefully) by looking for the central question the writer wants to answer, locating key terms, and understanding the reading's most important ideas. When you write a report, you often divide the larger topic you are explaining, like animal play, into categories such as playing with objects, playing with members of other species, etc. When you evaluate, you use criteria to analyze an item, an idea, or a policy.

1. Deciding How to Analyze the Topic

Analyzing may seem difficult because it isn't always clear how to break the larger problem or issue into smaller pieces. Typically, however, academic writing assignments ask writers to use one or more of the following questions to analyze:

- Why does/did X happen? (causes)
- What factors are involved in X? (factors related to X)
- For what reasons is X significant? (reasons)
- What will happen because of X? (effects)

The secret of a good analysis is to go beyond obvious or immediate reasons or causes for or effects of X. The example illustrates a good analysis.

Recent floods in the Midwestern states of the United States

Immediate/Obvious Causes

- unusually wet winter and spring with larger than normal snow- and rainfall

Underlying Causes

- changes in the ozone layer due to pollution (called "global warming")
- melting of the polar ice caps
- normal variations in climate over long periods of history
- overbuilding of the environment by humans and the usual ways that nature deals with climate changes

Immediate Effects

- loss of property and crops due to flooding
- economic devastation to the region

Long-term Effects

- better crop harvests in the future (due to flooding)
- changes in the primary economy of the region from farming to light industry
- change in the use of land in the region

Often causes and effects are interrelated in complex ways. This can be represented as a **cause-effect chain**. In this kind of chain, effects of one problem or situation can often become causes of another problem or situation. Here is an example:

more and more people own cars

levels of air pollution increase

the amount of carbon dioxide and other gases in the atmosphere increases

the temperature of the earth gets warmer

sea level increases

low-lying countries, such as the Netherlands, may flood

Activity 5-2 Explaining and Analyzing a Weather Pattern

Think of an interesting or unique weather pattern that occurs where you live now or in a place where you have lived. If necessary, conduct a subject search in the library or on the World Wide Web. For example, you might search under *tornadoes/Kansas, hurricanes/Florida,* or *tsunamis/Indonesia* or *Japan.* Explain this weather pattern to a partner, answering at least one of the three questions in *Deciding How to Analyze the Topic.* An example is provided.

Tsunamis are often called tidal waves, but they are not caused by ocean tides, which are influenced by the gravity between the sun and the moon. Tsunamis are actually caused by landslides, volcanoes, or earthquakes on the seafloor. When an earthquake occurs on the floor of the ocean, it moves the water, creating waves that move at 500 to 600 miles per hour. In open ocean tsunamis are not detectable, but as these waves get into shallower water closer to land, the height of the waves increases. The highest tsunami ever recorded occurred in 1971 in Japan and it was 278 feet high.

> Why do tsunamis happen? (causal chain of steps that create a tsunami)

Tsunamis can be very destructive. In 1983, a tsunami that started in the Sea of Japan killed 120 people. In 1946, the waterfront in Hilo, Hawaii was completely destroyed because of a tsunami that began off of Alaska. Waves that were 32 feet high flooded the business district and killed 159 people.

> What happens because of tsunamis?

Source: S. L. Harris, "Unstable Lands: The Terror of Tremblors and Volcanoes" in *Restless Earth: Disasters of Nature* (Washington, DC: The National Geographic Society, 1997, 176–179).

2. Writing Your Analytical Thesis

A thesis for a paper analyzing causes, factors, reasons, or consequences does not have to contain your opinion or an argument. But a thesis does contain:

1. the topic, problem, or issue your paper focuses on

2. an overview of the reasons, causes, factors, or consequences involved in the issue or problem

The following analytical thesis statements introduce causes. These thesis statements answer the question: *Why does/did X happen?*

> For the past two decades scientists have been working to improve their understanding of the climate system so that they can identify *long-term climate changes and the natural and human causes behind such changes.*

But as climate declined from the peak of the medieval warm period and slid into the trough of the little ice age, *it was damp and disease, not biting cold, that first set back the growth of western European civilization in the fourteenth century.*

Activity 5-3 Reviewing Thesis Statements

Examine the following thesis statements from the writing assignments in previous chapters. How are these similar to and different from the thesis statements in *Writing Your Analytical Thesis?* Consider how the topic is stated, whether there is an overview of factors or causes of the topic, and whether the thesis expresses an opinion or argument.

> In my opinion, catharsis does not work even when the conditions outlined in *The Great Catharsis Debate* by Carlson and Hatfield are met.
>
> Three common types of psychologically related problems that the elderly suffer from include depression, memory loss, and sleep disorders.
>
> The movie *Black Rain* portrays Japanese yakuza and their customs well. The *yakuza's* practices are shown accurately in the movie by introducing the relation between a boss and his followers.

Activity 5-4 Writing a Thesis Statement

Write a paragraph explaining the weather pattern you discussed in Activity 5-2. Find a sentence that could serve as the thesis statement for an essay analyzing this weather pattern. If you don't have a thesis sentence, write one that meets the criteria outlined above in *Writing Your Analytical Thesis.*

3. Organizing the Whole Analysis Paper

Another important task for anyone who writes an analysis is to organize the information into a meaningful and useful form. The overall shape of an analysis will vary depending on how you are analyzing the topic. In a paper analyzing causes, reasons, factors, or consequences, however, some of the basic components of the analysis will be:

- a brief introduction with a thesis statement that gives background about the topic and an overview of the reasons, causes, factors, or consequences you will discuss
- a paragraph that gives background about the topic (this is optional, if you have given enough background information in the introduction)
- several body paragraphs, each presenting a single cause, factor, reason, or consequence OR a cause-effect chain
- details, evidence, and examples that explain each paragraph's analytical point
- a conclusion that explains what you have learned from your analysis. You might discuss the importance of understanding the causes, give an informed opinion about the issue you have examined, or make a recommendation

Here is an example of an analytical essay. The topic is "parachute kids," or teenagers who have emigrated to the United States alone or with only one parent to attend high school. This essay was written by Timothy Lau, a student from Hong Kong. The essay shows clearly how reasons or causes are interrelated.

"Parachute kids," adolescents mostly from Hong Kong, have literally been "dropped" into American suburbs and high schools. Their parents buy homes and enroll their children in local high schools because they seek better educational opportunities for their kids. Unfortunately, these young people do poorly in school, often disobey their parents, and even get in trouble with police. <u>The reasons for the problems parachute kids face are related to their family situation in the U.S.</u>

Background on the topic of "parachute kids"

Thesis statement

It all started because of Hong Kong's reunion with the People's Republic of China. More and more families moved abroad in search of a clearer future, economically and politically. Often, however, the entire family did not move together. Most of the time, parents either left their kids with grandparents or other relatives in the United States or the mother alone emigrated with her children while the father stayed in Hong Kong because of financial reasons.

Reason 1—Hong Kong's reunification with China and the family structure of he families

Without both parents in the household, it is difficult to maintain the same degree of control over adolescent children as would be possible with two parents. As one of my interviewees said, "With only my mother here, I feel less pressure because whenever she wants to punish me, she always needs to consult with my dad in Hong Kong. That usually takes a long time, and meanwhile, I can continue to do what I please." This problem is

Reason 2—lack of authority in the household (a result of Reason #1)

worsened by the fact that, in typical Chinese families, the father is viewed as the head of the household. If the father is not present, children may feel less willing to listen to the mother.

Another factor that complicates discipline for these "parachute kids" is that the mothers often work outside the home. Most families are not wealthy enough to maintain two households, one in the U.S. and another in Hong Kong. The effect of this cannot be underestimated since parents can no longer devote time and attention to the child.

Reason 3—Mother's working outside the home (also a result of Reason #1)

When we are trying to devise a solution, we must first see how the problem originates. If we look at the problem of "parachute kids" as an educational problem or as a racial problem, we may overlook the part that family structure plays in the issue. It is probably unrealistic to suggest that families immigrate together or that wives devote themselves to their children. Neither of these solutions are financially possible. But, there is another way: mothers or grandparents might consider forming a social network among the families of their teenager's friends to oversee their behavior or take turns being the "supervising" household. If the teenagers know that many eyes are watching them and that a number of people care about them, they might do better socially and academically.

Conclusion—The writer states why it is important to understand the reasons that underlie the problem and offers a solution.

4. Organizing the Body Paragraphs of the Analysis Paper

There are two useful patterns for organizing information in the body paragraphs of the analysis paper. Here are two examples of how you might organize the body paragraphs in papers that discuss the causes of climate change (the first example) and the consequences of climate change on emigration (the second example):

Organization Option 1

Many people believe that the number of sunspots (as a measure of solar activity) influences our climate. The sunspot cycle of 11 and 22 years is a prime example of a belief in this particular forcing function. Sunspots go through periods when they are numerous or relatively few, and people searching for some explanation of weather variations have resorted to linking the two phenomena. Using solar activity as an indicator, they try to forecast rainfall amounts in the agricultural heartland of the United States—the Great Plains—or estimate grain prices in the world marketplace as a result of drought that may be sunspot-related.

Although many scientists are skeptical of the linkage, people who look for cycles in nature believe that every 20 to 22 years or so drought returns to the Great Plains. They use the 1930s Dust Bowl as ground zero and step off 20-year intervals from there in both directions: Droughts plagued the midsection of the United States during the 1870s, 1890s, 1910s, 1930s, 1950s, 1970s, and most recently the mid-1990s. Today there is renewed interest in the scientific community about the influence of solar activity on climate and weather.

A Single Cause or Factor: sunspot activity

In order to explain why climate changes, the writer has identified several natural causes and several human causes. The writer devotes one or two paragraphs to explaining each cause.

Organization Option 2

H. H. Lamb has suggested that the beginning of the end of the little optimum (a period of climate warming) may have been responsible for the emergence of the Mongol hordes out of Asia early in the thirteenth century. Just before Genghis Khan and his hordes swept out of Asia, the usually arid heartlands had, for a time, been relatively moist and productive, as part of the climatic pattern associated with the optimum. Populations increased as a result. The outburst of that population, to penetrate into European Russia, on the one hand, and as far as Beijing on the other,

Causal Chain

In order to explain why Genghis Khan invaded Europe and China, the writer explains a possible causal chain that might have led Genghis Khan to leave Mongolia.

1st—favorable climatic conditions in usually arid heartlands
⇓
2nd—population growth and spread in Mongolia
⇓

occurred just when high latitudes began to cool rapidly, and there was a great advance of sea ice southward near Iceland. There could, says Lamb, have been an invasion of cold Arctic air into the heart of Asia as part of this new pattern of climate, reducing the productivity of the land and forcing the people to follow their charismatic leader in a quest for survival.

3rd—invasion of cold Arctic air **and** population migration
⇓
4th—productivity of land dropped
⇓
5th—Genghis Khan leads followers out of Mongolia in search of a more favorable climate

LEARNER'S NOTEBOOK

Organizing a Causal Analysis

Write a paragraph that explains one of the causes of the weather pattern from Activities 5-2 and 5-4 or that explains the causal chain that leads up to this weather pattern. Have a partner read your paragraph and then determine which organizational pattern you are using. An example is provided.

Here is the causal chain that causes tsunamis and results from a tsunami:

1st: a landslide, earthquake, or volcano occurs on the seafloor
⇓
2nd: waves are created that move at 500–600 miles per hour
⇓
3rd: these waves move toward land and shallower water
⇓
4th: as the water gets shallower, the waves' height increases
⇓
5th: the waves hit the shore as tsunamis
⇓
6th: buildings near the shore are destroyed and people drown

FOCUSING

Introduction to Readings

Talking about the weather is often a way of making polite conversation with strangers or acquaintances. Because it seems to be such an insignificant topic, we may not realize how much weather influences our daily lives and even the course of our history. The readings in this chapter examine how the changes in the climate have influenced history and speculate on causes and consequences of future climate change.

Pre-reading Vocabulary

Activity 5-5   Verbs that Link Causes and Results

Some verbs link *causes* (expressed in the subject of the sentence) to *consequences* (expressed by the object). See page 360, Appendix B for more examples and information.

cause
consequence

Increases in population and improvements in agriculture **produced** wealth.

Use the following verbs to make sentences that relate causes and consequences of weather or climate patterns that you are familiar with. Change the verb form to agree with the subject or the verb tense where appropriate. An example is provided.

Cause	Verb/Verb Expression (The base forms of the verb are given. Be sure to make verbs agree with subjects.)	Consequence(s)
1.	**bring about**	
2.	**cause**	
3.	**contribute to**	
4. Eruptions of volcanoes in one part of the world	**create**	beautiful sunsets in other parts of the world.
5.	**lead to**	
6.	**be responsible for**	
7.	**increase**	
8.	**generate**	
9.	**produce**	

Pre-reading Activity

Activity 5-6   Discussing the Consequences of Weather Patterns

Look at the newspaper headlines below. Choose two of the headlines and, with a partner or in a small group, discuss the possible immediate and long-term consequences (personal, economic, social, political, or international) of the weather patterns. Use the verbs that link causes and results from Activity 5-5 in your discussion.

Plains States Brace for Runoff, "Historic" Flooding

Cold Damages Midwestern Fruit Crop

Thousands Killed in Powerful Quake in Iran

Antarctic Warming, Garbage Worry Scientists

Eastern U.S. Shivers

1 Dead After Tornadoes, Hail Pelt Texas

Past Flooding Blamed for North Korean Famine

Activity 5-7   Discussing Global Warming

In a small group or with a partner, discuss what you know about the problem of "global warming" (its causes, its possible consequences, and possible solutions for it). Take notes about your discussion and share your information with the class.

READING 1   CLIMATE SHIFTS: OMENS OF GLOBAL WARMING
(CHAPTER IN A POPULAR BOOK)

"Climate Shifts: Omens of Global Warming" appeared in a book published by the National Geographic Society. The writer examines climate change and what causes it. Because this book was not written for an academic audience, the author does not give a reference list at the end or list page numbers or years of sources he cites.

Activity 5-8   Verb + Preposition Combinations

Many verbs that are commonly found in academic writing are really verb + preposition combinations. That is, certain verbs combine with a preposition to form a unit.

> Climate change *can be defined* as variability, fluctuations, and change in the strictest sense of the word.

> The strictest definition of climate change *refers to* longer-term changes over many decades or centuries.

For a list of verb + preposition combinations, see pages 367–368, Appendix B.

In each of the following sentences from "Climatic Shifts: Omens of Global Warming," find and underline the verb + prepositions. Then, on a separate piece of paper, write your own sentences using five of the verb + preposition combinations. If you are unsure of the meaning of a verb + preposition combination, consult a dictionary. An example is provided.

1. Climate <u>is defined as</u> the average weather conditions in a certain place over a period of years.

   Inflation is defined as the overall rise in prices that consumers pay.

2. Many scientists and policymakers are concerned about the threat of global warming.

3. Until the 1960s, the study of climate was viewed as a necessary, but unexciting field.

4. Climatologists refer to any factor that influences the climate as a forcing function.

5. Forcing functions can be divided into external and internal factors.

6. Scientists attribute any change in global weather patterns to a combination of factors including sunspots, volcanoes, earth's orbit, and human influence.

7. Industrialized societies have contributed to climate changes by polluting the air and depleting the ozone layer with harmful chemicals.

8. Countries that desire economic growth often rely on burning fossil fuels to get energy to produce goods.

CLIMATIC SHIFTS: OMENS OF GLOBAL WARMING
Climate Change

Climate change can be considered objectively and subjectively. Objectively, it can be defined as variability, fluctuations, and change in the strictest sense of the word. Variability describes changes on a relatively short time scale, followed by a return to an average condition. Fluctuations represent nonpermanent changes that take place over decades. The strictest definition refers to longer-term changes over many decades or centuries, followed by a return to some expected average condition, or to a permanent change in average conditions prevailing for some period of time. Most policy makers today are concerned about this definition of climate change when they refer to global warming. The fear is that the climate regime is not just varying on some relatively short time scale but, in fact, is undergoing a permanent change.

Climate change can also be defined according to human perceptions. Humans tend to think in terms of shorter time scales, such as years and decades. Even if cooler or warmer years were to occur, people might view them as a permanent change in climate and not as variability or fluctuation.

Until the 1960s, an effective argument could have been made that studying climatology would be like watching grass grow: pretty dull and devoid of uncertainty or surprise. The field was viewed as a necessary but unexciting endeavor. In the early 1970s, fear of the resurgence of an ice age changed all that. After a few decades of relatively benign weather and climate, the period from about 1940 to the early 1970s was cooler than the preceding decades. The 1970s witnessed extreme adverse climate anomalies worldwide that, when linked with circumstantial and anecdotal information, suggested the earth was sliding toward the next ice age. For example, reputable scientists noted the following in support of a new ice age: The growing season in England was two weeks shorter than in previous decades; fish usually caught off the northern coast of Iceland were being found off its southern coast; hay production in Iceland had dropped by 25 percent because of cooler temperatures; armadillos that had migrated as far north

as Kansas were moving southward, and so on. Food production dropped drastically in the early 1970s, as did fish catches. To show just how serious the ice age fear was then, several books were published on the topic: *Fire or Ice*, *The Cooling*, and *The Weather Conspiracy*.

This view soon gave way to concern about global warming caused by human activities that heat up the atmosphere. For the past two decades scientists have been working to improve their understanding of the climate system so that they can identify long-term climate changes and the natural and human causes behind such changes. Just looking back at the past thousand years, climatologists have identified variability, fluctuations, and long-term trends. The warming that took place in the 11th and 12th centuries was a century-scale climate change. The little ice age from 1600 to about 1850 was a long-term trend toward cooling. The causes of these multicentury changes (trends) have not been identified with certainty. In the 20th century, there have been decades-long fluctuations: The 1900 to 1920 period was wet and cool; 1920 to 1940 was warm and wet; 1940 to 1970 or so was a cool period; from the mid-1970s the atmosphere has been heating up.

Change: Natural Causes

Several factors can bring about climate change. Scientists call them *forcing functions* because they make the climate system alter its behavior. They can be divided into internal and external factors: The former are inherent to the climate system; the latter are external to it.

External forcing functions include solar activity, variations of earth's orbit over very long time scales, and random volcanic activity. Global climate changes over the past thousand years have been attributed rightly or wrongly to one or a combination of these functions.

Many people believe that the number of sunspots (as a measure of solar activity) influences our climate. The sunspot cycle of 11 and 22 years is a prime example of a belief in this particular forcing function. Sunspots go through periods when they are numerous or relatively few, and people searching for some explanation of weather variations have resorted to linking the two phenomena. Using solar activity as an indicator, they try to forecast rainfall amounts in the agricultural heartland of the United States—the Great Plains—or estimate grain prices in the world marketplace as a result of drought that may be sunspot-related.

Although many scientists are skeptical of the linkage, people who look for cycles in nature believe that every 20 to 22 years or so drought returns to the Great Plains. They use the 1930s Dust Bowl as ground zero and step off 20-year intervals from there in both directions: Droughts plagued the midsection of the United States during the 1870s, 1890s, 1910s, 1930s, 1950s, 1970s, and most recently the mid-1990s. Today there is renewed interest in the scientific community about the influence of solar activity on climate and weather.

In the 1920s, Serbian mathematician Milutin Milankovitch proposed the idea that changes in earth's orbital pattern have a major influence on the development of ice ages. The orbit places parts of the earth at varying distances from the sun in a given season, thereby causing different climate patterns on geologic time scales of millennia and longer. Wallace Broecker of Columbia University succinctly stated Milankovitch's theory: "Changes in the tilt of the Earth's rotation axis and in the point in the annual cycle of the Earth's closest approach to the Sun alter the way solar radiation forces the climate."

Ice cores are providing evidence of variability in the timing of the ice ages, and this variability—on scales of hundreds and thousands of years—cannot be explained on the basis of orbital theory.

For its part, volcanic activity affects climate on the order of only a few years. It can make identification of a climate change "fingerprint" more difficult because its influence on the world's climate can temporarily mask climate trends. A series of volcanic eruptions, however, could have a major influence on the global climate regime for periods much longer than just a few years.

Change: Human Causes

Human activities have been altering the natural environment for thousands of years. Since the onset of industrialization, however, the effects have increased dramatically, particularly on the chemical composition of the atmosphere. Societies everywhere have witnessed and perhaps contributed to changes caused by air pollution, acid rain, and ozone depletion. For example, the burning of fossil fuels (coal, oil, natural gas) releases large amounts of carbon dioxide (CO_2), a greenhouse gas, into the atmosphere; such gases trap long-wave radiation re-emitted by the earth's surface.

Carbon dioxide is not the only greenhouse gas produced by human activities. Methane (CH_4) is emitted by wetlands, by termites and other animals, and during the cultivation of rice. Nitrous oxide (N_2O) when used as a fertilizer in agriculture, also is released into the atmosphere. Chlorofluorocarbons (CFCs) were developed in the 1920s and have been used as foam-blowing agents, refrigerants, electronic component cleaners, and as ingredients in aerosol sprays. Although CFCs are also a greenhouse gas, their overall effect is unclear.

As populations grow and economies industrialize, governments increase their energy consumption. Many of them rely more on fossil fuels in the absence of cleaner technologies. China, for example, has large coal reserves and plans to use them in its drive for economic development. Without other natural energy resources or the funds to import clean energy-related technologies, China must use its coal instead of expensive sources that do not produce carbon dioxide, such as solar or nuclear power. Other countries face a similar dilemma.

Another contribution to the gas buildup comes from tropical deforestation in South America, Southeast Asia, and Central Africa. Deforestation contributes about 15 percent of the human-induced increases in greenhouse gases released into the atmosphere. Cutting down trees destroys vegetation that pulls carbon from the air and stores it, and burning them releases stored carbon. Industrialized countries are largely responsible for deforestation: Japan, for example, is the world's major importer of tropical hardwoods.

The construction of cities and the concentration of energy usage in them have generated unnatural climates in urban settings. Some researchers have found that a heat island produces more precipitation within a city and downwind from it. St. Louis, the capital of the state of Missouri, was used to prove this hypothesis. The heat-island effect has meant that temperature recordings have to be adjusted for changes in records that followed the warming of the cities. Because of the effect, some cities are showing a 3°F warming.

Also, land-use changes—deforestation, clearing, cultivation—can alter local and regional climates. According to Russian scientists, certain farming practices increase rainfall. They believe that wide-scale irrigation can produce enough evaporation to favorably alter the local climate, making the air more humid.

Source: Michael H. Glantz, *Restless Earth: Disasters of Nature* (Washington, DC: The National Geographic Society, 1997, 246–253).

Active Reading

Activity 5-9   Outlining the Reading

An informal outline has been started for "Climate Shifts: Omens of Global Warming." Fill in all of the missing information. Compare your outline with that of a classmate.

Phenomenon _____

Natural Causes

Factor 1 _The number of sunspots, which is a measure of the sun's activity, may have influenced the world's climate._

Factor 2 _____

_____

_____.

Factor 3 _____

_____

_____ .

Human Causes

Problem 1: _Buildup of "Greenhouse" Gases in the Atmosphere_

Contributing Factor 1 _The burning of fossil fuels releases CO_2, and leads to gas buildup in the atmosphere. The same thing happens because of methane, nitrous oxide, and CFCs._

Contributing Factor 2 _____

_____

_____

Problem 2: Other Changes in Climate

Cause 1 _____

_____

_____ .

Cause 2 _____

_____

_____ .

Activity 5-10   Creating a Reference Page of Sources Cited

Pretend that you are Michael H. Glantz, the author of the chapter "Climatic Shifts: Omens of Global Warming" and that you have rewritten your chapter for an academic audience. Using the information below, write reference entries for each source and create the reference page for your article. Choose either APA or MLA format for the references.

> **GLR**   See pages 310–313, Section 4, of the GLR for more information.

1. **Author:** Raymond S. Bradley and Philip D. Jones, Editors
   Title: Climate Since AD 1500
   Type of Source: Book
   Publisher: Routledge
   Year/Date of Publication: 1992
   Place of Publication: London

2. **Author:** H. H. Lamb
   Title: Climate, History and the Modern World, 2nd Edition
   Type of Source: Book
   Publisher: Routledge
   Year/Date of Publication: 1995
   Place of Publication: London

3. **Author:** Keith Smith
   Title: Environmental Hazards: Assessing Risk and Reducing Disaster, 2nd Edition
   Type of Source: Book
   Publisher: Routledge
   Year/Date of Publication: 1996
   Place of Publication: London

READING 2   OF FROZEN MILK AND BISON HERDS
   (CHAPTER FROM A BOOK)

This chapter analyzes the causes of historical changes in 13th and 14th century Europe and China. The authors find that important historical events such as the conquests of Genghis Khan and the setback in the development of European civilization were due largely to changes in climate.

Activity 5-11   Using Time Expressions to Signal Chronological Organization

Writing about historical events is usually organized chronologically. To signal important time shifts to readers, writers use a variety of time expressions. Scan from the paragraph "Of Frozen Milk and Bison Herds" to find other examples of time expressions that the authors use to signal chronological organization.

Time Adverb + Sentence	Preposition + time period/date	Preposition + 2 time periods/dates
1. **just *when*** high latitudes begin to cool . . .	1. ***by*** 1300 ***or a little before*** . . .	1. ***between*** 1240 ***and*** 1362, . . .
2. _____ _____	2. *early **in*** the 13th century	2. _____ _____
3. _____	3. _____	
	4. _____	
	5. _____	
	6. _____	

Activity 5-12   Using Time Expressions to Signal Chronological Organization

Think of an important historical time frame or choose one from the following list. Write a paragraph about important events that occurred during the time frame you have chosen. Use four time expressions from "Of Frozen Milk and Bison Herds" to help your readers follow the chronological organization. An example is provided.

Historical Time Frames

A. 1750–1850—the Industrial Revolution

B. 1933–1945—World War II, Japanese expansion into China and Korea

C. 1950s and 1960s—independence movements in African countries

D. 1987–1990—the end of the Soviet Union, democracy movements

E. 1960s—civil unrest, wars

F. 1992–the present—war in the former Yugoslavia, worldwide economic and democratic changes

EXAMPLE

Between 1942 and 1945, Japanese Americans were sent to internment camps at various remote locations around the U.S. Just when the war in the Pacific theater was expanding, the United States Department of War issued an order to have all Japanese Americans rounded up. By the end of 1942, the U.S. government had forced Japanese Americans out of their homes and businesses and had relocated them to internment camps in various places in the United States. At the end of the war, these domestic prisoners were released, but the U.S. government made no attempt to pay them for their suffering and financial loss.

OF FROZEN MILK AND BISON HERDS

Although the Norse were the people who seem to have taken fullest advantage of the opportunities provided by the little optimum (*a period of warmer temperatures from approximately AD 800–1200 BC*), it 5 would be wrong to leave you with the impression that the benefits by-passed the rest of Europe entirely. The warmth in Europe seems to have continued until about 1300, a little later than in Greenland, and to 10 have coincided with the awakening of the form of European civilization that has continued to the present day. From the middle of the eleventh century onwards, there were increases in population and improvements 15 in agriculture, producing wealth which led to a great phase of cathedral building and to the Crusades, Europe's attempt to take control of the Holy Land from Arab hands. William's conquest of England, and the 20 subsequent development of a new kind of English culture, were a minor part of all this activity. But by 1300, or even a little before, this phase of European expansion was at an end. 25

Lamb (*a pioneering climatologist who has promoted the idea that climate change influences human affairs*) has suggested that the beginning of the end of the little optimum may have been responsible for the emergence of the Mongol hordes out of Asia early in the thirteenth century. Just before Genghis Khan and his hordes swept out of Asia, the usually arid heartlands had, for a time, been relatively moist and productive, as part of the climatic pattern associated with the optimum. Populations increased as a result. The outburst of that population, to penetrate into European Russia, on the one hand, and as far as Beijing on the other, occurred just when high latitudes began to cool rapidly, and there was a great advance of sea ice southward near Iceland. There could, says Lamb, have been an invasion of cold Arctic air into the heart of Asia as part of this new pattern of climate, reducing the productivity of the land and forcing the people to follow their charismatic leader in a quest for survival.

This, as Lamb acknowledges, is speculation—there is no direct proof that climatic change was an underlying cause of the outburst of the Mongol hordes. But their homeland was close to the region of China where there had been severe cold for some centuries (while the North Atlantic enjoyed its little optimum), and there is good evidence that at the end of the little optimum cold spread gradually westward from China to Europe. Lamb's Genghis Khan scenario exactly fits that picture. That wave of cold does not seem to have been caused simply by a shift of the circumpolar vortex (*circular winds that blow from west to east around the globe. They usually isolate a mass of cold air over the Arctic*) to a new position, but by an expansion of the whole vortex, as well. This eventually brought cold to high latitudes everywhere in the northern hemisphere—a little ice age that lasted from the middle of the fifteenth century to the middle of the nineteenth century, and which was at its worst in Britain and Europe in the seventeenth century. But as climate declined from the peak of the medieval warm period and slid into the trough of the little ice age, it was damp and disease, not biting cold, that first set back the growth of western European civilization in the fourteenth century.

Death and Desertion

The setback in the development of European civilization was heralded by an μincrease in stormy weather. In the thirteenth century, on four separate occasions disastrous sea floods took the lives of at least 100,000 people in Holland and Germany, the worst of these floods killed more than 300,000 people. Between 1240 and 1362, more than half the agricultural land (60 parishes) in the then-Danish diocese of Schleswig was swallowed by the sea; in other coastal regions sand, not water, was the problem, as the strong winds created marching dunes that enveloped many coastal villages and townships, including the port of Harlech, on the west coast of Wales.

Many historians mention bad weather in passing when describing the events of these centuries, but few acknowledge the possibility that the deterioration in climate played a key role in the deterioration of civilization. In his epic *Hutchinson History of the World,* for example, the Oxford historian J. M. Roberts says that the medieval economy was "never far from collapse," and that agriculture was "appallingly inefficient." So when two successive bad harvests in the early fourteenth century reduced the population of Ypres by a tenth, he blames the inefficiency of the infrastructure of society, not the bad weather—seeming to miss the point that in the preceding two centuries, during the little optimum, harvest failures had been rare, and that is why society had thrived and population had increased in spite of the "appalling inefficiency" of the farmers. No historian could fail to notice, however, that something dramatic happened in Europe in the fourteenth century. As Robert puts it:

> It is very difficult to generalize but about one thing there is no doubt: a great and cumulative setback occurred in the fourteenth century. There was a sudden rise in mortality, not occurring everywhere at the same time, but notable in many places after a series of bad harvests about 1320. This started a slow decline of population which suddenly became a disaster with the onset of attacks of epidemic disease which are often called by the name of one of them, the "Black Death" of 1348–59 (p. 550).

But why did the harvests fail? Because of bad weather. And why did people succumb to the Black Death (another name for bubonic plague)? Because they were weakened by malnutrition. In the late thirteenth century, life expectancy in England was about 48 years; at the end of the fourteenth century, it was less than 40 years. The Black Death was partly to blame, along with other killing epidemics of typhus, smallpox and even influenza which was still a major killer in the twentieth century; more people died of "flu in a great European epidemic just after World War I than had been killed on the battlefields of the Great War itself." In some regions, half the population was wiped out by these plagues; over the whole of Europe, the population fell by a quarter. Trouble produced more trouble—searching for scapegoats for the disasters, people often took to hunting witches or persecuting Jews; civil unrest brought uprisings in France in 1358 (the Jacquerie) and in England in 1381 (the Peasants' Revolt). And in many regions the land became depopulated as people deserted the villages and abandoned their fields.

But which came first—death or desertion? Traditional school history books lay the blame for depopulation of rural regions on the wave of plagues. But more recently researchers such as Martin Parry of the University of Birmingham, have pointed out that the records show that there were many villages with uncultivated land in every part of England in the year 1341, at the time of a great survey known as the *Nonarium Inquisitiones.* Farmland was being abandoned, not just in England but across Europe, *before* the plagues struck. Villages were being deserted before the Black Death did its grisly work on a weakened population, and the villages that were abandoned in the wake of the plague were just those which had been most weakened by the preceding famines, and had already lost two-thirds of their population before the disease set to work. Famine and depopulation *first,* and then the ravages of plague, has now clearly been established as the order in which desertion and death altered the face of rural Europe in the fourteenth century; and before the famine had come the detrimental change in climate.

Scotland suffered even worse than England. The favorable climate of the 12th and 13th centuries had allowed agriculture to develop far up the glens, and brought a golden age of civilization in the north, where many English exiles had retreated from the Norman invaders. But in the 14th century, crop failures and hunger stimulated clan warfare. In the 1430s, conditions were so bad that bread was made from the bark of trees, since there was no grain; and the civil unrest became so great that in 1436 King James I was murdered while out hunting near Perth. With the king no longer safe in his own lands, the court retreated to the fortified city of Edinburgh, 210 in the south of the country, which became Scotland's capital. In the same decade, further south, the severe weather brought the last recorded evidence of wolves being active in England.   215

The effects of the climate shift were also felt far away from Europe. In Africa, desert regions became drier and expanded during the fourteenth and fifteenth centuries, while in India various estimates of 220 the total population suggest that a peak of about 50 million was reached in AD1000, and that as the climate deteriorated, this fell to 200 million in 1200 (remember that the characteristic little ice age weather 225 drifted westward from China, and therefore hit India sooner than it did Europe) and 170 million in 1400, with a sharper fall down to 130 million by 1550. All this was caused by the development of a 230 stronger, larger circumpolar vortex around the Arctic region, and associated changes in monsoon rains and temperature patterns across the northern hemisphere. Closer to that expanded vortex, in North America, 235 the changes were even more dramatic.

References

Lamb, H. H. 1982. *Climate, History, and the Modern World.* London: Methuen.

Roberts, J. M. 1976. *The Hutchinson History of the World.* London: Hutchinson.

Source: John and Mary Gribbin, *Children of the Ice: Climate and Human Origins* (Cambridge, MA: Basil Blackwell, 1990, 140–144).

Active Reading

Activity 5-13   Identifying Causal Chains

Historical writing combines narrative with informational writing. In the following causal chain, the writers tell the sequence of events that led many villages to become depopulated and many people to die. The whole story, however, makes one point: Weather has an important influence on human civilization. In small groups, reconstruct the chain of causes and consequences found in either paragraph 7 or 8. An example from paragraph 6 is provided.

EXAMPLE

Paragraph from "Of Frozen Milk & Bison Herds"

Causal Chain

Paragraph 6 But why did the harvests fail? Because of bad weather. And why did people succumb to the Black Death (another name for bubonic plague)? Because they were weakened by malnutrition. In the late thirteenth century, life expectancy in England was about 48 years; at the end of the fourteenth century, it was less than 40 years. The Black Death was partly to blame, along with other killing epidemics of typhus, smallpox and even influenza. In some regions, half the population was wiped out by these

1st: Bad weather increased.

2nd: Harvests failed.

3rd: People suffered from malnutrition due to lack of food.

4th: Weakened people died in great numbers of the Black Death and other plagues.

plagues; over the whole of Europe, the population fell by a quarter. Trouble produced more trouble— searching for scapegoats for the disasters, people often took to hunting witches or persecuting Jews; civil unrest brought uprisings in France in 1358 (the Jacquerie) and in England in 1381 (the Peasants' Revolt). And in many regions the land became depopulated as people deserted the villages and abandoned their fields.

5th: There were persecution of Jews and witchhunts (to find someone to blame for these tragedies).

6th: Entire villages and regions were abandoned.

Analysis of Language: Using Informational Grammar to Write an Analysis of Causes

A. Verb Tense Shift in Academic Writing

Writers who analyze causes about past or present problems or events shift tenses frequently within one paragraph and between paragraphs because they are often presenting several types of information, each of which has a corresponding verb tense.

VERB TENSES IN ACADEMIC WRITING

Tense	Purpose in Writing	Examples
Simple present	generalizations, statements of theory, or definitions	Many people believe that the number of sunspots (as a measure of solar activity) *influences* our climate. (Paragraph 7, Climatic Shifts)
Present perfect	descriptions of past research or past events that have present results or are related to the present or to the topic being discussed	Since the onset of industrialization, however, the effects of human beings *have increased* dramatically, particularly on the chemical composition of the atmosphere. (Paragraph 12, Climatic Shifts)
	often used to introduce a topic	Climatology *has been viewed* as an uninteresting field.
Present perfect progressive	description of activities that began in the past but are ongoing	Human activities *have been altering* the natural environment for thousands of years. (Paragraph 12, Climatic Shifts)

Tense	Purpose in Writing	Examples
Present progressive	description of work (usually scientific) that is being done right now	Ice cores **are providing** evidence of variability in the timing of ice ages. (Paragraph 9, Climatic Shifts)
	description of an ongoing activity	The fear is that the climate regime **is** not just **varying** on some relatively short time scale but, in fact, **is undergoing** a permanent change. (Paragraph 1, Climatic Shifts)
Simple past	description of past research or past events (often used as examples)	The 1970s **witnessed** extreme adverse climate anomalies worldwide. (Paragraph 3, Climatic Shifts)
Past perfect	background for an event or phenomenon that is being explained	Hay production in Iceland **had dropped** by 25 percent because of cooler temperatures. (Paragraph 3, Climatic Shifts)
Past progressive	emphasis of one unusual or unexpected past action or event (compared with usual or expected past actions or events that are expressed in the simple past)	Fish usually caught off the northern coast of Iceland **were being caught** off its southern coast. (Paragraph 3, Climatic Shifts)
	interpretations or analysis of simple past events	The strange weather events in the 1970s, when linked with circumstantial and anecdotal information, suggested the earth **was sliding** toward the next ice age. (Paragraph 3, Climatic Shifts)
Modal auxiliaries in the verb phrase	predictions about future outcomes and results	A series of volcanic eruptions **could have** a major influence on the global climate regime for periods much longer than just a few years. (Paragraph 11, Climatic Shifts)
	explanations for unclear situations or to draw conclusions	Russian scientists believe that wide-scale irrigation **can produce** enough evaporation to alter the local climate, making the air more humid. (Paragraph 17, Climatic Shifts)

GLR   See pages 297–300 in the GLR for more information.

Activity 5-14 Identifying Verb Tense Shifts and Their Purpose

In order to understand better *when* and *why* writers shift verb tenses, reread paragraphs 4, 16, and 17 of "Climatic Shifts: Omens of Global Warming." Underline the verbs in these paragraphs. Fill in the chart below by writing in sentences containing as many of the various verb tenses as you can find. Explain the purpose of the verb tense in each sentence. An example is provided.

Tense	Purpose in Writing	Examples
Simple present		
Present perfect		
Present perfect continuous		
Present progressive		
Simple past		
Past perfect		
Modal auxiliaries in the verb phrase	explanations for unclear situations, events	Russian scientists believe that wide-scale irrigation can produce enough evaporation to alter the local climate, making the air more humid

Activity 5-15 Practice with Verb Tense Shift

Below is a list of recent weather-related events in the United States and a paragraph speculating about the causes of these events. Fill in the blanks with the appropriate verbs from the list below. Make sure that the verb tense corresponds to the information the verb is conveying. An example is provided.

January 1996: severe winter storms on the East Coast of the United States

Fall 1996: fires in California, Washington, and Oregon

Winter 1996: severe flooding in Oregon and northern California

January and February 1997: floods in Illinois, Kentucky, and Tennessee

- attempt   • continue   • occur   • rise
- be   • experience • overflow • vary
- believe   • make   • predict

Flooding in various states throughout the Midwest, northwest, and west
(1) _have been making_ headlines over the past six months. The most recent flooding
(2) _____ in the upper Midwestern states of North Dakota, Minnesota, and
Wisconsin this past April. Prior to this, in the months of February and March, the
Mississippi and Ohio Rivers (3) _____ their banks in states such as
Kentucky, Tennessee, and Illinois. Even before the floods in the Midwest, the American,
Sacramento, and Willamette Rivers (4) _____ well beyond their banks in
California and Oregon.

The United States (5) _____ other unusual climate patterns lately. In
recent years, weather patterns (6) _____ from extremely cold to extremely
dry conditions. Currently, scientists (7) _____ to understand why the
weather (8) _____ so erratic in the past five years. Some scientists
(9) _____ that global warming plays an important role. These experts
(10) _____ that the climate (11) _____ to change dramatically
in coming years.

B. Adding Information About Results with *ing* Verb Phrases

Academic writers pack a lot of information into sentences. One of the major differences between speaking and writing is that written sentences use a wider range of
vocabulary and more complicated grammar. One way of writing such academic sentences is to use what is called a "participle phrase." Section 7, page 342, of the GLR ⦿
explains more about participle phrases. In this activity we will work only with the *ing*
participle phrase. Here is an example of how the *ing* participle phrase is formed:

Cause	Sentence with *ing* participle phrase
The orbit places parts of the earth at different distances from the sun in a given season.	The orbit places parts of the earth at different distances from the sun in a given season, thereby **causing** different climate patterns on geologic time scales of millennia and longer.
Result	
This causes different climate patterns on geologic time scales of millennia or longer.	

Notice that the two sentences are combined by changing the second into an *ing* participle phrase. To make the *ing* phrase, the subject is dropped, and the main verb is changed to the *ing* form. The *ing* participle phrase follows the main clause and is set off from the main clause by a comma.

These sentences can be used to talk about causes and their results. The cause is given in the main sentence and the result in the *ing* participle phrase.

Activity 5-16   Identifying *ing* Participle Phrases

In each of the following sentences, underline the *ing* participle phrase that expresses a result of the action in the main clause. Briefly, state the cause and result in each sentence. Then, rewrite the original sentence as two separate sentences, one that expresses the cause, the other that expresses the result. Make sure that the second sentence has the appropriate subject. You will have to pick out the key noun from the first sentence to use as the subject of the second sentence. An example is provided.

1. Russian scientists believe that wide-scale irrigation can produce enough evaporation to favorably alter the local climate, <u>making the air more humid</u>.

   Cause: _____ evaporation _____   Result: _____ more humid air _____

   Russian scientists believe that wide-scale irrigation can produce enough evaporation to

   favorably alter the local climate. <u>This evaporation</u> can make the air more humid.

2. There could have been an invasion of cold Arctic air into the heart of Asia as part of this new pattern of climate, reducing the productivity of the land and forcing the people to follow their charismatic leader in a quest for survival.

   Cause: _____   Result: _____

   _____

   _____

3. From the middle of the eleventh century onwards, there were increases in population and improvements in agriculture, producing wealth which led to a great phase of cathedral building and to the Crusades.

   Cause: _____   Result: _____

   _____

   _____

4. The jet stream straddles North America, influencing the formation of weather systems and guiding their paths across North America as it flows west to east.

Cause: _____   Result: _____

_____

_____

Activity 5-17   Stating Causes and Results Using *ing* Participle Phrases

The left column contains causes and the right column contains results. Combine the two into one sentence with an independent clause that expresses a cause or reason and an *ing* phrase that expresses a result. An example is provided.

Causes	Results
1. Four separate disastrous sea floods hit Holland and Germany.	These floods killed 300,000 people. They left more than a million homeless.
1. Four separate disastrous sea floods hit Holland and Germany, killing 300,000 people and leaving a million more homeless.	
2. Strong winds created marching dunes.	The dunes enveloped many coastal villages and townships.
2.	
3. During the medieval warm period, harvests were plentiful and food was abundant.	Plentiful harvests and abundant food resulted in a population boom.
3.	
4. At the end of the fourteenth century, major epidemics such as typhus, smallpox, and influenza struck England.	These epidemics wiped out half of the population in some regions.
4.	

Activity 5-18   Writing Your Own Sentences with *ing* Participle Phrases

Think of a current situation or a local problem (an environmental, economic, or crime problem in your area). It should have some obvious consequences or results that can be expressed in participle phrases. Again, if you don't have enough information, conduct a subject search at a library or on the World Wide Web. Write four sentences about the situation using *ing* participle phrases. An example is provided.

EXAMPLE

Rebel forces took over the capital of Zaire, forcing President Mobutu to flee the country. For a long time, Mobutu used his country's money for his own purposes, causing unnecessary economic hardship to his people.

C. Creating Complex Noun Phrases: Noun + Relative Clause

Academic writers use many long, complex noun phrases to give detailed information about topics. One method for creating such complex noun phrases is to attach a complete sentence to a noun in the form of a *relative clause*. A relative clause is a sentence that has been changed so that it can be attached to a noun. Because a relative clause has a similar function to an adjective, these clauses are often called *adjective clauses*.

The villages **that** were abandoned because of the Black Death had been weakened by periods of famine.

Fluctuations in climate represent nonpermanent changes **that** take place over decades.

There are two types of noun + relative clauses:

Defining (restrictive) relative clauses: The sentence attached to the noun contains information that is essential to identify the person or thing being discussed. Notice there are no commas in this sentence.

Fluctuations in climate represent nonpermanent changes [**that** take place over decades].

Nondefining (nonrestrictive) relative clauses: The sentence attached to the noun contains extra information that is not necessary to identify the person or thing being discussed. Notice that *which* replaces the non-human noun (*that* is not used in nondefining relative clauses) and that there is a comma between the noun and the relative clause.

Leopards are good climbers, so the monkeys can escape them only by climbing out onto the smallest branches, [**which** are too weak to support a leopard].

GLR   See pages 291–293 in the GLR for more information.

Activity 5-19   Creating Complex Nouns with Relative Clauses

The first sentence in each of the following sets contains an important noun. As a writer, however, you wish to add more information to give it exactly the correct meaning. First, find that noun. Then, use the information in the second sentence to create a relative clause. Add that clause to the noun that you identified in the first sentence. Then, in the space provided, rewrite the first sentence including this new complex noun + relative clause. If the information you attach to the noun creates a nondefining relative clause, make sure to add a comma and use the appropriate relative pronoun. The first one is provided.

1. a. The warmth in Europe led to a new form of European civilization.

    b. This new form of European civilization has continued up to the present day.

    The warmth in Europe led to a new form of European civilization that has continued up to the present day.

2. a. The wave of cold eventually brought the famous Little Ice Age.

    b. The Little Ice Age lasted from the middle of the 15th century to the middle of the 19th century.

3. a. The farmland and villages were the most prosperous in England.

    b. Farmland and villages were abandoned during the Black Death.

4. a. The warming was a century-scale climate change.

    b. The warming took place in the 11th and 12th centuries.

5. a. China must use its coal instead of expensive sources of energy.

    b. Expensive sources of energy do not produce carbon dioxide.

PUTTING IT ALL TOGETHER

FINAL WRITING ASSIGNMENT

Your writing task is to write a paper analyzing the causes of one of the following:

- a weather pattern or problem that you are familiar with
- an historical event or situation in a country you are familiar with
- a current situation or problem that interests you

Work together in groups to write your analysis. Consult *The Basics of Writing an Analysis* on pages 159–166.

Audience and Purpose

Write for an audience of college students. Consider what your readers probably already know about this topic. Try to provide some information that the average reader might not know.

Preparing to Write

Complete the following diagram with your peers to gather information and think strategically about how to write this analysis and what to include in it.

Problem You Will Analyze: _____

_____

⇓

Analysis Question You Will Answer:

_____

⇓

Audience: Readers who may know about the obvious causes of the situation or problem, but whom you want to inform about the underlying causes of your topic.

⇓

Thesis (answer to the analytical question): _____

_____

⇓

Decide the Causes of the Problem:

Cause 1: _____

Evidence:

Cause 2: _____

Evidence:

Cause 3: _____

Evidence:

Sources to Consult: interviews with experts or people who have knowledge of the topic

writing letters to solicit information

surveys

books

popular magazines and newspapers

information from the World Wide Web

brochures and information from private organizations

government documents

⇓

Types of Evidence: case studies

personal experience from someone you interview

facts

statistics

laws and regulations related to the topic

research findings

examples

quotations from experts

⇓

ORGANIZATION

Background about your topic: _____

_____

Continued

> **Organization of Body Paragraphs: (choose one based on your content)**
>
> ____ each paragraph presents a single cause, factor, or reason
>
> ____ each paragraph presents a causal chain
>
> ⇓
>
> **Conclusion:**
>
> ⇓
>
> **Written Draft**

Self-editing Activity

1. Before giving your draft to a peer, read it again to make sure that it says what you intended and is organized in the best way for this particular writing task. Make any changes needed to improve meaning and organization.

2. Choose and edit your draft for two of the language features reviewed in this chapter. Where indicated, turn to the GLR ⬤ and use the recommended self-editing strategies.

   ☐ underline all the verbs in your paper that link causes and results. Are they used appropriately? Are there more places in your draft where you could use these? Consult Appendix B: Vocabulary in Academic Writing, if necessary.

   ☐ monitor the use and shifting of verb tenses to convey your intended meaning.

   ☐ use of *ing* participle phrases to write about results.

   ☐ use of relative clauses to create complex noun phrases.

   > **GLR** See page 300, Section 3, for more information on editing for verb tense shift and page 296 in Section 3 for information on editing relative clauses.

3. Edit your draft for one of the language features reviewed in the previous chapters that you think may need more careful attention in your writing. Consult the self-editing activities in the previous chapters.

Peer Response Activity

Exchange papers with a partner. Answer the following questions about your partner's paper:

1. What problem is the writer analyzing?

2. What causes are given for the problem in the paper? What new information did you learn about the causes or factors associated with this problem?

3. What is the most interesting cause the writer gives in the analysis? Why?

4. Ask the writer two journalistic questions about ideas that were unclear in the paper.

5. Make one suggestion to help the writer revise the draft.

LEARNER'S NOTEBOOK

Reflecting on Writing Analysis Papers

Report what you have learned about writing an effective analysis paper. Consider the way you wrote your analysis as well as the way your peers approached the writing task.

Revise

On your draft, list two changes that you will make to your analysis. Rewrite your paper, including these changes.

LOOKING AHEAD

With a partner or in a small group, read and then analyze the following assignment.

Introduction to Women's Studies

Give two reasons to explain why the sociological perspective might prove useful to feminists interested in describing women's realities. What is the distinction feminists make between sex and gender? Why focus on the difference? What is to be gained by thinking about women's realities in terms of gender as opposed to sex?

DISCUSSION

1. In what ways will this analysis differ from what you have learned about writing analysis papers? Describe specific differences that you notice.

2. What can you learn about the professor and his/her expectations by reading the assignment? Be specific in this audience analysis.

3. What problems do you anticipate for the person doing this analysis? What solutions can you offer?

Chapter 6

Problem-Solving

Privacy and Personal Information

GOALS

WRITING
- ◆ define a problem clearly
- ◆ offer several solutions and analyze the advantages and disadvantages of each

GRAMMAR
- ◆ practice structures that writers use to persuade:
    - sentences with *if, even if*, and *unless*
    - modals such as *can, must*, and *should*
- ◆ practice how writers use nouns in presenting solutions

CONTENT
- ◆ learn about ways in which your personal privacy can be invaded on the computer and by agencies that have personal information about you
- ◆ learn how you can protect your privacy

ACADEMIC FIELDS

Law
Computer Science
Medical Ethics

Sample Authentic College/University Writing Assignments

The problem-solving skills you will learn in this chapter can be used to complete college/university assignments and exam questions like the ones below.

Geography

Identify one problem related to allocation of resources that the world is currently experiencing. **Offer possible solutions, analyzing** the **advantages** and **disadvantages** of each solution.

Atmospheric Sciences

The human population on Earth is currently doubling about every 30 years. It has been suggested that overpopulation problems could be solved by colonizing the Moon or Mars. **Analyze** the **advantages** and **disadvantages** of this solution.

 CNN video support is available for this chapter.

GETTING READY

Warm-up Activity: Writing

In our personal lives, we confront problems that need solutions. Sometimes there are no easy solutions or there may be several possible solutions. In either case, problem-solving involves identifying possible solutions, considering each alternative carefully, and exploring the feasibility of each alternative. Finally, you will probably have to persuade others that one alternative is the most efficient or acceptable plan.

Identify a problem that needs solving at your school or in your local community. Write a memo to someone in a position to deal with the problem. In it, explain why the situation or issue you have identified is a problem and recommend two or more possible solutions. Possible topics include problems with transportation or parking, class registration procedures, academic counseling, or financial aid. Or you might discuss problems with traffic, crime, or some aspect of the neighborhood or environment in your community. Compare the situation or problem that you have written about with that of another classmate.

LEARNER'S NOTEBOOK

Examining a Solution's Advantages and Disadvantages

In your learner's notebook, write a paragraph explaining the advantages and disadvantages of each solution you recommended to the problem you identified in the warm-up writing.

Activity 6-1   Writing a Letter of Advice

Advice columns are the most common types of writing that communicate solutions to problems. Read the column below and work together with a partner or in a small group to write a letter recommending a solution to the letter writer's problem. Compare your response to those of other classmates.

Dear Ann:

My daughter, who recently divorced her husband of 15 years, is planning to remarry this summer. My husband and I are very supportive, but we are faced with a dilemma. Please help us make the right decision.

"Donna" has asked us to take the photographs of her first wedding off the family room wall so as not to offend her new fiancé. Our former son-in-law comes to the house quite often with the grandchildren. Since he was deeply hurt by the divorce, we have always made an extra effort to include him whenever possible and be especially cordial. If these photographs were removed, it would be noticed immediately and could damage our friendship.

Should we remove the pictures and risk an already strained relationship, or should I go out and purchase double picture frames and display photos of both past and present husbands?

DISTRESSED IN PEBBLE BEACH, CA.

The Basics of Writing a Problem-Solving Paper

Unlike the other types of writing you have done in this book, problem-solution papers require more of both the writer and the reader. Since problem-solution papers motivate readers to change their own behavior or become involved in solving a problem, the writer must think carefully about how the reader may view the problem or situation, what solutions for change the reader will find acceptable, and how best to persuade the reader to accept the proposed solution(s).

Academic problem-solving involves several skills that you have already learned. It includes:

- Investigating the problem to find out how it affects people and what is being done about it.
- Reporting your own experience or expertise about the problem and potential solutions.
- Analyzing the problem and giving reasons why it needs to be solved.
- Evaluating the advantages and disadvantages of various solutions.

1. Defining the Problem or Situation Clearly

Once you have decided on the problem or situation that you will consider, your task as a writer is to explain it clearly for your audience, helping them not only to understand *what* it is, but *why* it is a problem. This section of the paper convinces readers that the problem exists. The following explanation of the problem of garbage was written by a community college ESL student, Melissa Castro. The explanation:

- provides general background about the problem,
- gives a clear statement of the problem, and
- explains the problem in detail, providing evidence and further explanation of the problem.

Day by day, societies all over the world consume more and more stuff. They follow the example of first world nations, thus making the same mistakes. Garbage is the biggest of them all. It is known that the richer the country, the more waste it produces. The United States alone produces about <u>209 million tons of municipal waste per year</u>, which is <u>more than four pounds per person per day</u> (*Discover Magazine,* June 1997). This extends from harmless candy wrappings to giant sites where toxic wastes are dumped.

background about the problem

evidence of problem

<u>Garbage is our worst enemy</u>. In countries like the U.S., to open a snack package shows one of the infinite reasons why we have so much waste. First there is a regular carton. Then there is the plastic wrapping. And after that, you will still find a plastic or paper tray before you can actually reach your snack. It would be much easier for us and especially for mother nature if that same snack came in only a plastic or paper wrapping or even in a reusable package.

statement of the problem

further explanation & evidence of problem

Melissa Castro chose to write about a problem that we are all familiar with so she didn't need to provide lots of evidence or explanation to help the readers understand **what** the problem is and **why** it is a problem. Notice that the next writer needs to provide more background, explanation, and evidence about a less familiar problem: the invasion of privacy on the Internet.

Someone is watching you. Likely, several someones are—anyone from your boss to a nighttime employee at your Internet service provider, and possibly someone from the government. From the moment you connect to the Net, you are leaking information to the world about who you are, what you do, and what you are interested in. As private a pastime as surfing the Internet might seem, it's not. <u>The computers that make up the Net monitor and often record everything you do while online. And it isn't hard for a cybersnoop to find out more about you.</u>

background about the problem

statement of the problem

Giving It Away

Web sites commonly get information about you through an online registration form. Some sites offer a sample of their content to anyone who browses by, but reserve the best "stuff" for visitors who register with the site. Although there's nothing illegal about requiring you to register with a site, you should realize that the registration information usually goes into a marketing database that is sold to just about anyone

explaining the problem in more detail

willing to pay for it. A sports-oriented site might sell its list
of subscribers to a sports magazine, which may use it for an
e-mail ad campaign. If you've ever been barraged with junk
mail a few weeks after you registered at a new Web site, it's   evidence of problem
a good bet your name and address were sold to one or more
mailing-list companies.

Source: B. Mann, *Stopping You Watching Me,*
Internet World, April 1997, 42.

2. Stating Your Solutions and Analyzing Advantages and Disadvantages

The part of the paper in which you provide solutions is the heart of the paper. A good
solution section:

- clearly responds to the problem you have defined
- provides one or more concrete solutions vs. ones that are vague or simplistic
- presents the advantages and disadvantages of the proposed solutions

Here is an example of the solution section of a problem-solution article. It offers solutions to the problem of privacy on the Internet.

Now that you know how snoops can invade your privacy
online, what can you do about it? <u>There are several steps you</u>   general statement of the
<u>can take to protect yourself. Some are more cumbersome than</u>   solution
<u>others, and only you can decide when to make the trade-off of</u>
<u>convenience for security.</u>

Use the Anonymizer. The Anonymizer (http://www.   solution
anonymizer.com) is a Web site that acts as a middleman
between your browser and other Web sites and prevents the sites   advantages of the solution
you visit from learning anything about you.

One big disadvantage of the Anonymizer is that it adds
another step to the path information must travel to get from a   disadvantages of the
Web site to you. The Anonymizer loads the information for   solution
you, then transfers it to your browser, making everything you
do on the Web slower. You also must remember to use it,
although if you're willing to commit to using the Anonymizer
for all your Web browsing, you can configure your browser to
work that way. A third disadvantage is that the Anonymizer
doesn't work with everything you find online. Still, if you
want to surf the Web anonymously, the Anonymizer is an
effective way to do it.

Use Encryption. <u>The simplest and safest way</u> to prevent unauthorized people from reading your e-mail is to use encryption software. When both parties use the same software, messages sent from one person to another are readable only by the intended recipient. Whether you're sharing your marketing ideas for the next quarter or simply making vacation plans that will leave your home unoccupied, there are many reasons for keeping your private mail private.

author's preferred solution

Source: B. Mann, Stopping You Watching Me,
Internet World, April 1997, 42.

The writer has considered two solutions to the problem of safeguarding Internet privacy, and has stated the advantages and disadvantages of two of the approaches. The writer presents his preferred solution, the use of encryption software, last.

3. Identifying Your Audience and Focusing Your Solutions

The solutions a writer proposes and how specific they are depend largely on the audience. Reread "Use the Anonymizer" above. Notice the difference between that proposed solution and the one below. The author of "Use the Anonymizer" provides specific steps the reader can take to solve the problem of Internet privacy. He can do this because he knows that the audience can actually act on them immediately. The writers below, on the other hand, provide a general solution to the problem of confidentiality of medical records. The writers know that the audience, unless he or she is a member of the U.S. Congress, cannot take direct action.

Solutions [to the problem of ensuring the confidentiality of medical records] must come primarily from Washington. For only Congress can impose confidentiality laws governing interstate computer networks and prohibit the disclosure of medical information without a patient's consent.

statement of the solution

Congress can take a first step toward patient privacy by passing the proposed Fair Health Information Practices Act, introduced in January by Rep. Gary A. Condit (D-Ceres). Condit's bill doesn't address all of the ways in which the sophisticated medical records industry has learned to procure patient data. Those loopholes will have to be closed by future legislation. But unlike two confidentiality bills that died in Congress last year, Condit's bill more sharply limits disclosure of medical records.

disadvantages of the solution

advantages of the solution

Source: Editorial, Threat to Confidentiality of Personal
Medical Records, *Los Angeles Times,* March 14, 1997, B4.

Source: Drawing by S. Gross. © 1996 The New Yorker Magazine, Inc.

Activity 6-2   Identifying the Problem in a Cartoon and Proposing Solutions

Choose this cartoon or the one in Activity 6-17 and do the following:

1. Write an explanation of the problem it depicts. Make sure to give background about the problem and provide examples or evidence that will help your readers to understand that this is an important problem.

2. Develop one possible solution for the problem you have chosen.

3. Use the chart below to consider the advantages and disadvantages of that solution.

Solution 1: _____

Advantages	Disadvantages

LEARNER'S NOTEBOOK

Reading a Newspaper Article that Proposes Solutions

In the opinion or editorial section of your local or school newspaper, find an article that explains a problem and then provides solutions for it. In your learner's notebook, summarize the problem and the writer's solution(s). State whether you think the solution(s) respond(s) well to the problem. Share your summary and your opinion with a partner.

FOCUSING

Introduction to Readings

The widespread use of computers to store information has meant that more and more information about each one of us is easily accessible. Sometimes this makes our lives more efficient; at other times, such information is too readily available to people who may misuse it.

Pre-reading Activity

LEARNER'S NOTEBOOK

Defining Privacy

What is privacy? Write what privacy means to you and explain what factors might influence your definition of privacy. Consider such things as your cultural values, your family's concept of privacy, your socioeconomic position, or the availability of technology. Share your ideas with two other classmates.

Activity 6-3   A Privacy Quiz

Take the following "Privacy Quiz" to see how much you know about the privacy of your personal information. Circle T if the statement is true and F if it is false. Answers can be found on the last page of this chapter.

T   F   **1.** The United States Postal Service has the right to sell your name and address to private businesses that, in turn, place it on mailing lists.

T   F   **2.** The constitution of the United States contains an amendment that protects the privacy of personal information.

T   F   **3.** You are the only one with the legal right to access your credit history (the record of what you have purchased with credit and your payment or non-payment history).

T   F   **4.** If your name becomes part of a company's mailing list, you do not have the right to remove it.

T   F   **5.** It is illegal to intercept private electronic communications including e-mail, cellular phones, etc.

T   F   **6.** Your telephone number is the property of the phone company.

T   F   **7.** The personal information you provide to obtain a driver's license (such as address, height, weight, etc.) can be sold or provided to private businesses.

T   F   **8.** Today's presidential candidates are required by law to make their medical records public.

Pre-reading Vocabulary

Verb + Noun, Noun + Noun, and Adjective + Noun Combinations

Nouns often combine with other words to create set expressions. Here are some examples of nouns combined with other kinds of words:

Verb + noun = to safeguard information

noun + noun = a privacy issue

adjective + noun = private information

When you learn a new word, it is useful to notice the expressions it appears in.

It is sometimes especially difficult to identify verb + noun expressions because they can be separated by other words. To find the essential elements of a verb + noun expression, find the noun and then look before or after it for the nearest verb:

Accruing voluntary *information* from you isn't necessarily a privacy issue.

Information you *disclose* voluntarily does, however, become a privacy issue when it is combined with information obtained about you involuntarily.

Activity 6-4   Finding Word Combinations with Nouns

To prepare to read about privacy, write as many expressions as you can that contain the words *privacy* and *information*. Then scan the two readings, "Stopping You Watching Me" and "Confidentiality of Personal Medical Records" to find other verbs, adjectives, or nouns that appear with the words *privacy* and *information*. Add these to the chart also. Some examples are provided for you.

privacy/confidentiality	information
Verb + Noun Expressions	**Verb + Noun Expressions**
to be entitled to privacy	to safeguard information
Noun + Noun Expressions	**Adjective + Noun Expressions**
a clear invasion of privacy	detailed information

Activity 6-5   Practice Using Word Combinations

Go back to the Activity 6-3 and choose one of the privacy problems in the Privacy Quiz. Write two sentences using two of the different verb expressions, noun expressions, or adjective-noun expressions with *privacy* and *information* that you found in Activity 6-4. An example is provided.

Problem: Today's presidential candidates are not required by law to make their medical records public.

1. Without laws to force presidential candidates [to disclose information] about their health, people might run for office who are seriously ill and who could die in office.
2. While it is important for American voters to know if a future president is in good health, the press can easily [obtain information] that is none of the general public's business and would not impede a future president from doing his job well.

READING 1   STOPPING YOU WATCHING ME (MAGAZINE ARTICLE)

"Stopping You Watching Me" appeared in *Internet World,* a magazine published for people who enjoy "surfing," or searching the Internet.

Pre-reading Activities

Activity 6-6   Predicting the Contents of a Reading Passage

After reading the title and skimming the first paragraph of the reading, predict the problem that this article will address. Think of specific examples of the problem that the writer might include. Write these examples on a separate piece of paper.

STOPPING YOU WATCHING ME

Someone is watching you. Likely, several someones are—anyone from your boss to a nighttime employee at your Internet service provider, and possibly someone from the government. From the moment you connect to the Net, you are leaking information to the world about who you are, what you do, and what you are interested in. As private a pastime as surfing the Internet might seem, it's not. The computers that make up the Net monitor and   5
often record everything you do while online.

And it isn't hard for a cybersnoop to find out more about you; combining the information about the sites you visit, where you live, and the registration information many sites require, anyone with a sense of logic can build a quick and accurate profile on you.

Privacy on the Internet is an illusion unless you take active steps to ensure it. The first   10
step in protecting yourself is to learn how your privacy can be violated.

Giving It Away

Internet sites gather information from you in two ways: voluntarily and involuntarily. Accruing voluntary information from you isn't necessarily a privacy issue; if you don't want someone to have the information, you don't have to give it to them. Information you disclose voluntarily does, however, become a privacy issue when it is used in ways you didn't intend or when it is combined with information obtained involuntarily.

Web sites commonly get information about you through an online registration form. Some sites offer a sample of their content to anyone who browses by, but reserve the best "stuff" for visitors who register with the site. Although there's nothing illegal about requiring you to register with a site, you should realize that the registration information usually goes into a marketing database that is sold to just about anyone willing to pay for it. A sports-oriented site might sell its list of subscribers to a sports magazine, which may use it for an e-mail ad campaign. If you've ever been barraged with junk mail a few weeks after you registered at a new Web site, there's a good possibility that your name and address were sold to one or more mailing-list companies.

Taking It

Involuntary information gathering is what most people think of when the subject of online privacy comes up. That kind of information gathering is usually perfectly legal. But piecing together a detailed profile of you based on the Web sites you visited and information publicly available about you, for instance, would feel to most people like a clear invasion of privacy.

There are several ways snoops can gather information about you without your knowledge:

Newsgroup Postings. Messages you post to a newsgroup may seem to disappear after a while, but you can be sure they're stored somewhere. All a snoop needs is your name to use services like Deja News (http://www.dejanews.com) or AltaVista to look up virtually any message you ever posted and, thus, get a peek into your viewpoints and, depending on the newsgroups, your tastes.

Internet Directories. Public information is just that—public. Even if you have an unlisted phone number, there's a chance that you're listed in a public directory and some site on the Net has a gateway to it. Nationwide and worldwide phone directories abound, as do for-fee databases with more detailed information. Anyone can use one of these directories to find your address, phone number, birthday, and more. While all this information is publicly available through other sources, Internet directories make it cheap and easy for anyone to get it, and that makes many people uncomfortable.

E-mail Interception. While the previously discussed privacy threats are all legal, others are not. "Electronic mail is the most pro-surveillance technology ever invented," says Andre Bacard, author of the Computer Privacy Handbook, "with the possible exception of the microphone." A technically savvy snoop can capture e-mail messages as they pass through or stop at a computer to which he has access. The necessary equipment is minimal, and although most holes have been fixed, Unix's origin as an open, academic system makes it particularly vulnerable to prying eyes.

Reading your e-mail might not even be illegal. Your company probably has the right to read whatever messages you send and receive, especially if it has informed you of its right to do so in the employee handbook. And even if it didn't have the right, it certainly has the ability—and you would likely never be able to prove that you were passed up for promotion because of the things you said about your boss via e-mail to a friend.

Self-Defense

Now that you know how snoops can invade your privacy online, what can you do about it? There are several steps you can take to protect yourself. Some are more cumbersome than others, and only you can decide when to make the trade-off of convenience for security.

Ask About a Privacy Policy. Thanks to a combination of public concern and publicity about potential problems, many sites have adopted privacy policies. They typically describe the kind of information they collect and what it is used for.

Think Before You Register. Does the site have a privacy policy you like? If so, registering there is probably safe. If not, you often can find an alternative source for the information at a site that doesn't require registration. Consider whether you really need the information and whether the knowledge you gain is worth the privacy you lose.

Use the Anonymizer. The Anonymizer (http://www.anonymizer.com) is a Web site that acts as a middleman between your browser and other Web sites and prevents the sites you visit from learning anything about you.

One big disadvantage of the Anonymizer is that it adds another step to the path information must travel to get from a Web site to you. The Anonymizer loads the information for you, then transfers it to your browser, making everything you do on the Web slower. You also must remember to use it, although if you're willing to commit to using the Anonymizer for all your Web browsing, you can configure your browser to work that way. A third disadvantage is that the Anonymizer doesn't work with everything you find online. Still, if you want to surf the Web anonymously, the Anonymizer is an effective way to do it.

Use Anonymous Remailers. An anonymous remailer accepts an e-mail message from you, strips off any identifying information in the header of the message, and forwards the message to its destination with an address like "an1234@nowhere.net." All anyone knows about you is that you are using an anonymous remailer called nowhere.net. Most anonymous remailers are free.

While anonymous remailers offer privacy advantages, they have several disadvantages as well. First, not all remailers support two-way message delivery. You can send messages anonymously, but not receive responses. Second, anonymous remailers have a bit of an unsavory reputation: many people associate them with shifty types and may be wary of messages coming from an anonymous e-mail address. Third, because you are writing anonymously, people may not take you seriously. If you're unwilling to stand by what you write, why should anyone believe you?

Use Encryption. The simplest and safest way to prevent unauthorized people from reading your e-mail is to use encryption software. When both parties use the same software,

messages sent from one person to another are readable only by the intended recipient. 95
Whether you're sharing your marketing ideas for the next quarter or simply making vacation plans that will leave your home unoccupied, there are many reasons for keeping your
private mail private.

In Your Own Hands

In many ways, the Internet remains an untamed, chaotic place. The amount of privacy 100
you are entitled to online is still an open question. In the meantime, snoops of various sorts
are taking advantage of the situation, gathering and using information you may not want
them to have.

You must take your privacy into your own hands. Knowing some of the tricks used to
gather information about you allows you to take countermeasures to thwart most of them. 105
It's up to you to decide how much privacy you want and how hard you're willing to work
to get it.

Source: Bill Mann, Stopping You Watching Me,
Internet World, April 1997, 42–46.

Active Reading

Activity 6-7   Analyzing the Purpose, Tone, and Audience of a Reading Passage

Circle the answers that best reflect the intended audience, purpose, tone, and way the
writer arouses the reader's interest in "Stopping You Watching Me." You may choose
more than one answer, but you must be ready to defend your choice with sentences or
words from the reading.

	"Stopping You Watching Me"		
Audience	government policymakers	a general audience	experts in the field of computers
	individual computer users	companies that market products on the Internet	
Purpose	to inform to persuade	to entertain to propose a solution	to give advice
Tone	optimistic sarcastic	objective angry	concerned amusing
Strategy to engage readers' interest	statistics an intriguing first sentence asking a question a current news item	example cases	

Activity 6-8   Applying the Guidelines for a Problem-Solution Essay

Answer the following questions based on your opinion of how well the author of "Stopping You Watching Me" satisfies the guidelines for a well-written problem-solution paper. If you answer "yes" to any question, provide an example from the reading. If you answer "no" to any question, give a reason for your answer. An example has been done for you.

Basic Questions about a Good Problem-Solution Paper			Reasons/Examples
1. Has the writer explained the problem clearly and convinced you that this problem concerns you?	<u>Yes</u> No		1. "Internet sites gather information from you in two ways: voluntarily and involuntarily." "From the moment you connect to the Net, you are leaking information to the world about who you are, what you do, and what you are interested in. As private a pastime as surfing the Internet might seem, it's not. The computers that make up the Net monitor and often record everything you do while online."
2. Has the writer provided solutions that clearly respond to the problem discussed?	Yes No		2.
3. Are the solutions concrete?	Yes No		3.
4. In explaining the solutions, has the writer discussed the advantages and disadvantages?	Yes No		4.

READING 2   THREAT TO CONFIDENTIALITY OF PERSONAL MEDICAL RECORDS (NEWSPAPER EDITORIAL)

The following article appeared in *The Los Angeles Times*. It addresses a growing problem related to privacy and medical records.

Pre-reading Vocabulary

Activity 6-9   Using a Dictionary to Learn Key Words

Choose four of the vocabulary words that appear in italics in "Confidentiality of Personal Medical Records." Look each word up in an English-English dictionary. Find out its part of speech (noun, adjective, adverb, verb) and its meaning in the context of the sentence. Prepare to report this information to your classmates. The first italicized word is done as an example.

EXAMPLE

Act (noun)—a law that has been officially passed by the government.

LEARNER'S NOTEBOOK

Learning New Vocabulary

Review the vocabulary words that you have collected and learned in this chapter and in previous chapters. Consult pages 363–368, Appendix B: *Vocabulary in Academic Writing* for information about learning new vocabulary. In your learner's notebook, write about what you've discovered about learning vocabulary. Consider such things as how you best remember words, whether there is a difference between vocabulary for reading and for writing, and any other ideas you have about learning vocabulary. Share your ideas with two other classmates.

THREAT TO CONFIDENTIALITY OF PERSONAL MEDICAL RECORDS

Last year, the U.S. Congress passed the Kennedy-Kassebaum Health Insurance Portability and Accountability *Act*. This act contained a little-publicized *provision* asking health care providers to build a national database of patients' *medical records*. Americans have much to gain from such a database. With it, emergency room doctors could review the medical history of an unconscious accident victim before deciding on a method to revive him. Or researchers could try to determine whether medication given to pregnant women was associated with diseases in their children years later.

There are no federal laws, however, *ensuring* that medical records will be limited to professional hands like these. And so unless Congress acts *promptly* against *inappropriate* access, Americans stand to lose as much as they will gain from the *ongoing* computerization of medical records. Now many doctors are thinking twice about what information they include in patient records, for fear it could be used against a patient's best interest. And some people are *denying themselves* the benefits of genetic tests because they don't want insurers and employers to discover they have a *predisposition* to a particular disease.

One would think that patients already enjoy privacy of their medical records, but as a National Research Council panel warned earlier this month, "There are no strong *incentives* to safeguard patient information because patients, industry groups, and government regulators aren't demanding protection."

California is one of a few states offering a degree of medical confidentiality. Under section 56 of the state civil code, companies are allowed to see the medical records of their employees only if they can show that they need the information to make medical insurance contributions. But Beth Givens, project director of the non-profit Privacy Rights Clearing House in San Diego, says section 56 has a "*loophole* big enough for a Mack truck to drive through." It allows hospitals and other health care facilities to *release* a patient's key medical records unless the patient has forbidden release in writing. Moreover, under another act of the federal government, companies that develop their own medical plan are *exempt from* all state confidentiality laws.

Solutions must come primarily from Washington. For only Congress can *impose* confidentiality laws governing interstate computer networks and prohibiting the disclosure of medical information without a patient's *consent*.

Congress can take a first step toward patient privacy by passing the proposed Fair Health Information Practices Act, introduced in January by Representative Gary A. Condit (D-Ceres). Condit's bill doesn't *address* all the ways in which the sophisticated medical records industry has learned to procure patient information. Those loopholes will have to be closed by future legislation. But unlike two confidentiality bills that died in Congress last year, Condit's bill more sharply *limits* disclosure of medical records.

The Kennedy-Kassebaum Act gave Congress until late 1999 to *devise* a plan for ensuring medical confidentiality. Present dangers, however, *demand* action that is more prompt.

Source: Editorial Board, *Los Angeles Times*, March 24, 1997, B4.

Active Reading

Activity 6-10   Analyzing the Purpose, Tone, and Audience of a Reading Passage

Circle the answers in the following chart which best reflect the intended audience, purpose, tone, and way the writers arouse the reader's interest in "Confidentiality of Personal Medical Records." You may choose more than one answer, but you must be ready to defend your choice with sentences or words from the reading.

	"Confidentiality of Personal Medical Records"		
Audience	government policymakers	a general audience	medical experts
		healthcare workers	college students
Purpose	to inform	to entertain	to give advice
	to persuade		to propose a solution
Tone	optimistic	objective	concerned
	sarcastic	angry	amusing
Strategy to engage readers' interest	statistics		little-known facts
	quotes from experts		current news items

Activity 6-11 Applying the Guidelines for a Problem-Solution Essay

Answer the following questions based on your opinion of how well the authors of "Threat to Confidentiality of Personal Medical Records" satisfy the guidelines for a well-written problem-solution essay. If you answer "yes" to any question, provide an example from the reading. If you answer "no" to any question, give a reason for your answer. An example has been done for you.

Basic Questions about a Good Problem-Solution Paper		**Reasons/Examples**

1. Has the writer explained the problem clearly and convinced you that this problem concerns you?

<u>Yes</u> No

1. The authors are concerned about the federal government's decision to develop a national medical database. Although the database could be useful in some instances, the information contained in the records could possibly be used against the patient in some way.

Basic Questions about a Good Problem-Solution Paper			Reasons/Examples
			The authors convince readers that this is a problem by giving examples of how these computerized records affect doctors and patients: "Now many doctors are thinking twice about what information they include in patient records, for fear it could be used against a patient's best interest. And some people are denying themselves the benefits of genetic tests because they don't want insurers and employers to discover they have a predisposition to a particular disease."
2. Has the writer provided solutions that clearly respond to the problem discussed?	Yes No	**2.**	
3. Are the solutions concrete?	Yes No	**3.**	
4. In explaining the solutions, has the writer discussed the advantages and disadvantages?	Yes No	**4.**	

Activity 6-12   Writing a Study Summary Using New Vocabulary Words

Write a study summary of "Threat to Confidentiality of Personal Medical Records." Use at least four of the new vocabulary words from Activity 6-9. Review how to write a study summary on page 17 in Chapter 1.

Analysis of Language: Using Persuasive Grammar to Write About Problems and Their Solutions

A. Using Conditional Sentences to Persuade Readers

Academic writers often use conditional sentences to try to convince readers about logical relationships between causes and results, or between reasons and choices. Writers hope to convince readers that the relationship between the two parts of the statement is rational, logical, and true. This structure is common in problem-solution papers. The sentences often begin with *if, even if,* or *unless.* This *if* part of the sentence indicates conditions associated with a problem, argues for a certain solution, or gives readers choices about how to solve a problem. Here are some examples to show how writers use conditional sentences to try to persuade readers.

1. Meanings of Sentences with *if*

Indicating a choice or "conditions" that lead to an outcome or problem

Main clause—states the outcome or problem

Your company probably *has* the right to read whatever messages you send and
subordinate clause—states the condition

receive, especially *if* it *has informed* you of its right to do so in the employee handbook.

subordinate clause—states the condition   main clause—states the choice

If you *don't want* someone to have the information, you *don't have* to give it to them.

2. Meaning of Sentences with *unless*

Indicating that an "unfulfilled" condition will lead to a problem or given outcome

subordinate clause—states the "unfulfilled" condition

Unless Congress *acts* promptly against inappropriate access, Americans *stand* to
main clause—states the problem or outcome

lose as much as they will gain from the ongoing computerization of medical records.

3. Meaning of Sentences with *even if*

Indicating that, although a condition is met, the expected outcome is not guaranteed. (The condition won't affect the outcome.)

subordinate clause—states a condition that will not affect the outcome   main clause—states the problem or outcome

Even if you *have* an unlisted phone number, you*'re* probably listed in a public directory and some site on the Net has a gateway to it.

GLR   See pages 326–327 in the GLR for more information.

Activity 6-13   Locating Conditional Sentences in a Piece of Writing

Reread "Stopping You Watching Me" and "Threat to Confidentiality of Personal Medical Records." Find and write two sentences that contain *if,* two sentences that contain *unless,* and one sentence that contains *even if.* Underline the verbs in each part of the sentence and label the main clause and the subordinate clause. Then answer the following questions about the sentences you find:

- What is the writer trying to persuade the reader of?
- Are you persuaded?
- What's the problem if you are not persuaded?

Some examples are done for you.

If Conditional Sentences

EXAMPLE

                 subordinate clause   main clause
1. [If you don't want someone to have the information,] you don't have to give it to them.

   Analysis of Meaning: The writer is trying to tell readers that they have a choice about whether to release personal information over the Internet. He is trying to persuade readers that they have some responsibility for controlling the flow of personal information on to the Internet, too: we shouldn't just rely on technology or government regulation.

2. _____

   Analysis of Meaning: _____

   _____

   _____

   _____

3. _____

   Analysis of Meaning: _____

   _____

   _____

   _____

Unless Conditional Sentences

EXAMPLE

subordinate clause   main clause

4. [Unless Congress acts promptly against inappropriate access,] Americans stand to lose as much as they will gain from the ongoing computerization of medical records.

Analysis of Meaning: _____

_____

_____

_____

5. _____

Analysis of Meaning: _____

_____

_____

_____

6. _____

Analysis of Meaning: _____

_____

_____

_____

Even if Conditional Sentences

EXAMPLE

subordinate clause   main clause

7. [Even if you have an unlisted phone number,] you're probably listed in a public directory and some site on the Net has a gateway to it.

Analysis of Meaning: _____

_____

_____

_____

8. _____

Analysis of Meaning: _____

_____

_____

_____

Activity 6-14   Writing Persuasive Conditional Sentences

Because conditional sentences create connections between conditions and outcomes that are believable for readers, they must be accurate; writers must choose information carefully, use correct verb tenses in both parts of the sentence, and consider using adverbs and modals to control the tone of the statement. To practice this type of persuasive writing, do the following:

- Use conditional sentences with *if* and *unless* to discuss the conditions that create the problem discussed in each of the following privacy situations.
- Then think of potential solutions. Use conditional sentences with *if* and *unless* to discuss the specific conditions that will make a proposed solution work.

Compare your statements to those of other students to share ideas about ways to make accurate and persuasive statements. One example is provided.

| | **Privacy Situation** | **Conditional Sentences** |

Privacy Situation

1. We all receive a large amount of "junk" mail from direct mail marketers. This is because the U.S. Postal Service sells its national database that contains all of our names and addresses to direct mail companies. Carl Oppedahl, a practicing lawyer in Manhattan, spent several years trying to stop his mother from receiving such direct mail solicitations. Carl's mother responded to many of these direct mail ads and often provided the companies with her credit card number as she purchased items.

Source: Based on A.W. Branscomb, *Who Owns Information?: From Privacy to Public Access* (New York: HarperCollins, 1994, 9–11).

Conditional Sentences

Problem

If you give your name and address to one direct mail company, you will most certainly receive catalogs from five or six other companies who have bought your name and address.

Solution

Unless you change your address directly with the direct mail companies and people you do business with, you will continue to receive unwanted junk mail.

2. Willis Mog, an attorney in Illinois, was angry because his dinner hour was interrupted with telemarketing calls. He received as many as 15 calls during the dinner hour. He felt like he might have to go outside, go out for dinner, or disconnect the phone, missing potentially important business calls.

Problem

_____
_____
_____

Solution

_____
_____
_____

Source: Based on Branscomb, see above, 30–31.

3. About three months ago, Rebecca Smith went to the Department of Motor Vehicles to renew her driver's license. Within one week, she received unsolicited information from a company that provides weight loss programs. They sent the information to her based on the weight and height she put down on her driver's license application.

Problem

_____
_____
_____

Solution

_____
_____
_____

Source: Based on Branscomb, see above, 25.

B. Using Modals to Present Solutions

Modals such as *should, must, might,* and *may* are used to talk about solutions. Writers use them to vary the strength of the solutions they give.

Command: A company *must have* a clear and unambiguous policy about e-mail privacy.

Strong advice: A company's e-mail privacy policy *should be updated* regularly and communicated to all employees.

Option or choice: Companies *might consider* rewriting their E-mail privacy policy once a month and communicating this to all employees.

Solutions are also presented using *can.* Writers use *can* when they want to offer various options to the reader and to indicate that the reader has the ability to do something and sometimes even the "power" to do so.

Ability and power: There are several steps you *can take* to protect yourself.

Ability: With an anonymous remailer, you *can send* messages anonymously, but not receive responses.

GLR   See pages 315–321 in the GLR for more information.

Activity 6-15   Identifying Sentences with *Can*

Go back to the readings and find three more examples of sentences that use *can* to indicate ability and power. Write the sentences below.

EXAMPLE

There are several steps you *can take* to protect yourself.

1.

2.

3.

Activity 6-16   Using Modals to Write Solutions

Choose two of the situations related to the privacy of personal information from Activity 6-15. Write two sentences to propose solutions for each situation. Write one sentence using *can* to present readers with options and another sentence using *must* or *should* to give either strong advice or a command. Discuss how the meaning changes when the modal changes.

EXAMPLE

Situation 3: About three months ago, Rebecca Smith went to the Department of Motor Vehicles to renew her driver's license. Within one week, she received unsolicited information from a company that provides weight loss programs. They sent the information to her based on the weight and height she put down on her driver's license application.

1. The state legislature should pass a bill prohibiting the DMV from selling any of its databases.

2. Rebecca can write a letter to the DMV and ask them not to give her name to anyone.

Analysis of Language: Using Interactive Grammar to Write About Problems and Their Solutions

A. Addressing the Reader

Like speaking, writing is an act of communication. However, writers of academic English observe certain conventions when expressing their ideas to their audience. While in spoken conversation we usually address our audience by using pronouns such as *you* and *we*, academic writing tends to avoid these pronouns. Look at the following example.

> A good e-mail policy ensures that employees' privacy is not violated except for legitimate business purposes.

In non-academic writing, writers often seem to "talk" more directly to their readers. They address them using *you* or *we* and use questions to involve them more in the ideas. Here are some examples:

> **We** can all agree that **we** have a right to privacy in the restroom. That's an easy one. *But does an employee have the right to assume that a locker, a desk drawer, or an e-mail message is private?* That's not so clear," says Jeffrey Kingston, a partner with the San Francisco law firm of Brobeck, Phleget and Harrison, and author of *Privacy in Computer Networks.*

> Someone is watching *you.* Likely, several someones are—anyone from *your* boss to a nighttime employee at *your* Internet service provider, and possibly someone from the government.

You may have learned that you should never use *I* or *you* in academic writing. This, however, is probably an overgeneralization. Depending on the audience and purpose, even academic writers may use *we* and sometimes even *you* and *I.*

GLR   See page 313–319, Section 5, in the GLR for more information on modal auxiliaries.

Activity 6-17   Practice Addressing Different Readers

Some people have difficulty controlling the amount of television and the kinds of programs they view. Outline solutions for this problem in writing to two different audiences:

- A friend who you write via e-mail. Your friend watches too much television and has asked for advice about how to reduce his TV-watching.
- A professor in an introductory college course in communications. She has asked you to write a memo addressing ways that people can control their "addiction" to television viewing. See pages 41–42 in Chapter 2 to review the format and guidelines for writing memos.

Source: Copyright © 1972, Los Angeles Times. Reprinted by permission.

Activity 6-18 Analyzing How a Writer Addresses Different Readers

Exchange the two pieces of writing you did in Activity 6-17 with a partner and read your partner's work. Which is more interactive? Which is more informative? Underline words or phrases that indicate how the writer is addressing the reader. Is each piece of writing suited to its audience? Why or why not? Is one more persuasive than the other? Why or why not?

PUTTING IT ALL TOGETHER

FINAL WRITING ASSIGNMENT

Consult *The Basics of Writing a Problem-Solving Paper* on pages 195–198 and write an essay about one of the following topics that:

- explains the problem
- proposes possible solutions
- analyzes the advantages and disadvantages of each solution
- recommends one solution

Here are some possible topics:

1. A problem that you are currently experiencing in your life as a student, parent, neighbor, or apartment dweller. (See Warm-up writing.)

2. A problem portrayed in one of the cartoons in this chapter.

3. One of the following situations involving privacy and the release of personal information. Refer to Activity 6-14 for cases that illustrated some of these invasions of privacy:

   a. the release of credit or financial information

   b. the sale or release of names, addresses, and phone numbers to companies

   c. the unauthorized release of medical records

4. A problem-solution topic that you choose. Make sure to consult your teacher about this topic.

Audience and Purpose

Choose one of the following:

- *If your purpose is to influence* the actions or behaviors of individual readers, direct your essay to individual readers. Use interactive grammar (*I, you, we* questions) to do this.
- *If your purpose is to influence* a government or business policy, address your paper to an agency or person that has the power to solve the problem. Use modals to vary the strength of the solutions that you give.

Preparing to Write

The following diagram will help you to gather all of your information and think strategically about what and how to write.

A Well-Defined, Focused Problem: _____

_____

Evidence to Convince Your Reader of the Problem:

Types of Evidence: case studies
personal experience from someone you interview
facts
statistics
laws and regulations related to the topic
research findings
examples
quotations from experts
⇓

Sources to Consult: interviews with experts or people who have knowledge about the topic
surveys
books
popular magazines and newspapers
information from the World Wide Web
brochures and information from the government or private organizations
⇓

Audience/Purpose: _____

Possible Solutions: _____

_____

_____

⇓

Advantages of Each Solution	Disadvantages of Each Solution

Recommended Solution: _____

Reasons:

Citing Sources and Preparing a Reference Page

After you have written your draft, check that you have provided in-text citations for all quotations, paraphrases, and summaries you have used. Also, prepare a reference page. To review how to cite sources, consult pages 310–313 in the GLR ⬤ and page 91 in Chapter 3 for more information.

Self-editing Activity

1. Before giving your draft to a peer, read it again to make sure that it says what you intended and is organized in the best way for this particular writing task. Make any changes needed to improve meaning and organization.

2. Choose and edit your draft for two of the language features reviewed in this chapter. Where indicated, turn to the GLR ⬤ and use the recommended self-editing strategies.

   ☐ formation and appropriate use of sentences that contain *if, if not, unless* to convey your intended meaning

   ☐ use of the modals *should, must, might, may,* or *can* to vary the strength of solutions or provide options for the reader. Does each modal you use convey the strength of the solution to your reader in the way you wanted it to?

   ☐ use of vocabulary appropriate for academic writing rather than speaking

   ☐ use of *I, you,* or *we* to address the reader that is appropriate to your audience and purpose

   ☐ use of expressions combining adjectives + nouns

3. Edit your draft for one of the language features reviewed in the previous chapters that you think may need more careful attention in your writing. Consult the self-editing activities in the previous chapters.

Peer Response Activity

Exchange papers with a partner. Answer the following questions about your partner's paper. If you answer "yes," give an example from your partner's paper. If you answer "no," give your peer advice about how to improve this part of the paper.

Basic Questions about a Good Problem-Solution Paper			Reasons/Examples
1. Has the writer explained the problem clearly and convinced you that this problem concerns you?	<u>Yes</u> No		1.
2. Has the writer provided solutions that clearly respond to the problem discussed?	Yes No		2.
3. Are the solutions concrete?	Yes No		3.
4. In explaining the solutions, has the writer discussed the advantages and disadvantages?	Yes No		4.

LEARNER'S NOTEBOOK

Reflecting on Writing Problem-Solving Papers

Report what you have learned about writing an effective problem-solution paper. Consider the information in your paper, the organization of your paper, and the language you used to discuss your solutions.

Revise

On your draft, list two changes that you will make to your problem-solution paper. Rewrite your paper, including these changes.

L
O
O
K
I
N
G

A
H
E
A
D

With a partner or in a small group, analyze the typical college/university assignment below.

Criminal Law

Each year police pursuits of criminals in cars results in the deaths of hundreds of suspects and of dozens of civilians and policemen. Chasing the bad guys is an outmoded procedure that causes more problems than it solves. How can we devote our resources to using another set of tools that will catch suspects with less carnage?

DISCUSSION

1. In what ways will this problem-solving assignment differ from what you have learned about writing problem-solving papers? Describe specific differences that you notice.

2. What problems do you anticipate for the person doing this problem-solving assignment? What solutions can you offer? Make a list of three potential problems and solutions for each.

Chapter 7

Synthesizing

Business and Responsibility

GOALS

WRITING
◆ determine the writing strategies that apply to various writing tasks
◆ complete short writing assignments using the appropriate writing strategies

GRAMMAR
◆ review of features of informational writing:
    verb tense shift
    creating complex nouns using reduced relative clauses
◆ review of features of persuasive writing:
    using modals to vary the strength of judgments
    using subordination and coordination

CONTENT
◆ learn about the ethical dilemmas that can result from business decisions
◆ consider whether standards of business conduct in one country can or should be "exported" to other countries

ACADEMIC FIELDS
Business
Economics

Sample Authentic College/University Writing Assignments

In this chapter you will learn how to combine all the skills you have learned in the previous chapters so that you can complete college/university assignments like this:

Marketing

The purpose of this project is to **identify** and **investigate** a real, current example of product positioning. Identify the organization and the market segment being targeted. **Determine** the probable approaches to positioning being employed. **Gather evidence** to support your ideas. These can include news or magazine articles, copies of print ads or press releases, interviews with company executives, photos of displays or outdoor advertising, direct mail pieces, audio or videotapes of ads or public service announcements. **Evaluate** the organization's marketing strategy. Does it seem reasonable? Is it attractive? Why or why not?

Political Science

Write a ten-page paper, using at least three sources. In recent decades the U.S. has fallen behind other "First World" countries in educating its youth. There are many **problems** in our educational system, but no consensus about possible **solutions**. In this paper, **report** on when the United States lost its place in education. **Research** different reforms and reform theories. **How** would these work or have they worked in real schools? Why or why not? **Offer solutions** for the U.S. education system. Would you combine reforms or come up with a totally new idea?

 CNN video support is available for this chapter.

GETTING READY

Warm-up Activity: Writing

In life, we are often faced with complex decisions or situations that don't allow us to find a quick solution or obvious course of action. They require, instead, that we use many of the thinking skills that you have practiced in previous chapters. We need to synthesize. That is, we need to carefully:

- examine where we are *(Explaining)* and/or
- understand why or how we got to this point *(Analyzing causes, factors, or reasons)* and/or
- determine what our options are, and their advantages and disadvantages *(Problem-solving)* and/or
- choose the best solution or course of action based on how effective or workable it is *(Evaluating)*

Here is an example of a complex problem to consider: A friend who is married with three children recently discovered that two of her elderly relatives are suffering from terminal illnesses and need care. Complicating this situation is the fact that her relatives live in another state and do not have the financial resources to hire caregivers or go to a nursing home. To decide how to solve this problem, the friend, her immediate family, and her extended family got together and examined the problem. Solving this problem required the family to use many of the skills you have been studying.

Write a solution to this problem and a list of the skills you used to arrive at it.

LEARNER'S NOTEBOOK

Examining Your Approach to a Problem

In your learner's notebook, write about a major decision or complex situation that you have faced in your life (e.g., a decision for or against marriage, a decision to transfer to a different university, a decision about changing your job or major field of study, a serious financial problem, or a serious health problem). As you explain the situation and your response to it, mention the thinking skills from the list in *Warm-up Activity: Writing* that you used to find a solution to your problem.

The Basics of Synthesizing

1. Using Several Writing Strategies to Complete a Writing Task

The previous chapters have given you strategies for approaching the more common writing assignments that you will encounter.

- Summarizing and Responding
- Explaining or Reporting
- Investigating
- Evaluating
- Analyzing Causes, Factors, or Reasons
- Problem-solving

Certain writing assignments or tasks may require you to combine more than one strategy to successfully complete the assignment. The goal of this chapter is to help you think strategically about how to *synthesize* (to combine) several writing strategies to fully respond to an academic assignment or task.

This chapter presents various short writing assignments designed to give you practice in deciding which writing strategies you could use. You will not write a draft of every essay in the chapter. Instead, you will plan how you *could* write them in small groups.

This essay by Yumiko Okamoto combines several writing strategies to explain, analyze, and propose solutions for the problem of *nonprofit organizations*. These are organizations that do not have to pay the same taxes as profit-earning companies because they are supposed to work on projects that benefit the public good (society).

Whenever we hear the words "nonprofit organization," we assume that these companies are public benefit organizations with a genuine intention of doing good. This is a misconception. Today, nonprofit organizations look and act like normal companies—running businesses and making money. Yet, somehow, they maintain a tax-free status, thereby enriching their executives.   BACKGROUND

Across America, 1.1 million organizations claim tax-exempt status. Many of them are able to pay their executives millions of dollars while providing little charity and doing no research. In fact, they are so busy making money that they do not have time to do their presumably core mission. The National Geographic, a scientific and educational nonprofit institution, made $459.6 million in 1993, but contributed less than 5% to geography education in American schools. The   REPORTING
Institute for Advanced Studies in Medicine, another nonprofit, applied only $3,373 to research out of the $792,000 it raised in funds.

Continued

Don't all the numbers bother you? We should be asking, "Why are they 'nonprofit'?" "Why aren't they paying taxes?" Actually, the reason these companies don't pay taxes is because the criteria for being a nonprofit is so broad that it is very easy to claim tax-exempt status. In the Internal Revenue Code, Section 501(c) (3), a nonprofit is defined as "religious, educational, charitable, scientific, literary organizations, and organizations that test for public safety, foster national or international amateur sports competitions, or prevent cruelty to children or animals" (p. 114).

ANALYZING REASONS why so many companies can maintain tax-exempt status

The Internal Revenue Service (IRS) has been challenging abusive nonprofit organizations. For example, the Sierra Club was in lawsuits with the IRS over whether the income from the sale of their mailing lists was taxable. Local governments have also challenged abusive nonprofits, too. Hamot Health Foundation's tax-exempt status was reversed after the state of Pennsylvania accused the hospital of earning profits from paying patients while not donating enough services to the poor. However, the laws are vague and it is difficult to prove that a nonprofit is being abusive.

PROBLEM-SOLVING (Solution section)

Is there anything that we can do? Yes. It is form 990, the tax return that nonprofit organizations must file with the government. Nonprofits must make this form available for the public to inspect at their offices, and copies are available through the IRS. Form 990 tells us about postage expenses, income from fund raising, donations made by the company, and annual salaries for executives. For now, the only thing that can check the nonprofits is the actions of states and individual taxpayers.

PROBLEM-SOLVING

2. Deciding How to Approach a Topic: Purpose and Audience

The key to knowing which strategies to use is to understand your broader writing purpose. When you are able to choose the topic yourself, or are given a broad topic, you can decide what your purpose in writing will be, and thus, what approach to the topic you will take. Having a broad choice of topic may seem frightening, like having a blank piece of paper placed in front of you. Here are some hints that can help you:

A. If you know your purpose and audience:

- Phrase your purpose as a question that your paper will answer.

  EXAMPLE

  What's problematic about the current function of music now that modern technology has given us such free access to music?

- Decide which of the writing strategies will allow you to fully answer your question.

  EXAMPLES

  The function of music has changed *(Reporting & Summarizing,* perhaps - *Investigating).*

  The new function of music is problematic *(Formulating Criteria and Evaluating).*

B. If you don't have a clear idea about your topic or purpose:

- Find a broad topic that you have some information about.

  EXAMPLE

  Music is everywhere these days—even in institutions like banks, doctor's offices, or on the telephone, in elevators.

- Look at the different writing strategies. These may help you formulate a question that your paper will answer.

  Reporting—Where do you hear "institutional" music? What kinds of music are commonly played?

  Investigating—Why do stores like groceries and department stores play "institutional" music? Who provides this "music"?

  Analyzing causes, factors, or reasons—Why do people dislike "institutional" music?

  Evaluating—Is "institutional music" real music?

- Think about what your audience will be interested in knowing and what they already know about the topic.

- Combine several of the questions into one question that your paper will answer.

  EXAMPLE

  What has the effect been of having "institutional" music everywhere?

- Decide which of the writing strategies will allow you to fully answer your question.

The effect of "institutional" music *(Investigating and Reporting)*.

Is the effect positive or not? *(Formulating Criteria & Evaluating)*.

3. Deciding How to Approach an Assigned Topic

Assigned topics, either in essay exams or course essay topics, are often presented as a series of questions. When you get this kind of essay prompt, it is useful to think about the broader task your teacher is asking you to perform. That is:

What do the smaller questions add up to?

What is the broader question your essay will end up answering?

If you find the broader question, and use every paragraph in your essay to answer that question, then you will have produced a good piece of writing. You will also have answered all of the smaller questions in the process.

When you have determined the larger question that the series of questions will answer, then you must decide which of the writing strategies will allow you to fully answer that larger question.

A. Determine the larger question that the series of questions will answer.

Developmental History in the Far East

Discuss the role of Japan in Manchukuo and China from 1933 to 1937. Focus on the diplomatic and military events that led to the Marco Polo Bridge incident in 1937.

Larger Question: What were the key factors/events that led to Japan's political role in Manchukuo and China from 1933 to 1937?

B. Decide which of the writing strategies will allow you to fully accomplish the broader purpose.

Discuss the role of Japan in Manchukuo and China from 1933 to 1937 *(Summarizing or Reporting)*.

Focus on the diplomatic and military events that led to the Marco Polo Bridge incident in 1937 *(Analyzing factors/causal chain)*.

FOCUSING

Introduction to Readings

Companies affect people all over the United States as well as abroad. Because of their widespread influence, it is important to analyze the decisions that large corporations make in order to better form opinions about them and see how they indirectly or directly affect you. Each author in this chapter analyzes an aspect of widespread corporate practices.

Pre-reading Activity

Activity 7-1   Discussing Business Decisions

With a partner or in a small group, choose two of the following scenarios. Discuss which course of action you would take. Be prepared to give reasons for your choice. Share your response with the class.

1. If you left your company for a better position with a competitor, would you reveal to your new employers the confidential information about your old company?

2. If you knew you could double your money in two years by investing in a company whose activities you strongly disapproved of, would you do it?

3. If you had an idea so good that you knew you could either tell your boss about it and get a promotion, or leave and set up a profitable company of your own, which would you be more inclined to do? Would your final choice be based on thoughts about the desire for independence or loyalty to your employer?

4. If you had a great job at a wonderful company, and then accidentally discovered that for years management had been stealing money from the absentee owner, what would you do? How much would your actions be influenced by whether you liked the managers?

Source: G. Stock, *The Book of Questions: Business, Politics, and Ethics*
(New York: Workman Publishing, 1991, 67, 124, 166).

Short Writing Assignment 1

With a small group, identify a company policy that seems quite strict or harsh. You may choose your own or use one of the following options:

- mandatory drug testing before a new employee is hired
- a store's policy not to give cash back on returned merchandise

- extra service charges for paying bills late (for example, the phone company, credit card companies)
- a company's policy that fired employees must leave the building within two hours accompanied by a security guard

With your group members, complete Activity 7-2 to prepare to write a two- to three-page paper, explaining the policy and why the company might have such a strict policy. This is only preparation. **You will not actually write the paper.**

Preparing to Write

Activity 7-2   Discussing Possible Approaches to a Writing Assignment

In small groups, respond to these items as completely as possible to help you think strategically about completing the short writing assignment. Use a separate piece of paper.

1. Write as much as you know about the company policy.

   Identify the Policy:

2. Brainstorm potential reasons for the company policy.

3. Write any questions that you don't know the answers to:

4. Decide which sources to consult and write questions that you need to find answers to for each source:

   ❏ interviews with company owners or managers

   ❏ books or articles about business policies

   ❏ popular magazines and newspapers

5. Determine the larger question or broader purpose for writing this paper.

   Purpose for Writing: _to explain what the company policy is and give reasons for it._

6. Check the writing strategies that you will need to fully complete the writing task

   ❏ summarizing and responding

   ❏ explaining or reporting

   ❏ investigating

   ❏ evaluating

   ❏ analyzing causes, factors, or reasons

   ❏ problem-solving

LEARNER'S NOTEBOOK

Reflecting on Your Use of Writing Strategies

Now that you have planned this short paper, answer the following questions: Which of the writing strategies needed for the paper in Activity 7-2 do you think you have mastered? Which of the writing strategies do you still need to practice? Why are these challenging for you? Compare your answer with a partner.

READING 1   THE DOWNSIDE OF DOWNSIZING
(CHAPTER IN A POPULAR BOOK)

In "The Downside of Downsizing," the author examines a policy used by many businesses today: downsizing, or laying off workers to save money.

Pre-reading Vocabulary

Activity 7-3   Verbs Signaling Results

The verbs in the sentences below express results or consequences. Some of the verbs may have a negative meaning. Others are simply neutral. Determine whether the underlined verb seems to have a negative or neutral meaning. Two examples are provided.

1. Layoffs <u>breed</u> anxiety and a sense of betrayal.

   ("breed" has a negative meaning)

2. Downsizing <u>has often failed to achieve</u> the desired objectives.

3. Layoffs <u>undermine</u> trust and morale of employees who remain on the job.

4. The process of downsizing <u>creates</u> a self-protective mood among employees.

5. Downsizing also <u>increases</u> infighting among employees over shrinking monetary resources.

6. While 60% of the companies say that downsizing <u>resulted in</u> lower costs, only one third reported that it resulted in increased productivity or gave them a competitive advantage.

   ("result in" has a neutral meaning)

7. The combination of workforce and expanded production abroad <u>has contributed to</u> stagnant and declining living standards among the American middle class.

THE DOWNSIDE OF DOWNSIZING

[Innovators in American business], though still the daring minority, have been pursuing and implementing what has become known as "a high-performance strategy"—a strategy that not only puts their companies at the leading edge but also delivers the American people a high standard of living. ...

As Ford Motor Company learned, achieving high performance requires a redefinition of   5
work and of the relationships among people who work together. It means not only using the backs of workers but tapping their minds—and that entails giving more responsibility and autonomy to the ordinary worker and to the work team on the factory floor. ...

Trust ... is [an] essential ingredient for high performance, according to Motorola's long-time CEO, Bob Galvin. "To the degree that we can create a trusting environment, people   10
will respond," Galvin **emphasized**. "Trust is a tremendous motivator and a great energizer. If our people know that we believe in them, they will respond because they are trusted. That is a motivation factor that is unbeatable."

The pervasive job insecurity in America today, and the traditional adversarial tensions in many American companies, are barriers to the trust needed for a high-performance work-   15
place, according to Ray Marshall, now an economist at the University of Texas. "An adversarial system is not a good learning system," asserts Marshall. "I'm not going to share any information with you if I think that I'm going to lose in the process.... Most American workers believe that if they improve productivity, they lose their jobs. Well, that's not much of an incentive. And that's the reason job security becomes an important part of a high-   20
performance system." ...

The Downside of Downsizing

The current fashion of downsizing—deliberate, repeated layoffs—at some of America's most profitable corporations runs counter to the philosophy and strategy of the high-perfor-   25
mance workplace set out by Marshall and Galvin.

Experts differentiate the recent rash of corporate downsizing from earlier cutbacks and the massive restructuring of companies such as General Motors and IBM, which had to [restructure] after they had lost huge [amounts] of [money].

The waves of layoffs since 1992 reflect a different approach—a long-term strategy of   30
shrinking profit-making companies in good times. In fact, downsizing has become so pervasive that more than 85% of the Fortune 500 companies—profitable companies such as AT&T, BankAmerica, General Electric, Johnson & Johnson, NYNEX, Procter & Gamble, RJR Nabisco, Sears, and Xerox—have lopped off sizable numbers of employees in the past five years; 100 percent say they plan more layoffs in the next five years.   35

The downsizing strategy [completely reverses] the classic [assertion] of American industry voiced by Alfred P. Sloan, the former chairman of General Motors: "Growth is essential to the good health of an enterprise. Deliberately to stop growing is to suffocate."

Today, the corporate dogma is "Smaller is better."

Layoffs win points for corporate CEO's with Wall Street and boost the value of execu-   40
tive stock options, although recent experience, company by company, shows that, in prac-

tice, cutting staff typically has fallen dramatically short of making the improvement in competitive performance that money managers expect.

In corporate America today, downsizing is like dieting: Everyone is doing it, so people try it again and again, even though few achieve the desired results. As one [humorist] put it, 45 the fixation with downsizing has become the new "corporate anorexia."

Despite its popularity, downsizing in the late 1980s and early '90s has often failed to achieve its proponents' objectives, economists report, because typically slashing staff has not been "part of a thoughtful strategy to redesign the whole corporate structure and culture. Instead, it's an almost panicked reaction to pressures and problems . . . ." 50

In terms of achieving high performance in the long run, the problem with downsizing is that employees are treated as costs to be cut rather than as assets to be developed.

Layoffs undermine trust and the morale of employees who remain on the job; layoffs breed anxiety and a sense of betrayal. The sheer process of downsizing pulls decision-making power to the top of an organization, creates a . . . self-protective mood among employ- 55 ees, leaves managers averse to risk taking and less tolerant of failures, and increases internal infighting over shrinking resources, according to several studies. In such an atmosphere, teamwork becomes more difficult, and information—especially bad news—is not widely shared because of internal corporate fear and distrust.

While these intangibles may not show up immediately on the bottom line, all of them 60 hurt a company over the long run because they undermine the whole notion of employee empowerment and the crucial process of idea sharing that [America's innovative companies] have found most effective. In fact, many companies that have engaged in layoffs have discovered that their productivity was worse off afterward, even though they continued more rounds of downsizing. . . . 65

[A] survey of more than five hundred corporations done by Wyatt and Company, a management consulting firm, found that while 60% of the companies reported that downsizing resulted in lower costs, only one third reported that it resulted in increased productivity or competitive advantage. More than half the companies wound up replacing some of the dismissed workers. . . . 70

It is telling, moreover, that innovative companies such as Ford and Motorola have gone to great lengths not to resort to layoffs for the past several years, in the conviction that the security of their workforce is essential to high performance. Rather than focusing on cost cutting, Ford and Motorola have sought to expand into new lines of business in order to absorb workers displaced by efficiency measures, rather than laying people off. . . . 75

Finally, as a strategy of deliberate, long-term shrinking, downsizing has serious implications for the American economy.

It has already been painful to a wide swath of Americans, especially as American companies have expanded their production facilities abroad. The combination of workforce cutbacks at home and expanded hiring abroad by American companies has contributed to the 80 stagnant and declining living standards of much of the American middle class. It has pushed hundreds of thousands of well-paid blue-collar workers into lower-paying service jobs or part-time or temporary work. Nearly 20 percent of the Americans who lost their jobs from 1991 through 1994, for example, had not found work by November 1994, and nearly half of those who did find jobs were earning less than before. The constant pressure of job 85 cutbacks keeps wage levels down, so that the historic link between rising productivity and rising wages in American manufacturing has been broken. Productivity and profits continued to climb over the past twenty years, but the take-home pay of the average worker has gone down in real terms.

Some economists suggest, moreover, that the permanent strategy of layoffs, even in 90 good times, may actually hurt the long-term growth of the U.S. economy. For that strategy accentuates the income gap between the executive class and the working class in America, and some studies indicate that [this strategy cannot] stimulate growth.

In what have been the most rapidly growing capitalist economics in the world, the "miracle economies" of Hong Kong, Singapore, South Korea, Taiwan, and—until its recent 95 recession—Japan, the income levels of top corporate bosses have been much closer to the pay of ordinary workers than has CEO pay in America, and some economists see a connection between income equity and national economic growth.

There is little question that the relatively modest income disparities in Japanese industry contribute to the strong sense of social solidarity among the Japanese people and to their 100 willingness to accept belt tightening and extra devotion to the job in hard times for the sake of both company and country.

In America, it remains an open question how long rank-and-file workers who are falling behind economically will continue to tolerate growing disparities in earnings without social protest. The economic anxiety of Americans is a pervasive fact of life, widely reflected in 105 opinion polls. *Time* magazine summarized the American mood in a headline: "We're #1 and It Hurts ...."

Some corporate leaders and business magazines have commented that the social compact between employer and employee has been stretched to the breaking point in America, and that the bonds holding American society together have been frayed by the economic 110 tensions caused by downsizing.

Source: Hedrick Smith, *Rethinking America: Innovative Strategies
and Partnerships in Business and Education*, 409–412. © 1995
by Hedrick Smith. Reprinted with permission of Random House.

Active Reading

Activity 7-4   Identifying an Author's Writing Strategies

The author of "The Downside of Downsizing" provides answers to the following questions. In the blank, identify the writing strategy that the writer used to answer each question. Be prepared to explain your answer. An example is provided.

- summarizing and responding
- explaining or reporting
- investigating
- evaluating
- analyzing causes, factors, or reasons
- problem-solving

_____explaining or reporting_____ What is a "high performance" strategy?

_____ Why is it difficult to create a "high performance" workplace?

_____ What is downsizing?

_____ Why do companies engage in downsizing?

_____ What are the effects of downsizing on companies?

_____ What are the likely effects of downsizing on the American economy?

Activity 7-5   Annotating a Reading Passage

Annotate the part of "The Downside of Downsizing" that answers each of the questions in Activity 7-4. Review guidelines for annotating readings on pages 15–16 in Chapter 1.

Analysis of Language: Review of the Grammar of Informational Writing

A. Review of Reporting Verbs and Verb Tense Shift in Academic Writing

As you will remember from Chapter 5, writers often shift verb tenses between sentences because they are moving from generalizations to supporting examples, quotations, or paraphrases each with their corresponding verb tense. In informational writing (reporting, explaining, investigating), writers use reporting verbs such as _suggest, mention, assert,_ or _find_ to introduce quotations and paraphrases from experts and research findings.

> **GLR**   See pages 297–300, Section 3 and pages 308–309, Section 4 of the GLR; and pages 363–366, Appendix B, for more information on these topics.

Activity 7-6   Reviewing Reporting Verbs

In "The Downside of Downsizing," look for quotations or paraphrases from experts on economics and downsizing. Also look for research findings. Underline the reporting verbs that you can find. The reporting verb _emphasize_ has already been bolded in the reading.

Activity 7-7   Reviewing the Purpose of Verb Tense Shifts

Reread lines 52–69 of "The Downside of Downsizing." Underline the verbs in the three paragraphs. Fill in the chart below by writing in sentences containing as many of the various verb tenses as you can find. Explain the purpose of the verb tense in each sentence.

An example is done for you. For a review of the purpose in writing that each verb tense serves, consult the GLR (GLR) for more information.

Tense	Tense	Tense
simple present	"Layoffs undermine trust and the morale of employees."	Generalizations about layoffs
present perfect		
simple past		
modal auxiliaries in the verb phrase		

B. Review of Complex Noun Phrases in Academic Writing

As you know, academic writers often use complex noun phrases. One way that you have learned to add information to the central noun to is to create noun + *of*-phrases.

The economic anxiety of Americans is a pervasive fact of life.

Another way that you have learned is to attach a relative clause to a noun. To tighten the structure of this type of noun phrase, writers can delete the relative pronoun and part of the verb to create sentences that are less wordy. It is common for writers to delete parts of the relative clause when the sentence is in the passive voice. This deletion creates what is known as a *reduced relative clause*.

There are two types of relative clauses: defining (restrictive) relative clauses and non-restrictive relative clauses. Different guidelines apply for reducing each type of relative clause.

GLR   See pages 291–293, Section 3, of the GLR for more information on complex noun phrases with relative clauses.

1. Deleting information in relative clauses that add necessary information to the noun (defining relative clauses):

   The pervasive job insecurity in America today, and the traditional adversarial tensions in many American companies, are barriers to *the trust* *(that is)* **needed** for a high-performance workplace.

2. Deleting information from relative clauses that add extra information to the noun (non-defining relative clauses):

   The economic anxiety of Americans is *a pervasive fact of life*, *(which is)* widely **reflected** in opinion polls.

> **GLR** See pages 294–295, Section 3, of the GLR for other ways to delete words from relative clauses.

Activity 7-8   Practice Creating Complex Noun Phrases by Reducing Relative Clauses

Academic writing is characterized by the use of sentences that are packed with information. Noun phrases with reduced relative clauses are commonly used in such writing. To learn more about writing such sentences, reduce the following relative clauses. An example is provided.

1. Our concern is with the moral obligations of transnational corporations in dealing with difficult issues such as those [**that are**] raised by the marketing of drugs in third world countries.

2. One treatment for diarrhea is Lomotil, which is marketed by G.D. Searle.

3. Depo-Provera, a contraceptive that is taken by injection, protects women against pregnancy for three months or more.

4. The marketing of pharmaceuticals in the third world illustrates a dilemma that is faced by all transnational companies.

5. A survey of 500 corporations that was done by Wyatt and Company asked companies whether downsizing resulted in increased productivity.

6. Ford and Motorola have sought to expand into lines of business in order to absorb workers who have been displaced by efficiency measures.

Activity 7-9   Practice Writing a Study Summary Using Complex Noun + *of*-Phrases

Write a study summary of "The Downside of Downsizing" that answers the questions in Activity 7-4. Use at least five of the following complex noun + *of*-phrases from the reading. Review study summary writing in Chapter 1 on page 17.

- a redefinition of work
- the morale of employees

- the trend of down-sizing
- the growth of the U.S. economy

- the restructuring of companies
- a sense of worker solidarity

- the health of a company
- the declining income of American workers

LEARNER'S NOTEBOOK

Responding to the Opinion of Another

Read the following justification for downsizing by Robert E. Allen, a former CEO of AT&T, a major provider of telephone service. In your learner's notebook, write a response to Mr. Allen. To support your own response, use the ideas about downsizing found in "The Downside of Downsizing."

> Downsizing is inevitable in today's competitive business environment. I've taken criticism because I decided to reduce jobs at a time when AT&T is financially healthy and a market leader. But the time to act is when you are strong. Delaying would jeopardize the jobs of all AT&T people.

> Source: R. E. Allen, The Downside of Downsizing, *Newsweek*, April 8, 1996; 15.

Activity 7-10   Identifying Writing Strategies

Read the letter you wrote in the learner's notebook above to a partner. Check the writing strategy or strategies that your partner used. Which of your partner's points is the strongest response to Allen's opinion? Why? Where has your partner made the best use of "The Downside of Downsizing"? Why?

- ☐ summarizing and responding
- ☐ explaining or reporting
- ☐ investigating
- ☐ evaluating
- ☐ analyzing causes, factors, or reasons
- ☐ problem-solving

Short Writing Assignment 2

The following scenario describes a business policy that more and more companies are using to save money: moving manufacturing operations out of the United States to other countries where workers are cheaper. Like downsizing, this policy has decreased the number of available jobs in an important U.S. company. Imagine that you are an AT&T worker. Write a memo to the executives of AT&T explaining your reaction to this decision and suggesting several solutions the company might consider.

> AT&T, the largest telecommunications company in the U.S., is facing a big problem. Because of new government regulations, other international companies are now allowed to sell telephones in the U.S. As a result, AT&T has lost many customers because its phones are more expensive than those manufactured abroad.
>
> The company is proposing to close their U.S. manufacturing plants and open factories in places like Korea or Singapore, where people work for less money.
>
> Source: Committee on Comparative Cost Factors and Structures in Global Manufacturing, Manufacturing Studies Board, National Research Council, *Dispelling the Manufacturing Myth: American Factories Can Compete in the Global Marketplace* (Washington, DC: National Academy Press, 1992, 22–23).

Preparing to Write

Activity 7-11   Discussing Possible Approaches to a Writing Assignment

With a partner or in a small group, respond to the items below as completely as possible to help you think strategically about completing the short writing assignment. This is only preparation. You will not actually write the paper. Use a separate piece of paper.

1. Determine the larger question or broader purpose for writing this memo

   Purpose for Writing: _____

2. Check the writing strategies that you will need to fully complete the writing task. Fill in the blank after each strategy you choose with the kinds of information you would include. Examples are provided for you.

   ❏ summarizing and responding _____*my opinion that AT&T's plan is wrong*_____

   ❏ explaining or reporting _____

   ❏ investigating _____

   ❏ evaluating _____

   ❏ analyzing causes, factors, or reasons __*reasons for my negative opinion about the plan*__

   ❏ problem-solving _____

Activity 7-12   Discussing Possible Solutions

In your small groups, make a list of solutions to propose to AT&T to avoid closing the U.S.-based manufacturing plant. Include an analysis of advantages and disadvantages of those solutions. Present these advantages and disadvantages to your classmates.

READING 2   ETHICS IN INTERNATIONAL BUSINESS
(TEXTBOOK READING)

More and more, American companies have been conducting business abroad. Because business and advertising practices reflect cultural values, doing business abroad often raises important ethical questions. This textbook article analyzes the marketing of drugs in foreign countries by American companies.

Pre-reading Vocabulary

Activity 7-13   Finding Written Academic Expressions for Colloquial Language

In certain types of writing, academic writers will vary verbs that they use by substituting synonyms. In the left-hand column put the letter of the more academic synonym from the right-hand column that has the same meaning as the verb in bold. Consult a dictionary or thesaurus if necessary. An example is provided.

Common Words and Expression	Alternate Words and Expressions
_h_ 1. Many companies **do** business in foreign countries.	a. illustrate
___ 2. Problems with business ethics seem to **happen** for transnational companies.	b. employ
	c. advance
___ 3. The economic power of transnational companies **has caused** concern about their ethical standards in other countries.	d. give rise to
	e. accomplish
___ 4. We hope to provide guidelines to help companies **decide** appropriate ethical standards for marketing products abroad.	f. determine
	g. arise
___ 5. The problems that many drug manufacturers have had abroad **show** how difficult it is to do business in foreign countries.	~~h. engage in~~
	i. bring about
___ 6. Good reasons can be **given** to show that it is often morally right not to follow home country moral standards when doing business abroad.	
___ 7. Forcing other countries to follow our strict drug regulations will probably not **make** any significant change in medical practices in other countries.	
___ 8. Nigeria wants to strictly regulate the sale and marketing of drugs, but it does not have a government agency with enough power and money to **do** the task.	
___ 9. Companies must consider several important factors when deciding whether to **use** certain business practices in a foreign country.	

Activity 7-14   Practice Using New Vocabulary

Choose four of the words or expressions from the right-hand column in Activity 7-13 and use each to write a sentence about a company policy or decision that has affected you in some way. Consult page 361 in Appendix B. An example is provided.

EXAMPLE

Many companies engage in aggressive advertising campaigns, promising customers large savings if they buy a product before a certain date.

ETHICS IN INTERNATIONAL BUSINESS

Although many firms engage in business abroad, most of the ethical issues in this area arise for the transnational corporation, or TNC, which is generally defined as a firm that has a direct investment in two or more countries. The emergence of TNCs in the second half of the twentieth century has had a profound effect on developed and undeveloped countries alike. Their wealth and power have given rise to concern about the impact on local   5
economies and about the capacity of governments to regulate them effectively. The pharmaceutical industry, more than any other, has been criticized for its activities abroad. Although prescription and over-the-counter drugs have done much to alleviate suffering and increase the well-being of people around the globe, the major drug companies are also faulted for many of their practices.   10

Different Instructions

One of the most heavily criticized practices is promoting drugs in the third world with more suggestions for their use and fewer warnings about side effects than in developed countries. The following are some typical examples.

Diarrhea is a mild inconvenience in developed countries, but it is a life-threatening con-   15
dition in the third world and the major killer of children under the age of three. One treatment for diarrhea is Lomotil, marketed by G.D. Searle. This drug does not treat the underlying causes of diarrhea, however, but merely relieves the symptoms. Consequently, the World Health Organization (WHO) has declared Lomotil to be of "no value" in the treatment of diarrhea and a waste of time and money. The drug is also dangerous for young chil-   20
dren and should not be prescribed to children under the age of two. But Searle has recommended the drug for diarrhea in children as young as one year in Indonesia and in infants between three and six months in Thailand, the Philippines, and Central America.

Drug Dumping

Another charge against pharmaceutical firms is that they engage in drug dumping, a   25
practice of selling abroad drugs which have not been approved in the country where they are manufactured. Combination antibiotics (two or more drugs in a fixed ratio) have been banned from the U.S. market as a result of findings by the Food and Drug Administration (FDA) that the drugs can interfere with each other and that the fixed ratios prevent doctors

from prescribing the proper dose for each patient. Combination antibiotics are still marketed 30
in most developing countries, however, and even command high prices. Perhaps the most
controversial allegation of drug dumping concerns Depo-Provera, a contraceptive, taken by
injection, that protects women against pregnancy for three months or more. In the early
1970s, the FDA refused to approve Depo-Provera because tests conducted since 1965
showed that it can cause extended and even permanent infertility and possible breast tumors 35
and cervical cancer. All the time, Upjohn was promoting this contraceptive outside the
United States with no warnings about its side effects. American companies are forbidden by
the Food, Drug, and Cosmetic Act of 1938 to export drugs not approved for use in the
United States, but many means are available for evading this restriction. Upjohn, for example, was able to manufacture Depo-Provera legally by shifting production to plants in 40
Belgium.

Developing an Ethical Framework

The marketing of pharmaceuticals in the third world illustrates a dilemma faced by all
transnational corporations; namely, deciding which standards of ethics to follow. Should
TNCs follow the laws and prevailing morality of the home country and, in the case of 45
American corporations, act everywhere as they do in the United States? Should they follow
the practices of the host country and adopt the adage, "When in Rome, do as the Romans
do"? Or are there special ethical standards that apply when business is conducted across
national boundaries? And if so, what are the standards appropriate for international business? Unfortunately, there are no easy answers to these questions. 50

"No Double Standards!"

Let us consider, first, the position taken by some critics of TNCs: that business ought to
be conducted in the same way the world over with no double standards. In particular, United
States corporations ought to follow domestic law and a single code of conduct in their business dealings everywhere. This position might be expressed as, "When in Rome or any- 55
where else, do as you would at home." A little reflection is enough to show that this high
level of conduct is not morally required of TNCs in all instances and that they should not
be faulted for every departure from home country standards in doing business abroad. Good
reasons can be advanced to show that different practices in different parts of the world are,
in some instances, morally justified. 60
First, the conditions in other parts of the world are different in morally important ways
from those in the United States and other developed countries. If Rome is a significantly different place, then standards that are appropriate at home do not necessarily apply there. Drug
laws in the developed world, for example, are very stringent, reflecting greater affluence and
better overall health. The standards in these laws are not always appropriate in poorer, less 65
developed countries with fewer medical resources and more severe health problems.
In the United States, the risk of prescribing an antidiarrheal drug such as Lomotil to
children is not worth taking. But a physician in Central America, where children frequently
die of untreated diarrhea, might evaluate the risk differently.
Second, the fact that a drug has not been approved in the home country of a transna- 70
tional does not automatically mean that it is unsafe or ineffective. A drug for a tropical
disease might never have been submitted for approval, since there is no market for it in the

country where it is manufactured. Other drugs might not be approved because of concerns that are unfounded or open to question.

The FDA acted conservatively in refusing approval for Depo-Provera, for example; 75 many countries of Western Europe and Canada, with equally strict drug testing requirements, permit the use of this drug as a last resort contraceptive. Also the approval of drugs in the United States is a lengthy process. Companies convinced of the safety of a drug might be justified in rushing it to market in countries where it is legally permitted, while waiting for approval at home, especially if there is a pressing need abroad. 80

Third, many factors in other countries, especially in the third world, are beyond the control of TNCs, and they often have little choice but to adapt to local conditions—if they are going to do business at all. This position can perhaps be expressed as, "We do not entirely agree with the Romans, but we sometimes find it necessary to do things their way." For example, physicians in the third world often prefer to prescribe multiple drugs for a single 85 illness. Hence, the demand for combination antibiotics. Although this practice is disapproved by the American medical community, extending the United States ban on such drugs to the rest of the world is unlikely to bring about any significant change. If combination antibiotics were not sold, many doctors would continue to issue prescriptions for several different drugs to be taken simultaneously, very possibly in the wrong proportions. 90

"When in Rome ..."

The opposite extreme—that the only guide for business conduct abroad is what is legally and morally accepted in any given country where a TNC operates—is equally unacceptable. "When in Rome do as the Romans do" cannot be followed without exception. In order to see this, however, we need to examine one important argument used to support this position. 95

This argument is that the people affected have the right to decide. Where different standards exist, the right of a host country to determine which to apply should be respected. According to this argument, the primary responsibility for setting standards properly rests on the government and the people of the country in which business is being conducted. 100

Although there is some merit in the argument, "the people affected have the right to decide," it cannot be accepted without considerable qualification. For instance, just because physicians in some less developed countries routinely sell free samples does not make the practice right. Even when the practice is legal in the country in question and condoned by the local medical community, the indirect payment that physicians receive by selling free 105 samples makes it possible for drug companies to bribe physicians. This practice can still be considered as morally wrong.

A respect for the right of people to set their own standards does not automatically justify corporations in inflicting grave harm on innocent people, for example, or violating basic human rights. In deciding whether to employ a practice that is regarded as wrong at home 110 but is legal in a host country, a number of factors must be considered.

First, some countries lack the capacity to regulate transnational corporations effectively. The governments of these countries are, in many instances, no less committed than the United States and Western Europe to protecting their people against harm from prescription and over-the-counter drugs, but they do not always have the resources—the money, skilled 115 personnel, and institutions—to accomplish the task.

The law in Nigeria, for example, prohibits the marketing of any drug in a way that is "false, or misleading, or is likely to create a wrong impression as to its quality, character, value, composition, merit, or safety." Such a law cannot be effective, however, without an agency such as the FDA to acquire information about the vast number of drugs that enter 120 the country and issue detailed guidelines for their use.

Second, some countries with the capacity to regulate transnationals lack the necessary *will.* Often, the local medical community and powerful segments of the population benefit from the unethical marketing practices of the giant drug companies and willingly permit and even encourage their use.   125

Special Standards for International Business

Our results so far have been largely negative. The two extreme positions—"When in Rome, do as the Romans do" and "When in Rome or anywhere else, do as you would at home"—are both inadequate guides in international business. However, the discussion of these positions suggests some principles that can be used to make decisions in difficult cases. 130

Minimal and Maximal Duties

What principles might help companies engaged in international business define their obligations? Two have been proposed. One is the principle of *negative harm,* which holds that in their dealings abroad, corporations have an obligation not to add to the deprivation or suffering of people.   135

A second principle, proposed by Thomas Donaldson, is that corporations have an obligation to respect certain rights; namely, those that ought to be recognized as fundamental international rights. TNCs are not obligated to extend all the rights of United States citizens to people everywhere in the world, but there are certain basic rights that no person or institution, including a corporation, is morally permitted to violate. Of course, the main problem 140 with a principle to respect fundamental international rights is specifying the rights in question. Everyone has a right to subsistence, for example, but TNCs may be under no obligation to feed the hungry in a country where it operates. It has an obligation, however, not to contribute directly to starvation by, say, converting cultivated land to the production of an export crop.   145

Source: J. Boatright, *Ethics and the Conduct of Business*
(Englewood Cliffs, NJ: Prentice Hall, 1993, 411–421).

Active Reading

Activity 7-15   Identifying an Author's Writing Strategies

The author of "Ethics in International Business" provides answers to the following questions. In the blank, identify the writing strategy that the writer used to answer each question. Be prepared to explain your answer. An example is provided.

- summarizing and responding
- explaining or reporting
- investigating
- evaluating
- analyzing causes, factors, or reasons
- problem-solving

_____ What problem has arisen because transnational companies do business in developing countries?

_____ What practices have pharmaceutical companies been criticized for?

___analyzing___ What are the two ethical approaches that companies can take to selling their products in third world countries?

_____ Why might companies adopt different standards for selling drugs abroad than those they follow at home?

_____ Why might companies want to follow one standard wherever they do business?

_____ What principles should companies follow when marketing products abroad?

Activity 7-16   Writing a Study Summary

Reread the article and write a study summary that includes the answers to the questions in Activity 7-15. Review how to write a study summary in Chapter 1, page 17.

Analysis of Language: Reviewing the Grammar of Persuasive Writing

A. Using Modals to Vary the Strength of Judgments

In addition to using modals to vary the strength of generalizations and solutions, writers use modals such as *can, should, ought to,* and *must* to vary the strength of judgments that they make about an issue or practice.

EXAMPLES

Some critics of transnational companies believe that business *ought to be conducted* in the same way the world over with no double standards. **Strong judgment**

TNCs *should not be faulted* for every departure from home country standards in doing business abroad. **Strong judgment**

The practice of selling free drug samples *can still be considered* as morally wrong even though it is condoned by the local medical community. **Judgment with moderate strength**

GLR See pages 315–321, Section 5, of the GLR for more information about modal auxiliaries.

Activity 7-17   Evaluating a Business Policy

In a small group, choose **one** of the following business problems. Write a paragraph in which you judge the company's decision or action. After writing, edit the grammar carefully for effective use of modals. An example has been started for you.

Problem 1: AT&T decided to manufacture its phones in developing countries, thereby closing its manufacturing operations in U.S. communities.

Problem 2: In the course of her job, Mary Y. discovered that the company she works for has been cheating on its income tax. When she reported this to the Internal Revenue Service, her company fired her.

Problem 3: As the supervisor of a chain of 28 pizza restaurants and 500 workers, John J. O'Brien thought he would soon be promoted to regional vice president. He had worked for the company for 10 years and had received excellent work evaluations. However, one day his boss called him into his office to fire him, saying that John had been seen taking drugs at a weekend party. (Boatright, *Ethics and the Conduct of Business*, 182.)

EXAMPLE

Problem: The company's decision to fire Mary for reporting her company's tax evasion

Mary did the right thing by going to the Internal Revenue Service. Her company ought not have been able to fire her for reporting a serious violation of the law. In fact, no company should ...

B. Using Subordination and Coordination to Persuade Readers

As you saw in Chapter 4, writers use a variety of sentence types to show the logical connections between ideas within and between sentences. When evaluating or arguing about something, academic writers use subordination and coordination to show that their arguments are reasonable because they have considered the other side's opinion.

1. An independent clause + a dependent clause with a subordinator:

    Although there is some merit in the argument, "the people affected have the right to decide," it cannot be accepted without considerable qualification.

2. Combining two independent clauses with a conjunction:

    The governments of these countries are as committed as the United States and Western Europe to protecting their people against harm from prescription and over-the-counter drugs, *but* they do not always have the money, skilled personnel, and institutions to accomplish the task.

> **GLR**   See pages 261–270, Section 1 of the GLR for more information on expressing logical relationships.

Activity 7-18   Using Subordination and Coordination in an Argument

Pretend that you have just been appointed as the president of a pharmaceutical company that does business in another country whose medical practices are different from your own. Choose the approach to marketing drugs abroad presented in *Ethics in International Business* that you think your company should follow. Give reasons for your decision. Use subordination and coordination in sentences to show that your position is reasonable. An example has been started for you.

EXAMPLE

Our company should follow the practices and policies regarding drugs established in the country where we do business, even if it differs from practices and regulations in the U.S. because . . .

Short Writing Assignment 3

Imagine that you are an expert on standards of international business. You have been hired by a major cigarette company to help solve the following problem:

Because of strict government regulation of cigarette advertising in the U.S. marketplace, a major cigarette company is planning to begin selling its cigarettes in third world countries, where such regulations do not exist. They must decide if they will keep or remove the labels that warn of health risks on the cigarette packages that are sold abroad.

Based on your expertise, write a two- to three-page memo to cigarette company executives, explaining the two approaches that the company can take. Present the advantages and disadvantages of taking each approach. Base some of your ideas on *Ethics in International Business.* Review the guidelines and format for writing memos on pages 41–43 in Chapter 2.

Preparing to Write

Activity 7-19   Discussing Possible Approaches to a Writing Assignment

Together in small groups, respond to the following items as completely as possible to help you think strategically about completing the short writing assignment. Again, this is only preparation. You will not write a draft of this paper.

1. Determine the larger question or broader purpose for writing this memo.

   Purpose for Writing: _____

2. Check the writing strategies that you will need to fully complete the writing task. Fill in the blank after each strategy you choose with the kinds of information you would include.

   ❏ summarizing and responding _____

   ❏ explaining or reporting _____

   ❏ investigating _____

   ❏ evaluating _____

   ❏ analyzing causes, factors, or reasons _____

   ❏ problem-solving _____

Activity 7-20   Discussing the Advantages and Disadvantages of Solutions

In small groups, summarize the two approaches the cigarette company can take and the list the advantages and disadvantages of each. Present these to your classmates.

LEARNER'S NOTEBOOK

Reflecting on Your Learning and Use of Writing Strategies

Now that you have planned this short paper, answer the following questions: Which of the writing strategies identified in Activity 7-19 do you think you have mastered? Which of the writing strategies do you still need to practice? Why are these strategies challenging for you? Compare your answer with a partner.

PUTTING IT ALL TOGETHER

FINAL WRITING ASSIGNMENT

Choose one of the short writing assignments that you planned in a small group. Using the pre-writing that you did with your group members, write a draft of the paper to the specified audience. Work alone or in a group. Use several of the approaches/ strategies you have studied and practiced in this textbook. Consult "The Basics of Synthesizing" on pages 227–230 and Appendix A.

Self-editing Activity

1. Before giving your draft to a peer, read it again to make sure that it says what you intended and is organized in the best way for this particular writing task. Make any changes needed to improve meaning and organization.

2. Choose two of the language features reviewed in this chapter and edit your draft for them. Where indicated, turn to the GLR (GLR) and use the recommended self-editing strategies.

   ☐ use of the modals *can, should, ought to,* or *must* to vary the strength of an evaluation

   ☐ use of subordination and coordination to persuade.

   ☐ review your use of verb tenses and verb tense shift to appropriately convey your meaning to your reader.

   ☐ use and formation of complex noun + *of*-phrases.

   ☐ use of reporting verbs when incorporating quotations and paraphrases

   > **GLR** See pages 270–271, Section 1, for more information on editing sentences for transitions, subordination, and coordination and page 300, Section 3, for more information on editing for verb tense.

3. Edit your draft for one of the language features reviewed in the previous chapters that you think may need more careful attention in your writing. Consult the self-editing activities in the previous chapters.

Peer Response Activity

Exchange papers with a partner. Answer the following questions about your partner's paper:

1. What business problem is this writer addressing in the paper?

2. Check the writing strategies that the writer used to complete the writing task. Fill in the blank after each strategy with the kinds of information the writer included.

❑ summarizing and responding _____

❑ investigating _____

❑ explaining or reporting _____

❑ investigating _____

❑ evaluating _____

❑ analyzing causes, factors, or reasons _____

❑ investigating _____

❑ problem-solving _____

3. What is the most interesting part of the writer's paper? Why?

4. Ask the writer two questions about ideas that were unclear in the paper.

5. Make one suggestion to help the writer revise the draft.

LEARNER'S NOTEBOOK

Reflecting on Using Many Writing Strategies to Complete an Assignment

Report what you have learned about using many writing strategies in one paper. Consider the strategies that you used in writing your paper as well as the strategies your peers used. Which strategies seem to be the most useful or the most widely used in your paper and your peers' papers?

Revise

On your draft, list two changes that you will make to your paper. Rewrite your paper, including these changes.

• •

**L
O
O
K
I
N
G

A
H
E
A
D**

With a partner or in a small group, analyze the typical college/university assignment below.

ENVIRONMENTAL HEALTH
Written Report

The purpose of this assignment is to allow you, as a student, to learn more about a specific environmental health problem and to inform you of the sources of information available. Use at least four references on the topic; these include books, journal articles, government publications, or other acceptable published materials. Your paper should include:

I. A clear statement of the problem—who is affected, and its magnitude (number of people affected and seriousness of the effect).

II. Detailing the "science" of the problem—describe the agent (chemical, biological, or physical), how it affects health, and how people interact with it.

III. Control of the problem—discuss any applicable local, state, or federal laws; who is responsible for taking care of the problem, if anyone; what can they do, or what are they doing?

IV. Future needs—in your opinion, what should we do in the future to eliminate this problem?

DISCUSSION

1. What is the purpose of this assignment?

2. Which of the writing strategies that have been presented in previous chapters will you use to complete this assignment?

3. What problems do you anticipate for the writer of this assignment? What solutions can you offer?

Grammar
and
Language
Reference

The examples in this section are based on the readings in the textbook or on academic textbooks used in U.S. universities.

CONTENTS

Section 1 Grammar Common to All Types of Academic Writing

1A Basic Sentence Structure

SIMPLE SENTENCES

At the most basic level, English sentences have one independent clause, the main clause. A **clause** consists of a subject and a verb. It can also contain an object or a complement, depending on the verb. Some clauses stand alone. These are called **simple sentences.**

MAIN CLAUSE

Subject	Verb	Object
Bad deeds	escalate.	
Anger	begets	anger.

Subject	Verb	Complement
She	seems	young for her age.

PHRASES

We can expand a simple sentence in several ways. One way is to add a phrase that clarifies or modifies the meaning of the main clause. A phrase is made up of several words, but is not a complete sentence because it lacks a subject and a verb.

Phrase	Main Clause
Without rules for controlling anger,	it can slip into emotional anarchy.
In many societies,	the first step is to do nothing.

COMPOUND SENTENCES

Another type of sentence joins two independent clauses together with one of the following **coordinating conjunctions:** *and, but, or, so, for, yet,* and *nor.* This forms a compound sentence.

   Punctuation: A comma is placed at the end of the first clause before the coordinating conjunction.

Independent Clause	Coordinating Conjunction	Independent Clause
They extend sympathy and a willing ear to the enraged spouse for a while,	**but**	eventually they expect the person to "shape up" and "get on with it."
The victim may grouse and mutter about the loss of sympathy,	**but**	actually the friends and relatives are doing what any decent tribe would do.

COMPLEX SENTENCES

Complex sentences consist of two clauses connected by a subordinating word, such as *because, although,* or *while.* The clause that begins with the subordinating word cannot stand alone as a simple sentence. This clause is, therefore, called a **dependent** or **subordinate clause.**

   Punctuation: When the sentence begins with the dependent clause, the dependent clause is followed by a comma to set it apart from the main clause. When the sentence begins with the independent clause, no comma is necessary.

	Adverb Clause	
Independent Clause	Subordinator	Dependent Clause
Good manners melt resentment	**because**	they maintain respect between the two disagreeing parties.

Complex sentences express either a time or a logical relationship between the ideas in the two clauses.	**Time Relationship: When** Anglo-Americans are angry, they tend to proceed in stages from small steps to larger ones.
	Logical Relationship: At the time of the Samurai knights, these rules [about anger] had considerable survival value **because** a Samurai could legally execute anyone who he thought was not respectful enough.

COMPOUND-COMPLEX SENTENCES

Compound-complex sentences combine complex and compound sentences. They consist of at least three clauses. Two clauses are independent, joined by a coordinating conjunction. One or more clauses are dependent, joined by a time or logical subordinator.

Punctuation: Because these are usually long sentences, there are two considerations when punctuating them: 1) A comma is placed at the end of the first clause <u>before</u> the coordinating conjunction. 2) When the complex part of the sentence begins with a dependent clause, a comma is placed at the end of this clause and before the independent clause.

Subordinator + Dependent Clause	Independent Clause	Coordinating Conjunction	Subordinator + Dependent Clause	Independent Clause
If they try to change nature,	she will swiftly destroy them,	**but**	**if** they relax and accept the bounty of nature,	they will be taken care of.

Independent Clause	Coordinating Conjunction	Independent Clause	Subordinator + Dependent Clause
Layoffs win points for corporate CEO's with Wall Street,	**and**	they boost the value of executive stock options,	**although** recent experience shows that cutting staff typically has fallen dramatically short of expectations.

1B   Expressing Logical Relationships Through Coordination, Subordination, and Transition Words

Writing flows when it combines both short and long sentences. While short sentences allow writers to emphasize information, long sentences convey complex logical relationships between ideas. Writers produce long sentences by combining clauses using either coordination or subordination. Writers can also show logical relationships between sentences by placing a transition word or expression between them.

COORDINATION

When sentences are combined through coordination, two independent clauses are joined by a coordinating conjunction *(for, and, nor, but, or, yet, so)*. This type of sentence combining creates a compound sentence. When writers combine two clauses with a coordinating conjunction, they may be signaling that: 1) each clause is equally important; or 2) that each clause is new information for the reader. *Yet* often appears between two separate sentences that are connected through a logical relationship.

Independent Clause	Coordinating Conjunction	Independent Clause
Productivity and profits continued to climb over the past 20 years,	**but**	the take-home pay of the average worker has gone down in real terms.
Madison Avenue's goal is to manipulate rather than to educate,	**so**	the media merchandisers promote the crudest impression of ethnics held by the public.
Psychotherapy, of course, takes place within a culture	**and**	psychotherapists must have a thorough knowledge of the culture's rules about anger.
In Europe and America, an early-retirement culture has taken root.	**Yet**	over the past few years many governments have had to rethink.

SUBORDINATION

When sentences are combined through subordination, an independent clause is joined to a dependent clause that begins with a subordinating word or phrase such as *although, after, because, even though, despite the fact that, while.* This type of sentence combining creates a complex sentence. When writers choose to combine two clauses with a subordinating word, it is because there is some sort of logical relationship between the two and the writer wants to clearly signal that relationship.

Meaning	Subordinating Word/Phrase	Dependent Clause	Independent Clause
concession	**While**	they are not necessarily avid churchgoers,	most centenarians seem to have some sort of religious life.
concession	**Despite the fact that**	she tried periodically for an hour,	Norma the elephant was never able to swing.
time (*the action in clause 1 occurs at the same time as clause 2*)	**As**	each buffalo skidded to a halt,	it let out a loud bellow.

TRANSITION WORDS AND EXPRESSIONS

Transition words and expressions show a logical relationship between ideas within parts of a sentence or between sentences. When writers choose to combine two clauses or sentences with a transition word or expression, they want to make sure the reader understands the logical relationship between the ideas expressed in the two sentences or clauses.

Logical Connection	Sentence 1	Transition Word or Expression	Independent Clause
contrast	At the outset, he recognizes, as did many southern moderates, that "the Yankees are better equipped than we."	**However,**	Butler later heroically enlists in the Confederate army.

Continued

result/effect	Scheming southern women have long been a popular focus of fiction (Lillian Hellman's *The Little Foxes,* for example).	**Thus,**	Scarlett O'Hara's famed conniving and fierce independence are often seen as just another instance of literary fantasy.
addition (of similar information)	Marketing executives are less interested in your personal information than what you buy.	**Moreover,**	there are laws and regulations designed to make sure it stays that way.

MEANINGS AND FUNCTIONS OF CONJUNCTIONS, SUBORDINATORS, AND TRANSITION WORDS

Although conjunctions, subordinators, and transition words are each used to combine clauses and sentences differently, they often share the same or similar meanings. See the following pages for explanations and examples of those most commonly found in academic writing.

SIGNALING CONTRASTING RELATIONSHIPS

Contrast words indicate that the information in one clause or sentence differs in some way from the information in another. There are several types of contrast that can be signaled with transition words, conjunctions, and subordinators: 1) a contrast; that is, the information in one clause is opposite or different from the information in another clause; 2) a concession; that is, the information in one clause is true, but the information in the second clause must be acknowledged. When writers use these sentences, they want to convince a reader that the logical relationships are accurate.

CONTRAST

Subordinator	Conjunction	Transition Words
whereas **while**	**but**	**in contrast** **by comparison** **conversely** **on the other hand** **however**
A maximal duty or obligation, he says, is one whose fulfillment would be "praiseworthy but not absolutely mandatory," **whereas** a minimal duty is one that must be met or the corporation would lose its moral right to exist.	The Electronic Communications Privacy Act (ECPA) of 1986 establishes clear guidelines for monitoring e-mail messages sent over public systems such as MCI Mail or CompuServe. **But** no such regulations govern the monitoring of internal e-mail messages sent on a company-owned system.	Depressingly, the WHO also found that "the speed at which information is processed [by older workers] usually slows down substantially in older individuals." **On the other hand,** "while older managers take more time to reach decisions, they... appear to be as competent as younger managers in overall decision-making."

CONCESSION OR COUNTERARGUMENT

Subordinator	Conjunction	Transition Words
even though **although** **while** **despite the fact that**	**but** **yet**	**however** **nevertheless** **nonetheless**
While having some kind of e-mail guideline is better than having none, a poorly written policy can create new problems.	In Europe and America, an early-retirement culture has taken root. **Yet,** over the past few years many governments have had to rethink. "Some companies may be afraid to address the issue [of e-mail privacy] for fear of employee backlash," observes Bill Moroney. **But** by doing nothing, he adds, companies open themselves to employee dissatisfaction and to possible litigation.	Although Selznick consulted with the NAACP (National Association for the Advancement of Colored People), he **nevertheless** concentrated on his white audience, not the black protesters, and the film reflects his attitude.

SIGNALING THE ADDITION OF INFORMATION

Conjunctions, subordinators, or transition words signal several kinds of added information: 1) more information, either a new idea or one similar to the previous idea; 2) surprising or emphasized information; 3) examples or clarifying information.

ADDING NEW OR SIMILAR INFORMATION

Subordinator	Conjunction	Transition Words
New Information **in addition to the fact that**	**and**	New Information **in addition** **also** **moreover** **furthermore**
Similar Information **like** **in the same way as** **much as**	**or**	Similar Information **similarly** **likewise** **in the same way**
Like most women of her time, Scarlett found herself forced by economic necessity into a male domain.	We see what the dog intends. **And** the dog, too, gets a clear glimpse into our minds and knows what we want.	The take-home pay of the average worker has gone down because of downsizing. Some economists suggest, **moreover,** that the permanent strategies of layoffs, even in good times, may hurt the U.S. economy. But by doing nothing about e-mail privacy, companies open themselves to employee dissatisfaction and to possible litigation. **In addition,** until a larger number of companies do establish policies, the issue will remain murky and ripe for legislation.

ADDING SURPRISING OR EMPHASIZED INFORMATION

Subordinator	Conjunction	Transition Words
even though **although** **while** **despite the fact that**	**and even**	**moreover** **furthermore** **in fact** **actually**
In fact, many companies that have engaged in layoffs have discovered that their productivity was worse off afterward, **even though** they continued more rounds of downsizing.	Combination antibiotics are still marketed in most developing countries, however, **and even** command high prices.	All of the negative effects of downsizing hurt a company over the long run because they undermine the whole notion of employee empowerment and the crucial process of idea sharing. **In fact,** many companies that have engaged in layoffs have discovered that their productivity was worse off afterward, even though they continued more rounds of downsizing.

ADDING EXAMPLES OR CLARIFYING INFORMATION

There are no subordinators or conjunctions in this category.

TRANSITION WORDS

Examples **for example** **for instance** **in particular** **to illustrate**	This in turn means that conscious awareness is more likely when the activity is novel and challenging; striking and unexpected events are more likely to produce conscious awareness. **For example,** Janes (1976) observed nesting ravens make an enterprising use of rocks.
Clarification **namely** **specifically** **that is** **in other words**	The marketing of pharmaceuticals in the Third World illustrates a dilemma faced by all transnational corporations; **namely,** how companies should decide what ethical standards to follow.

SIGNALING CAUSE-EFFECT OR REASON-RESULT RELATIONSHIPS

These conjunctions, transition words, and subordinators indicate that the cause or reason, effect or result is stated in a second clause. There are two basic meanings of these words: 1) cause or reason and 2) effect or result.

SHOWING CAUSE OR REASON

Subordinator	Conjunction
because **since** **as** **due to the fact that**	**for**
In the early 1970s, the FDA refused to approve Depo-Provera **because** tests conducted since 1965 showed that it can cause extended and even permanent infertility and possible breast tumors and cervical cancer. A drug for a tropical disease might never have been submitted for approval, **since** there is no market for it in the country where it is manufactured.	Some economists suggest, moreover, that the permanent strategy of layoffs may actually hurt the U.S. economy. **For** that strategy accentuates the income gap between the executive class and the working class in America.

SHOWING EFFECT OR RESULT

Subordinator	Conjunction	Transition Words
so that **so** + adj. or adv. **+ that** **such** + noun phrase **+ that**	**so**	**therefore** **as a result** **thus** **for this reason** **consequently**
The constant pressure of job cutbacks keeps wage levels down **so that** the historical link between rising productivity and rising wages in American manufacturing has been broken. In fact, downsizing has become **so** <u>pervasive</u> **that** more than 85% of the Fortune 500 companies have lopped off sizable numbers of employees in the past five years.	Madison Avenue's goal is to manipulate rather than educate, **so** the media merchandisers promote the crudest impression of ethnics held by the public.	This drug does not treat the underlying causes of diarrhea, but merely relieves the symptoms. **Consequently,** the World Health Organization (WHO) has declared Lomotil to be of "no value" in the treatment of diarrhea. Monkeys climb into trees when they sense a leopard is approaching, but they must hide on smaller outer branches, where another enemy, the martial eagle, can easily attack them. **Thus** the tactics that help them escape from a leopard make them highly vulnerable to a martial eagle.

STEPS TO EDIT TRANSITION WORDS AND SUBORDINATION AND COORDINATION	EXAMPLES
Transition Words STEP 1: Underline all transition words that you have used. STEP 2: If there is a transition word in every sentence, perhaps you have used too many. You might try deleting transition words when the logical relationship between sentences is clear without it.	

Continued

STEP 3: Make sure that the transition word signals the logical relationship between sentences that you intended. Think about the logical connection between the two sentences and change the transition word if necessary.

STEP 4: Look for sentences whose logical relationship is complex and important for the reader to understand. Try adding a transition word here and see if it makes the relationship between the two ideas clearer.

There is a scene where the American player is riding a train with his interpreter, and he is smoking in the train. Despite the fact that there are many people around him, no one complains to him to stop smoking. <u>Indeed</u>, the film's makers researched Japanese society well because "pretending not to see and care" is typical behavior of the Japanese. (Kawamoto, 1997)

Subordination and Coordination

STEP 1: Put brackets [ ] around all sentences or clauses that begin with a subordinating word such as *although*, *while*, *because*. Does the subordinating word signal the appropriate logical relationship between the two clauses? If not, find a better subordinator.

STEP 2: Make sure that sentences that contain a subordinator have **both** a dependent clause (one that begins with a subordinating word) and a main clause (that does not begin with a subordinating word or a coordinating word such as *but*).

[Although there are some movies that portray Japanese culture], most of them are not contemporary. (Kawamoto, 1997)

[Although the movie is a comedy], the portrayal of the main character *in Mr. Baseball*, an American baseball player who tries to integrate himself into the Japanese culture, is serious. (Kawamoto, 1997)

STEP 3: Underline all sentences that contain two independent clauses connected with a coordinating word like *and*, *but*, or *yet*. Does the coordinating word signal the appropriate logical relationship between the two clauses? Would another word be better? Would a subordinator convey the meaning better?

STEP 4: Put double slash marks [//] between the sentences in one or two of your paragraphs. If you notice that many sentences are short, try combining them using subordination or coordination.

<u>There is a scene in the film where the American player enters into a Japanese-style bath before he washes his body,</u> **and** <u>he starts washing his body with soap once he enters the bath, just as it is done in America.</u> (Kawamoto, 1997)

1C   Verb Tense and Form

SUBDIVISIONS OF THE VERB SYSTEM

The English verb system has three major subdivisions: the present tense verbs, the past tense verbs, and the modal auxiliary verbs. The present and past tense verbs will be discussed in this section. For information on modal auxiliaries, see pages 315–321 in Section 5.

Present tense verbs include simple present tense, present progressive, present perfect, and present perfect progressive. In this section, all verbs are underlined <u>twice</u>.	As Ford Motor Company learned, achieving high performance <u>requires</u> a redefinition of work and of the relationships among people who work together. In 1990, there were more than 60,000 centenarians in the United States, and their numbers <u>are</u> rapidly <u>increasing.</u> Very few biologists or psychologists <u>have discussed</u> animal thoughts and feelings. Biologists <u>have been</u> too busy <u>studying</u> animal behavior to worry about animal thinking and feelings.
Past tense verbs include simple past tense, past perfect, past progressive, and past perfect progressive.	In the 1980's, doctors often <u>suggested</u> that waving your anger like a flag <u>was</u> good for the head, and cleansing for the soul. My mother <u>was sitting</u> next to my father holding my baby brother. Kelly's father <u>had heard</u> that there was work in South Dakota (before they left their home in Nebraska in a covered wagon). Villagers <u>had been expecting</u> to die in a war, but instead, they were killed by the Black Death.
The modal auxiliaries are *can, could, may, might, must, shall, should, will,* and *would.*	At the time of the Samurai knights, a knight *<u>could</u>* <u>execute</u> anyone who did not show him the proper amount of respect.

VERB PHRASES WITH SINGLE WORDS OR COMBINATIONS OF WORDS

English verb phrases in sentences are either single verbs or they are combinations of auxiliaries and a form of the main verb.

Single word verb phrases include the simple present tense and the simple past tense.	As Ford Motor Company learned, achieving high performance <u>requires</u> a redefinition of work and of the relationships among people who work together. In the 1980's, doctors often <u>suggested</u> that waving your anger like a flag was good for the head, and cleansing for the soul.
All other verb phrases in sentences combine two or more verbs to make a verb phrase.	In 1990, there were more than 60,000 centenarians in the United States, and their numbers <u>are</u> rapidly <u>increasing.</u> Very few biologists or psychologists <u>have discussed</u> animal thoughts and feelings. At the time of the Samurai knights, a knight <u>could execute</u> anyone who did not show him the proper amount of respect.

SIMPLE PRESENT TENSE

Form Note that verbs in the *present tense* change form. Certain subjects require that *s* be added to the verb. See pages 301–303 in Section 3 for information about *Subject-Verb Agreement*. Subjects are underlined once and verbs twice.	As Ford Motor Company learned, <u>achieving high performance</u> <u>requires</u> a redefinition of work and of the relationships among people who work together. <u>It</u> <u>means</u> not only using the backs of workers but tapping their minds.
Certain time expressions (adverbs) often occur with the simple present tense. These include: *generally, normally, often, frequently, sometimes, everyday, occasionally, seldom,* and *rarely.* Because simple present tense is often used to make generalizations, many writers add adverbs of frequency to make sure that the general statement has exactly the right meaning, and doesn't sound like an overgeneralization. Without the adverb, the statement means "always," so the writer uses the adverb to control the strength of the generalization.	This position can perhaps be expressed as, "We do not entirely agree with the Romans, but <u>we</u> *sometimes* <u>find</u> it necessary to do things their way." <u>The otter</u> *usually* <u>eats</u> while floating on its back.

PRESENT PROGRESSIVE TENSE

Form To form the *present progressive*, use *is* or *are* plus the *ing* form of the verb. This tense indicates that the action is ongoing in the present.	In 1990, there were more than 60,000 centenarians in the United States, and <u>their numbers</u> <u>are</u> rapidly <u>increasing.</u>
Verbs in this tense often occur with time expressions that clearly indicate a period of time in the present. These include *now, presently*, and *this semester/year/month*. Time expressions appear in italics.	At Duke, <u>Williams</u> has studied the long-term effects of hostility for years, but *now* <u>is</u> also <u>trying</u> to determine the day-by-day events that contribute to heart disease. For one thing, [<u>Williams</u>] says he<u>'s finding</u> that blood pressure goes up when people are exposed to violence.

PRESENT PERFECT TENSE

Form This verb is a two-part verb. It consists of the auxiliary *have/has* + the past participle of the main verb.	The single most influential interpretation of the Civil War in twentieth-century popular culture, <u>the film</u> <u>has defined</u> that war for a mass audience.
***have/has* + regular verbs** *have* visited *has* experienced *has* studied	<u>Very few biologists or psychologists</u> <u>have</u> <u>discussed</u> animal thoughts and feelings.
***have/has* + irregular verbs** *has* gone *have* taken *have* written	Invasion of privacy of the Internet <u>has</u> <u>become</u> a serious concern. Continued

Verbs in this tense often occur with time expressions that clearly indicate a period of time that began in the past, but is not finished (*since 1975, for a long period of time,* etc.). These also occur with time expressions that signal a time period that is not yet completed or has just ended (*yet, still, long, up to now, just so far*). Other time expressions indicate repeated actions at an unspecified time (*several times, often*). Time expressions in examples appear in italics.

It is telling, moreover, that innovative companies such as Ford and Motorola <u>have gone</u> to great lengths not to resort to layoffs *for the past several years,* in the conviction that the security of their workforce is essential to high performance.

Despite its popularity, <u>downsizing in the late 1980s and early '90s</u> <u>has</u> *often* <u>failed</u> to achieve its proponents' objectives, economists report.

SIMPLE PAST TENSE

Form
Most verbs add *ed* to form *the past tense.* These are called **regular past tense verbs.** However, some of the most common verbs have **irregular past tense** forms. It is necessary to memorize these. The forms of the verb are always the same no matter what the subject.

In the 1980s, <u>doctors</u> often <u>suggested</u> that waving your anger like a flag was good for the head, and cleansing for the soul.

<u>The scientists</u> also <u>drew</u> blood to test stress hormone levels.

Verbs in this tense often occur with time expressions that clearly indicate a time or period of time in the past. These include: *when he was a child, during the war, 200 years ago, in 1975, on that date, after they were married,* and *at that time.*

At the time of the Samurai knights, <u>these rules</u> <u>had</u> considerable survival value.

PAST PROGRESSIVE TENSE

Form To form the **past progressive,** use *was* or *were* plus the *ing* form of the verb. This tense indicates that the action was ongoing in the past.	<u>My mother</u> <u>was sitting</u> next to my father holding my baby brother.
Verbs in this tense often occur with time expressions that clearly indicate a period of time in the past. These include *during the war*, and *while I was in college, all the time.*	*During the spring and summer months of 1890,* <u>the Kelly family</u> <u>was traveling</u> from Saunders County in eastern Nebraska, near Omaha, where the children were born, northwest to the Black Hills of South Dakota.

PAST PERFECT TENSE

Form This verb is a two-part, or combination verb. It consists of the simple past form of the auxiliary *had* + the past participle of the main verb.	<u>Kelly's father</u> <u>had heard</u> that there was work in South Dakota (before they left their home in Nebraska in a covered wagon).
***had* + regular verbs** *had* visited *had* experienced *had* studied	<u>Villagers</u> <u>had been expecting</u> to die in a war, but instead, they were killed by the Black Death.
***had* + irregular verbs** *had* gone *had* taken *had* written	For example, it was once believed that those who achieved the age of 100 would tend to be calm, serene "Type B" personalities <u>who</u> <u>had led</u> relatively stress free lives. Continued

Verbs in this tense often occur with time expressions that clearly indicate a time or period of time in the past such as *before, ever since, already, just* and *before then.* ***Before*** *he went to China, he had never entertained the idea of learning Chinese.* ***Ever since*** *she was a teenager she had wanted to own her own car. He had* ***just*** *finished his experiment when the lab blew up. She'd* ***already*** *visited her client three times in the county jail when she was taken off the case.* Time expressions in the examples are in italics.	*By the 1970s,* <u>ethnicity</u> <u>had become</u> a subject of popular interest, enough so to attract the attention of the mass media. Nearly <u>20 percent of the Americans who lost their jobs from 1991 through 1994,</u> *for example,* <u>had not found</u> work *by November 1994.* Suddenly, I felt an extraordinary surge of energy, felt my spirit begin to part from my body. <u>I</u> <u>had</u> *never* <u>felt</u> so blissfully free.

1D   Noun Phrases, Articles, and Determiners

Nouns combine with articles and determiners to create noun phrases with three different types of meaning. Noun phrases can have definite meaning, indefinite meaning, or generic meaning.

GENERIC REFERENCE

Academic writers often communicate about groups of people or classes of things or ideas rather than about particular objects or people. Especially when making generalizations, writers are communicating about the kind of idea or thing or person rather than about a particular one. All three types of articles, *the, a/an,* and no article *(ø)*, can signal a generic reference noun phrase.

Generic reference nouns refer to a whole class or group of people, things, or ideas or a representative person, thing, or idea from a whole class. A possible test to determine if a noun phrase is generic reference is to put the words *all* or *many* in front of the noun phrase, or the phrase *in general* after it.	**(ø) Elephants,** both Indian and African, are particularly playful. **(ø) Animals** (in general) may also play with **objects.**
Plural Nouns in Generalizations Plural nouns with *ø* are used when the noun phrase refers to classes or groups. Plural nouns without an article often occur in descriptions of general characteristics with *have* or *be.* Nouns that appear in the plural form in generalizations are always count nouns.	What do **(ø) monkeys, (ø) dolphins, (ø) crows,** and **(ø) ants** think about? Or do **(ø) nonhuman animals** experience any **(ø) thoughts** or **(ø) subjective feelings.** One consideration can help us understand the presence of conscious thought. Continued

***The* + Singular Noun in Generalizations** *The* with a singular noun indicates that the noun is a representative of a class or group. *The* + a singular noun is used with particular types of nouns that include machines, inventions, plants, and animals. Usually a plural form of the same noun can be substituted and have the same meaning.	generic *the*, an invention **The laptop computer** has changed the way people do their work. **Laptop computers** have changed the way people do their work.
***A* + Singular Noun in Generalizations** *A* with a singular noun can also indicate that the noun is a representative of a class or group. *A* + a singular noun usually describes a generalized instance of the group or class. *A* + a singular noun often occurs in definitions, descriptions, and generalizations.	generalized instance 1) What is it like to be **an animal?** 2) Of course to interpret the thoughts, or their equivalent, which determine generalized instance **an animal's behavior** is difficult, but this is no reason for not making the attempt to do so. generalized instances, description 3) **An anonymous remailer** accepts generalized instances, description **an e- mail** message from you, strips off any identifying information, and sends the message to its destination.
Noncount Nouns in Generalizations For generic meaning, noncount nouns do not have articles.	noncount noun, general reference **(ø) Privacy** on the Internet is an illusion unless you take active steps to ensure it. noncount noun, general reference Web sites commonly get **(ø) information** about you through an on-line registration form.
Count Nouns vs. Noncount Nouns in Generalizations When writers make generalizations, they use either count nouns or noncount nouns. When they use count nouns with generic meaning, these nouns often appear in the plural form and do not have an article in front of them. Noncount nouns have only one form; they are never plural. When they have a generic meaning they are not preceded by an article.	What do **(ø) monkeys**, **(ø) dolphins**, **(ø) crows**, and **(ø) ants** think about? Or do **(ø) nonhuman animals** experience any **(ø) thoughts** or **(ø) subjective feelings?** One consideration can help us understand the presence of **(ø) conscious thought.**

INDEFINITE VS. GENERIC MEANING

Indefinite Meaning *A* and *an* are used with singular count nouns to signal indefinite meaning. Nouns are indefinite when they are mentioned for the first time and, therefore, are not known by the reader. Nouns are also indefinite if they refer to one member of a group of class. If you can substitute the word *one*, then the noun has an indefinite meaning. Usually when the same noun is mentioned a second time, the noun phrase changes to *the/this* + singular count noun.	Perhaps the most controversial allegation of drug dumping concerns Depo-Provera, First mention, indefinite **a contraceptive** taken by injection, that protects women against pregnancy for three months or more. All the time Upjohn was promoting Second mention, definite **this contraceptive** outside the United States with no warnings about its side effects.
Generic Meaning *A* and *an* are also used with singular count nouns for generic meaning. Instead of referring to an unknown or unspecified object, person, or idea, *a* or *an* with a generic noun phrase refers to a generalized instance of the group or class. If this type of noun is mentioned a second time in a paragraph, it <u>does not change</u> to *the*.	And it isn't hard for **a cybersnoop** to find out more about you; combining the information about the sites you visit, where you live, and the registration information many sites require, **a clever cypersnoop** can build a quick and accurate profile on you.

DEFINITE REFERENCE

Definite reference noun phrases consist of *the* + a plural noun, *the* + a singular noun, *the* + a noncount noun. Noun phrases marked with *the* refer to actual objects, people, or ideas. Here are some contexts which make nouns definite.

Second and Subsequent Mention A writer often starts with indefinite reference using *a* or *an* or no article + plural noun phrase because the reader does not share the same information. When the noun is used a second time, and if it is <u>not</u> a generic reference noun phrase, the writer changes to *the* because the information is shared with the reader.	Perhaps the most controversial allegation of drug dumping concerns Depo-Provera, First mention, new information **a contraceptive** taken by injection, that protects women against pregnancy for three months or more. All the time Upjohn was promoting Second mention, shared information **the contraceptive** outside the United States with no warnings about its side effects.

Continued

Phrases or Clauses A writer can make a noun definite by adding a following phrase (usually an *of-* or other prepositional phrase after the noun) or a clause (usually a relative clause).	Often, the local medical community and powerful segments of the population benefit from **the unethical marketing practices** <u>of the giant drug companies.</u> Second, **the fact** <u>that a drug has not been approved in the home country of a transnational</u> does not automatically mean that it is unsafe or ineffective.
Superlatives/Numbers/Unique Adjectives Certain adjectives usually occur with *the:* superlatives—*the largest, the most beautiful, the lowest* sequence—*the first, the next, the final* Other adjectives often occur with *the:* unique—*the same, the only, the one, the major, the main*	The ***first* step** in protecting yourself is to learn how your privacy can be violated. When both parties use **the *same* software,** messages sent from one person to another are readable only by the intended recipient.

STEPS TO EDIT NOUN PHRASES AND ARTICLES	
STEP 1: Underline all the nouns or noun phrases you have used. STEP 2: Check for nouns that generally require *the* (for example, names of particular countries such as ***the*** **United States** or bodies of water such as ***the*** **Atlantic Ocean** or uses with superlatives or sequencing words such as ***the*** **first year of his life**) STEP 3: Check next for forms based in their meanings (generic, indefinite, or definite). a. Check generalizations for generic noun forms. Use the following test: Put *all* in front of the noun or the phrase and *in general* after it, and if it makes sense, the noun is a generic noun form.	**Generic Meaning** Not very long ago, ~~the~~ longevity [in general] for most ~~of the~~ people [in general] was **[an]** ~~the~~ impossible thing to attain. <u>Living condition[s]</u>, which includes <u>the weather,</u> ~~the~~ <u>housings,</u> and ~~the~~ <u>dietary habits,</u> are <u>an important factor</u> that could contribute to <u>longer lives.</u> Continued

To mark the noun as having generic meaning, you must first decide whether the noun is count or non-count.

If the noun is **countable,** you have two choices: 1) add *s* to the noun, but do not put an article in front of the noun; 2) put *a/an* in front of the singular form of the noun.

If the noun is **noncount,** you do not need an article in front of the noun, and the noun does not add *s*.

b. Check statements that have definite meaning (these include specific examples that support generalizations) to be sure that count nouns are either singular or plural and that noncount nouns appear without *s*. All nouns with definite meaning are preceded by *the*.

Definite Meaning

To keep active, Roy Miller, now 100 years old, works one day every week for

first mention, indefinite meaning
a philanthropic organization.

second mention, specific reference
The organization helps homeless people find jobs. Roy enjoys helping the people get back on their feet.

1E   Nouns, Pronouns, Determiners, and Cohesion

AGREEMENT IN GENDER AND NUMBER BETWEEN NOUNS AND PRONOUNS

Personal pronoun is the name given to pronouns like *I, you, she, he, it,* and *they*. These nouns have subject forms that are used as subjects of sentences and object forms that are used as objects of a sentence or of a preposition.
Subject pronouns—*I, you, he, she, it, we, they*
Object pronouns—*me, you, him, her, it, us, them*
Possessive pronouns (+ noun)—*my, your, his, her, its, our, their*

When Anglo-Americans are angry, **they** tend to proceed in stages from small steps to larger ones.

Centenarians set high standards and follow **them** rigorously.

As you might expect, frustrated men and women were far more aroused than **their** peers. **Their** hearts raced and **their** systolic blood pressure shot up.

Continued

Because academic writing can involve long, complicated sentences, writers have to be careful to help readers determine which pronoun is referring to which noun. The rules are fairly simple, but can be fairly complicated to apply in long pieces of writing.

Singular with singular: Singular nouns are replaced with singular pronouns. Notice that *each* and *neither* in the second example refer to singular nouns and if pronouns replace these words, they must be singular pronouns: *his culture, her culture, or his/her culture.*	<u>Roy Miller</u> worked one day a week with the poor. **He** also was president of a philanthropic club. <u>The Arab,</u> who now likewise felt shamed, furiously hit <u>the Japanese student</u> before the teacher could intervene. Shame and anger had erupted in a flash, as *each student* dutifully obeyed the rules of **his culture**. *Neither [student]* could imagine, of course, that **his rules** might not be universal.
Plural with plural: Plural pronouns are used to refer to plural nouns.	<u>Louis Kelly's parents</u> followed the new wave of jobs over several states. From Nebraska **they** moved to the Black Hills of South Dakota.
Pronouns must also match the nouns they refer to in **gender:** *he* for masculine nouns, *she* for feminine nouns, *it* for things, animals, and, in academic writing, ideas and concepts. For more information about cohesion, see GLR pages 287–289.	<u>Roy Miller</u> reports that **he** never felt old. <u>Billy Earley</u> keeps active. **She** traveled to Washington, DC and Hawaii in the same year. For some groups in America, <u>anger</u> is an effective way to get your way; for others, **it** is the last resort. In the Frustration group, <u>the experimenter</u> repeatedly interrupted and harassed the subjects for counting too slowly. **He** made them start over three times. Finally, **he** insisted that the subjects' attitudes made further testing impossible. What makes <u>a cat</u> a good hunter? Part of the answer is **its** *age.* Old cats get lazy; the younger <u>the cat,</u> the more animals **it** catches.

MAKING THE PRONOUN REFER TO THE RIGHT WORD

Pronouns occur often in writing to replace nouns that are previously mentioned. When replacing a noun with a pronoun, it is important to remember to: • choose the appropriate pronoun to replace the noun • make sure that the noun the pronoun refers to is clear to the reader. That is, the pronoun should occur fairly near the noun it refers to. In the example, the writer substitutes the pronoun *it* for the noun **achieving high performance** in the second sentence because using the same noun again would sound repetitive and the noun it refers to is clear. But, because the second sentence contains a lot of information, the third time the writer refers to **high performance,** the noun is repeated.	When <u>Anglo-Americans</u> are angry, **they** tend to proceed in stages from small steps to larger ones. <u>Walter Forbes</u> of CUC International has a dream. A customer—one of 60 million he has in 21 countries—will log onto **his** Internet sales network to buy a dress. As Ford Motor Company learned, <u>achieving high performance</u> requires a redefinition of the relationships among people who work together. **It** also requires not only using the backs of workers, but tapping their minds—and that entails giving more responsibility and autonomy to the ordinary worker and to the work team on the factory floor. Trust is an essential ingredient for high performance, according to Motorola's long-time CEO, Bob Galvin.

DEMONSTRATIVE PRONOUNS

The words *this, these, that,* and *those* replace nouns or noun phrases, but they also specify them or point to them. *This/that* and *these/those* can occur alone, or they can precede a noun.

This and *that* replace **singular nouns** that refer to a person, a thing, or in academic writing, a concept or idea that has already been mentioned. *These* and *those* replace **plural nouns** that refer to people, things, or concepts.	<u>Animals may also play with objects.</u> **This** can be seen even in some animals that are known to play with other animals. Cynthia Moss may have spoken for biologists when, watching African elephants <u>play in the rain—running, twirling, flapping ears and trunks, spraying water at each other, flailing branches, uttering loud play trumpets</u>—she wrote in her notes, "How can one do a serious study of animals that behave **this** *way!*" <u>Well-learned behavior patterns</u> may not require the same degree of conscious attention as **those** the animal is learning how to perform. <div align="right">Continued</div>

	As with other ethnic groups, in the last several decades, <u>Italians</u> have moved in noticeable numbers into government service, political life, the professions, and the arts. It can be argued that **these** *people* usually do less sensationally horrifying things than gangsters.
Sometimes, *this/these* refer to some idea or thing that follows it.	The absence of laws inevitably leads to confusion, anger, and mistrust when an employer's actions run counter to an employee's expectations. Consider **this** scenario: <u>A network administrator routinely monitors e-mail traffic to make sure the system doesn't get overloaded.</u>
In speaking, *this/these* refers to what is "near," "here" or "now." *That/those* refers to what is "far away" or "in the past." These words are used in a somewhat similar manner in writing, but there is also a difference. Writers use *this/these* to keep the noun being replaced "here" and "now" in the reader's mind. Writers use *this/these* to refer to or replace an idea or concept that has just been mentioned or discussed at length. As in speaking, writers may use *that/those* to indicate that the noun being replaced is "far away" or "in the past." That is, the noun may refer to an old idea, practice, etc., one that people no longer believe to be true. *That/Those* can also emphasize a contrast between two nouns, the noun that is the subject of the sentence and the second or "other" noun. *Those* also refers to people.	Customized retailing via cyberspace is only one of scores of new ways computers and the Internet are making life quicker and more convenient for consumers. But, as with everything else, there's a cost: <u>Companies and people you're not familiar with have access to more personal information about you than ever before.</u> **This** is something entirely new. Magazines, direct mailers, and department stores all have exchanged mailing lists and customer information for decades. An impressive example is the use of small stones by <u>sea otters</u> to detach and open shellfish. **These** *intelligent aquatic carnivores* feed mostly on sea urchins and mollusks. <u>Well-learned behavior patterns</u> may not require the same degree of conscious attention as **those** (<u>other behaviors</u>) the animal is learning how to perform. We make inferences about <u>people's feelings and thoughts,</u> especially **those** of very young children.

1F   Relative Clauses and Appositives to Give Information About Experts and Interviewees

See pages 110–112 in Chapter 3, Investigating, for examples and exercises on this topic.

Section 2 Past Time Narrative

2A   Overview of Past Time Narrative Grammar

One of the first types of writing we all learn is storytelling or narrative. Narrative, however, is not just found in fiction; it is an essential element of many other types of writing. Most narratives are an account of events that happened in the past. Writers use these past time narratives as an example of a general point they want to make. Writers of history use them to discuss events that happened at a certain place and time. Writers of psychology and sociology use them to present case studies of individuals and groups. Scientific writers use them to explain how experiments were conducted. Introductory college textbooks use historical narratives often when they present the history of a field or discipline—the history of psychology, the history of genetics.

Narratives usually include the following grammar: • past tense verbs • time words and phrases to show the order of events • proper nouns and personal pronouns (he, she, they) to refer to the characters in the story This sample shows how these features interact in this type of writing. Subjects in the example are underlined once. Past tense verbs are underlined twice. Time expressions appear in italics. Pronouns are in boldface.	Pamela, a young college student, was traveling to a country in Africa on Quantum Airlines, but *first* **she** had to take a connecting flight from Denver to Los Angeles, the international flight's city of departure. **She** arrived at the Denver airport only to find that the flight to Los Angeles had been canceled *earlier,* thereby forcing **her** to miss **her plane**. The arrival time of the later plane, however, was dangerously close to the departure time of the Quantum flight to Africa. *Upon arriving at the Los Angeles airport,* Pamela ran to catch the departing flight. As **she** arrived at the gate, **she** saw the door closing. *When* **she** asked the gate attendant to let **her** board the plane, the airline employee said, "Sorry ma'am, but once the gate has been shut, we're no longer allowed to board any passengers. You'll have to get the next flight." Pamela *usually* cried when **she** was angry, but this time, **her** face reddened and **her rage** was visible.

2B   Past Tense Verbs

VERBS IN PAST TENSE NARRATIVE

Generally, the most frequent verb tense in past tense narratives is the **simple past tense.** Occasionally, verbs in a past tense narrative may be in **past progressive** or **past perfect.** Putting a verb in past progressive or past perfect emphasizes it in some way. This shift in tense between simple past and these two other tenses is marked by **chronological organizers,** such as *suddenly, by early last year.* These words and phrases indicate either a shift from an action or event at a fixed time in the past to an ongoing event in the past. They also indicate a shift to a different time period—either earlier or later.	*In 1890,* the Kelly family <u>was traveling</u> from Saunders County in eastern Nebraska, near Omaha, where the children <u>were born,</u> northwest to the Black Hills of South Dakota. Louis's Father <u>had heard</u> there was work on the railroad *then under construction* near what is now Custer National Park. "We <u>would camp</u> along the way," Louis continues. "My parents <u>slept</u> in a tent at night with the baby. My sister and I <u>slept</u> in the wagon. It <u>was</u> a converted farm wagon, not the Conestoga type or prairie schooners so often <u>pictured</u> in Western movies.
The **past perfect** has limited use. Primarily, writers choose to use the past perfect when they want to tell the events in a past experience or event **out of chronological order** or want to add additional information to the story. Notice in the example that the basic idea of the past event is that General Motors had to restructure. The writer adds the reason that they had to restructure and puts it in the **past perfect tense.**	Experts differentiate the recent rash of corporate downsizing from earlier cutbacks and the massive restructuring of companies such as General Motors and IBM, which <u>had</u> to restructure *after* they <u>had lost</u> huge amounts of money.
Past progressive is used when the writer wants to add additional information to the past experience or event. Using the **past progressive** allows the writer to emphasize the ongoing or co-occurring nature of an event in the past. Often the **simple past** form can be used instead of **past progressive.**	In the early 1970s, the FDA <u>refused</u> to approve Depo-Provera because tests <u>conducted</u> since 1965 showed that it can cause extended and even permanent infertility and possible breast tumors and cervical cancer. All the time, Upjohn <u>was promoting</u> this contraceptive outside the United States with no warnings about its side effects.

2C   Proper Nouns, Pronouns, and Cohesion

PROPER NOUNS: REFERENCE AND COHESION

Since stories usually involve a set of characters or people, proper nouns are used often in past time narratives. Writers do not usually repeat proper nouns in every sentence. Proper nouns play an important role in cohesion. **Cohesion** means that a piece of writing "sticks together"; the sentences move smoothly from one to another and the reader is never lost in following the writer's thoughts. Cohesion is achieved in several ways: 1) Sometimes writers vary the proper noun they use to refer to a thing or person or place. 2) Writers replace the proper nouns with pronouns. 3) Writers use words such as *this, these, that,* and *those.*

<table>
<tr>
<td>

In this example, there are three "characters:" the Dutch people, the dikes (protective walls that separate the sea from the land), and the sea itself. Look at all the ways the writer refers to the same noun. For example, in the first paragraph he first uses "many people" and then "more than a million Dutch citizens" to describe the same Dutch people. His references to the sea are in italic boldface and to the dikes in bold.

</td>
<td>

<u>Many people</u> were awakened by the air-raid sirens. <u>Others</u> heard church bells sounding. Some probably sensed only a distant, predawn ringing and returned to sleep. But before the end of that day—February 1, 1953—<u>more than a million Dutch citizens</u> would learn for whom these bells tolled and why. In the middle of the night, a deadly combination of winds and tides had raised the level of ***the North Sea*** to the brim of **the Netherlands' protective dikes,** and ***the ocean*** was beginning to pour in.

As nearby <u>Dutch villagers</u> slept, ***water*** rushing over **the dikes** began to eat away at **those earthen bulwarks** from the back side. Soon ***the sea*** had broken **through the seawall,** and ***water*** freely flooded the land, eventually extending ***the sea*** inward as far as 64 kilometers from the former coast.

<small>Continued</small>

</td>
</tr>
</table>

When proper nouns in a narrative refer to humans, writers pay careful attention to how they refer to them the second or third time they mention them so that the reference is clear to readers. In the example, the writer refers to two different males. To help the reader follow which "he" is being talked about, the writer only substitutes *he* or *his* for one of the nouns in the same sentence or the next sentence. When switching the reference to the other male character in the narrative, the writer has carefully chosen proper nouns: the Japanese or the Arab. These help the reader follow which person is being discussed.	The class was basic English for foreign students, and an Arab student, during a spoken activity, was describing a tradition of **his home country**. Something **he** said embarrassed a Japanese student in the front row, who reacted the proper Japanese way: **He** smiled. The Arab saw the smile and demanded to know what was so funny about Arab customs. The Japanese, who was now publicly humiliated as well as embarrassed, could reply only with a smile and, to **his misfortune, he** giggled to mask **his shame.** The Arab, who now likewise felt shamed, furiously hit the **Japanese student** before the teacher could intervene.
Some proper nouns are the names of people. It can be difficult to determine if a name is the family name or first name. It is also difficult to know if the person is a male or a female. If you are unsure about a proper noun you want to use, look it up in a dictionary or ask a teacher or someone else who knows English well.	For example, Janes (1976) observed nesting ravens make an enterprising use of rocks. **He** had been closely observing ten raven nests in Oregon, eight of which were near the top of rocky cliffs. Janes and companion climbed up the crevice and inspected the six baby ravens. As **they** started down, both parents flew at them repeatedly, calling loudly, then landed at the top of the cliff, still calling.
Sometimes writers will refer to animals with human names and then refer to them with the personal pronoun *he* or *she,* depending on the animal's gender.	When Norma, a young elephant, saw children swinging she was greatly intrigued. Before long **she** went over, waved the children away with her trunk, backed up to a swing, and attempted to sit on it. **She** was notably unsuccessful, even using **her tail** to hold the swing in place. Continued

Proper nouns can also refer to manufactured items, government agencies, and companies. These are all replaced by the pronoun *it* or *they*.	In the early 1970s, the FDA refused to approve <u>Depo-Provera</u> because tests conducted since 1965 showed that **it** can cause extended and even permanent infertility and possible breast tumors and cervical cancer.
This is probably the most common demonstrative in academic writing. It replaces **a singular noun** that refers to a person, a thing, or **a noun phrase** that refers to a concept or idea that has already been mentioned.	We decided to make <u>an intensive study</u> in the small Bedfordshire village. **This** began with a survey to see how many domestic cats there were in the village and whether their owners would be willing to participate. In addition, we recorded many catches for which there were no remains. Thus, <u>if a cat was seen to eat the entire specimen,</u> **this** was recorded as an "unknown."

REPLACING PROPER NOUNS WITH PRONOUNS

Many narratives focus on people and their actions. These narratives require the use of personal pronouns to refer to the various people involved in the action. Keeping the pronoun reference clear for the reader can be a challenge. Notice how this writer has plural forms for the subjects in the experiment and the singular masculine for the experimenter. See Section 1, pages 282–284, for more information on making the pronoun refer to the right word.	<u>Men and women</u> were randomly assigned to one of the three different conditions: <u>Some subjects</u> had a chance to verbally aggress. **They** were asked to fill out, in the experimenter's presence, a brief questionnaire evaluating <u>the experimenter's</u> capabilities as an experimenter, including the way **he** related to subjects. <u>Other subjects</u> had to physically aggress against **him.** **They** were given 10 opportunities to shock him. Most of **them** depressed the shock plunger eight times.

Section 3: Informational Writing

3A   Overview of Informational Grammar

Informational writing is found in almost everything you read in academic courses. This type of writing presents generalizations, theories, data, facts, and definitions.

As the short sample demonstrates, informational writing is characterized by many structures, all of which work together.

- complex noun phrases (in bold)
- long sentences made up of several clauses that are connected with subordination, coordination, transition words, and *ing* participle phrases
- the simple present tense to indicate a generalization
- the present perfect tense to introduce a topic or to show that something has happened and is still happening
- shifts in verb tense
- passive sentences to focus on a process or object rather than on the person doing an action

All verbs in the example are underlined twice.

Although many firms <u>engage</u> in business abroad, **most of the ethical issues in this area** <u>arise</u> for the transnational corporation, or TNC, [which is generally defined as a firm that has a direct investment in two or more countries.] **The emergence of TNCs** in the second half of the twentieth century <u>has had</u> a profound effect on developed and undeveloped countries alike. Their wealth and power <u>have given rise to</u> concern about **the impact on local economies and about the capacity of governments** to regulate them effectively. The pharmaceutical industry, more than any other, <u>has been criticized</u> for its activities abroad. Although prescription and over-the-counter drugs <u>have done</u> much to alleviate suffering and increase the well-being of people around the globe, the major drug companies <u>are also faulted</u> for many of their practices.

One of the most heavily criticized practices <u>is</u> **promoting drugs in the third world** with more suggestions for their use and fewer warnings about side effects than in developed countries. The following are some typical examples.

3B   Making Complex Nouns Using Relative Clauses

RELATIVE OR ADJECTIVE CLAUSES

In sentences like these examples, the words *who, whom, whose, which,* and *that* are called **relative pronouns.**	As Ford Motor Company learned, achieving high performance requires a redefinition of work and of the relationships among <u>people</u> *who* **work together.** Many <u>companies</u> *that* **have engaged in layoffs** have found that their productivity decreased. Although many firms engage in business abroad, most of the ethical issues in this area arise for the transnational corporation, or <u>TNC,</u> *which* **is generally defined as a firm that has a direct investment in two or more countries.**
Writers use them to add more information to a noun by attaching another sentence or clause to the noun. This second sentence is called a **relative** or **adjective clause.** These clauses usually come directly after the words they describe.	Many companies [*that* have engaged in layoffs] **have found that their productivity decreased.**
There are two types of relative or adjective clauses: • **Defining** (restrictive) **relative clauses** contain information that is essential to identify the person or thing being discussed. • **Non-defining** (non-restrictive) **relative clauses** contain extra information that is not necessary to identify the person or thing being discussed. Notice that writers put commas around these to indicate to their readers that they are adding extra information.	Recent experience, company by company, shows that, in practice, cutting staff typically has fallen dramatically short of <u>making the improvement in competitive performance</u> *that* **money managers expect.** <u>This area,</u> *which* **has been a problem for transnational corporations,** is examined first to illustrate the many problems encountered in international business.

DEFINING (RESTRICTIVE) RELATIVE CLAUSES

Adding a relative clause to a noun often means that some part of the clause must be changed or deleted. Relative pronouns *replace* some part of the second, or modifying, sentence. The relative pronoun plays a grammatical role in the relative clause; it can be a subject, object, or object of a preposition.

Function of the Relative Pronoun In the example, the noun modified by the relative clause is underlined. The relative pronoun is in italics. The relative clause itself is in bold. Any noun or phrase that is deleted is crossed out.	
subject of the relative clause In the first example, *who* is the subject of the relative clause and replaces the noun *people* in the relative clause. *Who* is used when the noun being replaced refers to a human. In the second example, *that* replaces the noun *company* and functions as the subject of the relative clause. *That* is always used in defining relative clauses when the noun being replaced refers to nonhuman subjects.	As Ford Motor Company learned, achieving high performance requires a redefinition of work and of the relationships among people *who* **work together.** Many companies *that* **have engaged in layoffs** have found that their productivity decreased.
object of the relative clause In the examples, *that* replaces the object of the relative clause, but it is placed right after the noun it refers to, not in the relative clause. Also, the noun is not repeated in the relative clause.	Recent experience, company by company, shows that, in practice, cutting staff typically has fallen dramatically short of making the improvement in competitive performance *that* **money managers expect** ~~improvement~~. Even when the practice is legal in the country in question and condoned by the local medical community, the indirect payment *that* **physicians receive** ~~indirect payment~~ **by selling free samples** makes it possible for drug companies to bribe physicians.
possessive in the relative clause In the example, *whose* replaces the possessive "its obligation."	Many experts criticize companies *whose* ~~its~~ **obligation is to help people it has harmed.** Continued

object of a preposition in the relative clause
In the example, the noun that is being replaced by a relative pronoun is part of a prepositional phrase *(in + this country)* in the relative clause. The relative pronoun is *in which,* a *preposition + which* combination. Notice that *which,* not *that,* is used when the relative clause is the object of a preposition.

A relative pronoun that functions as the object of a preposition will contain a *preposition + which (to which, of which, for which,* etc.). To decide which preposition you need, reconstruct the full prepositional phrase that you are replacing in the relative clause.

The primary responsibility is on the country *in which* **business is being conducted ~~in this country~~.**

NON-DEFINING (NON-RESTRICTIVE) RELATIVE OR ADJECTIVE CLAUSES

Function of the Relative Pronoun
In the examples, the noun modified by the relative clause is underlined and the relative pronoun is in italics. The relative clause is boldfaced.

subject of the relative clause
In the first example, *which* replaces a noun that has already been identified or is specific. It is the subject of the relative clause. In the second example, *who* replaces a person who is identified by his full name. In each example, the information provided in the relative clause is added information. We don't need it to know what the noun refers to.

Notice that *which* is used in a non-defining relative clause when replacing a nonhuman subject. *Who* is used in both defining and non-defining relative clauses to replace human subjects.

Although many firms engage in business abroad, most of the ethical issues in this area arise for the transnational corporation, or TNC, *which* **is generally defined as a firm that has a direct investment in two or more countries.**

Dr. Redford Williams of Duke University, *who* **has been studying about 100 lawyers for decades in an ongoing look at stress,** has found that the attorneys who said their anger levels were high in their years as students were four to five times more likely to die in their 50s than their somewhat calmer colleagues.

object of the relative clause
Which is placed right after the noun it refers to, not in the object position of the relative clause. Also, the noun is not repeated in the relative clause.

Increases in sea level could be expected to come about for various reasons, all tied to the heating of the earth's surface, *which* **most experts view ~~the heating~~ as a consequence of "global warming."**

REDUCING RELATIVE CLAUSES TO MAKE MORE CONDENSED SENTENCES

Writers often delete the relative pronoun to create sentences that are less wordy and stylistically more condensed.	Our concern is with the moral obligations of TNCs in dealing with difficult issues such as those ~~that are~~ **raised** by the marketing of drugs in third world countries.

Defining relative clauses can be reduced in two general ways: 1) just the relative pronoun is dropped and the rest of the clause remains the same; 2) both the relative pronoun and part of the verb phrase are dropped. There are some guidelines for reducing relative clauses.

The relative pronoun can be dropped if it is <u>not</u> the subject of the relative clause. In the first example, *that* is the object of the relative clause, in both examples.	The indirect payment ~~that~~ physicians receive by selling free samples makes it possible for drug companies to bribe physicians.
	Some companies have not made <u>the improvement</u> in <u>competitive performance</u> ~~that~~ financial experts expect.
The subject relative pronoun can be dropped only if part of the verb can be dropped, too. If the verb is a combination or two-part verb that begins with *be* (passive, present progressive, or past progressive), the subject pronoun and the *be* verb can be dropped. In this example, notice that the verb in the relative clause is passive.	Depo-Provera, a contraceptive ~~that is~~ **taken** by injection, protects women against pregnancy for three months or more.

REDUCING NON-DEFINING RELATIVE CLAUSES TO MAKE MORE CONDENSED SENTENCES

Non-restrictive relative clauses can be reduced only when both the pronoun and the verb can be removed.

Unlike defining relative clauses, you cannot drop relative pronouns that are not the subject of the clause. *Whom* and *which* cannot be dropped in these examples.	Maude Pratt Managhan, *whom* **the writer interviewed in 1989,** is probably dead now. Aging, *which* **everyone fears,** is inevitable.
Non-defining relative clauses can be reduced if: • the relative pronoun is the subject of the relative clause and the verb is *be* followed by a predicate noun phrase. • the relative pronoun is the subject of the clause whose verb is passive or present progressive and, therefore, contains *be* auxiliary.	The downsizing strategy completely reverses the classic assertion of American industry voiced by Alfred P. Sloan, ~~who was~~ the former chairman of General Motors. Most of the ethical issues regarding firms that sell internationally arise for the transnational corporation, or TNC, ~~which is~~ generally **defined as** a firm that has a direct investment in two or more countries.

NON-DEFINING RELATIVE CLAUSES WITH PROPER NOUNS

When the noun being described is a proper noun, you use commas to separate the relative clause from the rest of the sentence to indicate that extra information has been added; this information is not necessary to identify the person or thing being discussed. Writers use these types of non-restrictive clauses to add information that serves to add weight and credibility to the quotations or sources they cite.	The downsizing strategy completely reverses the classic assertion of American industry voiced by Alfred P. Sloan, **who was the former chairman of General Motors.** When the nonrestrictive relative clause that identifies the person contains the verb *be,*
the relative pronoun and the verb *be* can be deleted. The article that comes before the noun in the relative clause can also be deleted. These reduced relative clauses are also called *appositives.* The downsizing strategy completely reverses the classic assertion of American industry voiced by Alfred P.	Sloan, ~~who was~~ (the) **former chairman of General Motors.** A survey of more than five hundred corporations done by Wyatt and Company, ~~which is~~ **a management consulting firm,** found that only one third of companies reported that downsizing resulted in increased productivity.

STEPS TO EDIT RELATIVE CLAUSES

STEP 1: Find nouns that you have made complex by using a relative clause. Underline the noun and put brackets [ ] around the relative clause. Find other clauses that begin with *who, that, which,* or *where.* Put brackets around the entire clause and find the noun it modifies and underline it.

There are <u>several factors</u> [that contribute to extending the life of elderly people].

STEP 2: Make sure that the relative clause is located as close as possible to the noun it modifies. If not, move the additional information in the relative clause next to the noun. Delete or move other words/phrases.

<u>The result</u> of research showed that <u>the attorneys</u> had a greater than 50% chance of dying in their fifties [who said their anger levels were high in their years as law students].

STEP 3: Determine the function of the relative pronoun. Delete or change words in the relative clause if necessary. Make sure to add a preposition to the relative pronoun if necessary.

Angry people seem to face <u>prob-lems</u> *for* which they don't have solutions [~~for these problems~~].

In order for your yoga to make sense, you need to choose <u>the best place</u> ~~that~~ *where* you can concentrate.

STEP 4: Determine if the relative clause adds essential information to the noun (defining) or if it adds extra information (non-defining). If the relative clause is non-defining, put commas around it to indicate that to your readers.

<u>The living conditions of the elderly,</u> [which include the weather, housing, and dietary habits,] are important factors that contribute to longer lives.

STEP 5: Decide if you can or want to delete parts of the relative clause for stylistic reasons.

3C   Complex Noun Phrases with Prepositional Phrases

See pages 146–151 in Chapter 4, Evaluating, for information, examples, and exercises on this topic.

3D   *ing* Participle Phrases

See pages 182–185 in Chapter 5, Analyzing, for information, examples, and exercises on this topic.

3E   Verbs in Academic Writing

Correct use of verbs is important in a number of ways for academic writers:

- Academic writing usually contains both generalizations and evidence and examples to support them.
- Verbs help state rules and theories.
- When academic writers refer to the published work of other writers, they use verbs such as *report, mention, demonstrate,* and others to introduce these references.
- Verbs give the correct meaning to supporting information including facts and examples.
- Verbs indicate the current status of research and studies published in the past.
- Some academic writing uses past tense narratives. Examples are history textbooks and materials that recount the history of academic disciplines. Past tense is often used to tell about a past research project.

Notice in the following examples that certain verb tenses have very predictable functions in academic writing.

VERBS IN GENERALIZATIONS

Simple present tense is the most commonly used verb when stating theories, facts, and other generalizations that are currently accepted as true.	When Anglo-Americans <u>are</u> angry, they <u>tend</u> to proceed in stages from small steps to larger ones: First, they <u>hint</u> around...Then they <u>talk</u> to neighbors and friends of [their neighbor].
Simple past tense can be used to signal that a given generalization is no longer accepted as true.	Not long ago, letting rage out <u>was</u>, well, all the rage. Now, studies suggest that venting may up the heart attack risk.
Present progressive is sometimes used to communicate about work that is in progress.	At Duke, Williams has studied the long-term effects of hostility for years, but *now* <u>is</u> also <u>trying</u> to determine the day-by-day events that contribute to heart disease. For one thing, [Williams] says he'<u>s finding</u> that blood pressure goes up when people are exposed to violence.

VERBS IN EXAMPLES AND SUPPORT OF GENERALIZATIONS

Many examples are given using **past tense** verbs. In these examples, the central action will be in the simple past tense. **Past perfect** indicates that an action is completed before the central action. **Past progressive** indicates that a past action occurred at the same time as the central action.	generalization - present tense Animals also <u>play</u> with objects. past tense A wild alligator in Georgia <u>spent</u> forty-five minutes playing with the drops of water falling from a pipe into a pond.
Sometimes evidence consists of statements of facts. These facts are written with **present tense** verbs, if they are true now or believed to be true.	The main reason that employers <u>do not hire</u> older workers is that they <u>suspect</u> them of not being up to the job. Again there may be a grain of truth in this. A World Health Organization (WHO) study of older people's working capacity recently concluded that physical performance, at a peak in the early 20s, <u>declines</u> gradually thereafter. Eyesight <u>deteriorates</u> and hearing <u>gets worse.</u>

VERBS TENSE SHIFTS WITHIN A PIECE OF WRITING

Some students have the idea that they should use only one tense per paragraph. That would be like driving a car in first gear all the time. In fact, writers often shift tenses within paragraphs. However, these shifts always reflect some change in meaning.	
The first example contrasts something that was believed true in the past with something different that is currently believed. Notice that the writer signaled that a shift would occur by using the adverb *now.*	Not long ago, letting rage out <u>was</u>, well, all the rage. *Now,* studies <u>suggest</u> that venting may up the heart attack risk.
Another verb shift occurs when a writer reports a general truth that past researchers or people believed.	The downsizing strategy (of today) completely reverses the classic assertion of American industry <u>voiced</u> by Alfred P. Sloan, the former chairman of General Motors: "Growth <u>is</u> essential to the good health of an enterprise." Continued

A third example shows how verbs change when a generalization is stated that is based on research done in the past.	A World Health Organization (WHO) study of older people's working capacity recently <u>gathered</u> together the biological facts and <u>concluded</u> that physical performance, at a peak in the early 20s, <u>declines</u> gradually thereafter. Eyesight <u>deteriorates</u> and hearing <u>gets</u> worse.
A fourth example shows how verbs change when a generalization is supported by an example from the past.	By talking with centenarians, we <u>begin</u> to realize just how long 100 years actually is, and we <u>begin</u> to develop an appreciation for the tremendous changes that have occurred in America during their life times. Take for example, Louis Kelly, 103, of Scottsdale, Arizona, whose earliest memory <u>imparts</u> a vivid image of the way people lived and traveled long ago. "I can see it in my mind's eye. I <u>was standing</u> in a covered wagon looking out the back; my younger sister <u>was asleep</u> on the bedding on the floor beside me. I <u>realized</u> that my father <u>was driving</u> the team of horses and that this wagon <u>belonged</u> to us.

THE PRESENT PERFECT IN ACADEMIC WRITING

Present perfect verbs are used to communicate about time relationships. They can indicate that something happened during a period of time that started in the past and continues until now. This use is sometimes called the "indefinite" past because you do not know exactly when the action occurred—it was just before now.	Once a volcanic kind of guy himself, Williams said he <u>has learned</u> to ask questions about his anger. At Duke, Williams <u>has studied</u> the long-term effects of hostility *for years*.
Because of this basic meaning, present perfect verbs are often used to introduce a topic. After the introduction, the main content of the writing is in another verb form.	Today's workers <u>have begun</u> to think it will be their turn to retire next. In France, for example, new rules introduced in the 1970s <u>allowed</u> many people to retire at 60. In 1982 the pension age itself <u>was reduced</u> to 60.
Because the present perfect verb indicates that the action is closely tied to the present time, the present perfect is often used in academic writing to indicate that a theory or some research is still valid.	Innovators in American business, though still the daring minority, <u>have been pursuing and implementing</u> what <u>has become known</u> as "a high-performance strategy."

STEPS TO EDIT FOR VERB TENSE SHIFT	
STEP 1: Highlight or underline the verbs you have used in one paragraph. Make sure to highlight or underline the entire verb, including modals or other auxiliaries. Only highlight or underline verbs that have a subject. STEP 2: When you have switched verb tenses, can you explain why? Will your reader know why you switched or will the switch confuse him/her? In other words, have you signaled the tense shift to your readers — most importantly, a switch from present to past tense? STEP 3: Examine the verbs you have used to make sure the verb tense you have chosen matches the meaning you intend to convey. SIMPLE PRESENT—generalizations, statements of theory, or definitions PRESENT PERFECT—descriptions of past research or past events that have present results or are related to the present or to the topic being discussed; often used to introduce a topic or description of activities that began in the past but are ongoing PRESENT PROGRESSIVE—description of work that is being done right now; description of an ongoing activity SIMPLE PAST—description of past research or past events used as examples PAST PERFECT—background for the event that is being explained; when you are telling past events out of chronological order	The author of *The Anger Factor* <u>reports</u> that angry people <u>can</u> more than <u>double</u> the risk of a heart attack. Research <u>has shown</u> that anger <u>shortens</u> one's life span. In one research study, attorneys who <u>said</u> they <u>got</u> angry often when they <u>were</u> law students <u>were</u> four to five times more likely to die in their 50s than their colleagues who <u>did not</u> get angry. I <u>agree</u> with this generalization. When I ~~got~~ <u>get</u> very angry, I ~~heard~~ <u>hear</u> my heart pulsating like a nail driven on the wall. I ~~experienced~~ <u>experience</u> shortness of breath and my face ~~turned~~ <u>turns</u> crimson red. These symptoms <u>lead</u> to physical harm such as a heart attack. The following story is one such tragedy. My uncle <u>passed away</u> because he <u>was unable</u> to keep control of his anger over his son's misconduct and subsequently <u>died</u> of a heart attack.

3F   Subject-Verb Agreement

SUBJECT-VERB AGREEMENT: VERBS THAT REQUIRE THE CHANGE TO *s*

When certain subjects combine with present tense verbs, the verb must add an *s*. This change in the base verb is called **subject-verb agreement.**

The strange thing about English is that plural subjects have verbs *without* the *s*. Singular subjects have verbs with the *s*. In the examples, subjects are underlined once and verbs twice.	Richard Friedman, a professor of psychiatry at the State University of New York at Stoney Brook, said <u>these stud-ies and others leave</u> little doubt that <u>episodes of anger</u> <u>are</u> dangerous. At Duke, <u>Williams has studied</u> the long-term effects of hostility for years.
SIMPLE PRESENT TENSE	<u>A study by Dr. Murray Mittleman and his colleagues at Harvard Medical School suggests</u> that an angry outburst can more than double the risk of a heart attack in some people.
PRESENT PERFECT	Once a volcanic kind of guy himself, Williams said <u>he</u> <u>has learned</u> to ask questions about his anger.
PRESENT PROGRESSIVE	In the 1980s, doctors often suggested that waving your anger like a flag was good....Now, though, <u>the advice is</u> <u>changing.</u>
PRESENT PERFECT PROGRESSIVE	<u>Dr. Redford Williams of Duke University</u> who <u>has been</u> <u>studying</u> about 100 lawyers for decades in an ongoing look at stress....
PRESENT TENSE FORMS OF *BE*	Richard Friedman, a professor of psychiatry at the State University of New York at Stoney Brook, said these stud-ies and others leave little doubt that <u>episodes of anger</u> <u>are</u> dangerous.
PAST TENSE FORMS OF *BE*	Not long ago, <u>letting rage out was</u> "all the rage."

SUBJECTS THAT REQUIRE SUBJECT-VERB AGREEMENT

Any subject that is not clearly plural is treated as singular and the verb adds *s*. Such singular subjects express concepts and are often found in academic writing that presents information or generalizations. Instead of having people or objects as their subject, these sentences contain abstract subjects.

SINGULAR COUNTABLE NOUN	What's more, the dose of violence triggers a higher blood pressure surge when <u>an on-screen argument turns</u> into an arm-swinging wrestle.
NONCOUNT NOUN	Now, though, <u>the advice is changing.</u>
NOUN PHRASES (NOUN + *OF* + NOUN) Noun phrases often consist of a noun + *of* phrase. These subjects are more difficult because there are two nouns that the verb might agree with. In fact, the verb only agrees with the *first* noun and not the noun in the *of* phrase. To find the first noun, cross out the *of* phrase and you will be left with the noun that the verb should agree with. If the first noun is singular, the verb requires *s*.	Richard Friedman, a professor of psychiatry at the State University of New York at Stoney Brook, said these studies and others leave little doubt <u>that episodes ~~of anger~~ are</u> dangerous. ~~<u>The current fashion of downsizing at some of America's most profitable corporations</u>~~ <u>runs counter to</u> the philosophy and strategy of the high-performance.
THIRD PERSON PRONOUN	Once a volcanic kind of guy himself, Williams said **he** <u>has learned</u> to ask questions about his anger.
NOUN PHRASES WITH RELATIVE CLAUSES Subject-verb agreement is also tricky with these subjects because there are several nouns that the verb might agree with. As with noun + *of* + noun phrases, the verb only agrees with the *first* noun and not other nouns in the clause. To find the first noun, cross out the *that* clause and you will be left with the noun that the verb should agree with. If first noun is singular, the verb must add *s*.	"The notion ~~that letting it out is protective,~~" he said, "<u>is</u> not <u>borne out</u> in science."

Continued

INFINITIVES To + base form of the verb. Infinitives are treated as singular subjects.	<u>To</u> deliberately <u>stop growing is</u> to suffocate.
GERUNDS These look like verbs, but they are *ing* forms of nouns. They are singular subjects and therefore the verb adds *s*.	In the 1980s, doctors often suggested that <u>waving your anger like a flag was</u> good for the head.
NOUN CLAUSE	"<u>What we've developed is</u> a market that is open 24 hours a day, seven days a week—a market where price and content are supreme," says Forbes. "<u>What we have developed here is</u> the perfect market."

STEPS TO EDIT FOR SUBJECT-VERB AGREEMENT

STEP 1: Underline the subject of each clause or sentence and double underline the verb.

STEP 2: If the subject is not clearly plural, it is treated as if it were singular. Can the noun phrase be replaced by *he/she/it?* If so, add *s* to the verb. If the verb is *be*, change it to *is*. If the verb is *have*, change it to *has*.

STEP 3: If the subject is a noun phrase consisting of a noun + *of*-phrase or a noun + prepositional phrase, the verb agrees with the *first* noun and not the noun in the *of*- or prepositional phrase. To find the first noun, cross out the *of*- or prepositional phrase and you will be left with the noun that the verb should agree with. If first noun is singular, the verb must add *s*.

STEP 4: Be careful of subjects that always add *s*—these include:
- *infinitive phrases* (<u>To forgive someone who has hurt you</u> **is** divine)
- *gerund phrases* (<u>Enabling others to do their best work</u> **is** the mark of a good manager)
- *noun clauses* (<u>What really makes me angry</u> **is** that the company never even apologized)

In conclusion, <u>one ~~of many people's fantastic dreams are~~ is</u> becoming true. <u>People ~~who used to think that life span cannot be extended~~ are</u> now <u>changing</u> their minds. Elderly people can still enjoy healthy lives. Although <u>the ~~explorations of Professor Roy Walford and some other scientists~~ have not reached</u> a definite conclusion, <u>their research</u> still <u>points to</u> possible ways to prolong life. <u>Getting good results mobilizes</u> other researchers to persevere in this difficult area of research.

3G   Passive Sentences

In most sentences, the subject of the sentence is also the "doer" or performer of the action expressed by the verb. These are *active sentences*.	We <u>undertook</u> an intensive study in the small Bedfordshire village.
In *passive sentences,* on the other hand, the subject of the sentence receives the action expressed by the verb. The "actor" appears in a *by* phrase or does not appear at all, but is understood from the context. For more information about the functions of passive voice, see pages 67–70 in Chapter 2.	An intensive study of cats <u>was undertaken</u> in the small Bedfordshire village.

<u>Form</u>

The passive form of a verb is a combination, or a two-part verb. It consists of: *be* + past participle of the main verb.

    Passive verbs can appear in all the major tenses, just as active verbs do. Notice that the verb *be* marks the tense.

Simple Present:	*is/are* done
Present Continuous:	*is being/was being* done
Present Perfect:	*has been/ have been* done
Simple Past:	*was/were* done
Past Continuous:	*was being/were being* done
Past Perfect:	*had been* done
Future Past:	*would be* done

Play, which seems to be both a

present perfect passive verb

sign and a source of joy, <u>has been</u> increasingly <u>studied</u> in recent years.

If a cat <u>was seen</u> to eat the entire

past tense passive verb

specimen, this <u>was recorded</u> as an "unknown."

Passive sentences can also contain modals and semi-modals:

Modals

Present Time Reference:	*might be* done
	should be done
	could be done
Past Time Reference:	*might have been* done
	should have been done
	could have been done

Semi-Modals

Present Time Reference:	*had to be* done
	ought to be done
Past Time Reference:	*had to have been* done
	ought to have been done

The drug is also dangerous for young children and <u>should not be prescribed</u> to children under the age of two.

A drug for a tropical disease <u>might never have been submitted</u> for approval, since there is no market for it in the country where it is manufactured.

Let us consider, first, the position taken by some critics of TNCs: that business <u>ought to be conducted</u> in the same way the world over with no double standards.

Continued

Common Passive or Passive-like Verbs in Academic Writing

Certain verbs appear frequently in the passive form or in a passive-like form. They usually describe or express the location of the subject. Sentences with these passive or passive-like verbs do not contain *by* phrases.

to be composed of
to be called
to be known for
to be regarded (as)
to be considered (as)
to be founded
to be interested in
to be involved in
to be exposed to
to be concerned about/with
to be located near/in/at
to be supposed to

These celebrated e-mail controversies are not isolated incidents. They are, in fact, indicative of the confusion surrounding employees' and employers' rights where e-mail is concerned.

"If I'm exchanging e-mail messages about a proposal that's due and I go to the hospital, it can create problems if my mail is considered strictly private," says Ulrich.

In deciding whether to employ a practice that is regarded as wrong at home but is legal in a host country, a number of factors must be considered.

STEPS TO EDIT PASSIVE VS. ACTIVE VOICE

STEP 1: Underline all the verbs you have used in each paragraph.

STEP 2: Check that any passive verbs you have used are in the correct form to signal to the reader that they are passive (auxiliary *be* + past participle of the verb). If you notice, for example, that some verbs end in *ed,* but the rest of the verbs in the paragraph are in present tense, you might have forgotten to add the *be* auxiliary. If you notice an auxiliary *be* + a verb that has no *ed,* check to see if the verb should be passive and add *ed* to the main verb.

STEP 3: Wherever you have used a passive verb, check first to see that it fits the functions outlined in Chapter 2. Otherwise, consider if the active form of the verb would be better.

STEP 4: Common verbs that appear in the passive form should have a *be* auxiliary and appear in the past participle form.

We should *[be]* concern*[ed]* about how far the court has protected the photographers' right to self-expression.

I spent most of my time growing up in an Asian country, where the teachers are the rulers. The teachers *[are]* allow*[ed]* to hit children who are lazy.

Inflicting pain either physically or psychologically in the process of learning *[was]* found to be the best way to educate somebody.

You can solve this problem because you *[are]* supposed to breathe in when muscles expand and stiffen while doing yoga.

Section 4 Reporting Other People's Words and Ideas

4A   Quotations

The writing you do represents your ideas and, therefore, should be done in your "voice." In academic writing, however, you are usually balancing your voice with the ideas, research, and theories of other people. You will incorporate quotations from these experts into your writing. Maintaining your voice while using the ideas and words of experts is a balancing act. Therefore, writers are careful about how and what they quote.

Writers use quotations:

- to do justice to exceptionally memorable quotations
- to strengthen arguments by referring to acknowledged authorities on the topic
- to avoid changing the meaning of the original passage
- to capture the original flavor of the speech used by the person who said the words originally. (This use is prominent in investigative reports.)

INTEGRATING QUOTATIONS INTO YOUR WRITING

Quotations must fit into a paragraph made up of your own sentences. One way to ensure that a quotation connects well to your sentences is to use a signaling phrase such as *according to the professor* or reporting verbs such as *he said, the author notes.* This is how quotations most frequently appear.

Often the signal phrase or reporting verb appears before the quotation. Notice the use of commas and quotation marks and periods.
 	
    The reporting verb can also appear at the end of the quotation. Notice that a comma sets off the phrase containing the reporting verb and that the comma is inside the quotation marks.
 	
    The reporting verb can also occur in the middle of the sentence or between two sentences said by the speaker. The reporting verb is set off by commas. Notice that the first comma is set inside the quotation marks.
	Anthropologist Edward T. Hall <u>maintains</u> that "culture confers deep biases and built-in blinders on its members."
	
	"It is your responsibility to care for an old mother-in-law," **the Chinese psychiatrist <u>said</u>**.
	
	"The notion that letting it out is protective," **he <u>said</u>,** "is not borne out in science."
	
	"You have to effectively understand your feelings," **he <u>suggests</u>,** "and find a means of calming yourself down."

Sometimes you may not want to use the whole quotation, but only the most memorable parts or those that best support your own idea. These "partial" quotations must be integrated into the grammar of the whole sentence.	Anthropologist Edward T. Hall speaks of the **"deep biases and built-in blinders"** that every culture confers on its members. Continued

If the segment of the sentence you are quoting is a **dependent clause,** create an independent clause of your own and attach the dependent clause quotation to it. Begin the quote with a subordinator *(when, because, although)*.	Lila Hoover believes ordinary people became sensitive to racial injustice during the Depression and World War II, **"when people of all races suffered together."**
If the segment you are quoting is a **noun phrase,** it can be inserted either in the subject position or the object position of your own sentence.	Anthropologist Edward T. Hall speaks of the **"deep biases and built-in blinders"** that every culture confers on its members.
If the segment of the sentence you are quoting is an **adjective phrase,** insert it where you would normally put an adjective in your own sentence. Notice that the sentence is interrupted by quotation marks.	101-year-old Roy Miller notes that his **"young at heart"** character is one of the secrets to his reaching the century mark.
If the segment you are quoting is a **complement,** create a sentence that includes the subject and a linking verb, most commonly *be*, and add the quoted complement. Be sure to begin the quote with the adjective or adverb.	Despite its popularity, downsizing in the late 1980s and early '90s has often failed to achieve its proponents' objectives, economists report, because typically slashing staff has not been **"part of a thoughtful strategy to redesign the whole corporate structure and culture. Instead, it's an almost panicked reaction to pressures and problems."**
Avoid trying to insert an entire sentence quotation in your own sentence. Instead, use a partial quotation. One way to do this is to first label the subject, verb, object, and other parts of speech of your own sentence. Then make sure the portion of the original quotation that you want to use fits grammatically into the sentence.	***Original Quotation:*** "It appears that marked physical and mental decline is typical of the majority of centenarians." (Erdmore Palmer, Ph.D., author of *The Encyclopedia of Aging*) ***Your Sentence:*** While many centenarians do not look or act their age, <u>others</u> <u>suffer</u> **"marked physical and mental decline,"** according to demographic statistician Dr. Erdmore Palmer, author of *The Encyclopedia of Aging*.

4B   Reporting Verbs

VERB TENSE AND REPORTING VERBS

Either simple present tense, present perfect, or simple past tense can be used to report information. Usually the verb tense used within the whole piece of reported information is the same.	Carolyn Bowden, of the DC Office on Aging, **says** that improvements in public health have contributed to increases in longevity. "People <u>are</u> more knowledgeable about things that would encourage longevity."
Sometimes, however, the reporting verb is in the past tense and the reported information is in the present tense. In the second example, the reporting verb is in the past tense because the study is completed. The reported information is in present tense because it is a generalization that the researchers made from their research.	A World Health Organization (WHO) study of older people's working capacity recently gathered together the biological facts and **concluded** that physical performance, at a peak in the early 20s, <u>declines</u> gradually thereafter.
The third example shows a common pattern in academic writing. The verb which introduces the findings is in present perfect. The findings themselves are often in simple present tense.	Dr. John Thompson, a physician and researcher at the Sanders-Brown Research Center on Aging at the University of Kentucky in Lexington, **has concluded** that old people <u>don't exhibit</u> as uniform a physical or emotional profile as some investigators had expected.
Notice in the fourth example that the work is still in progress and is reported using the present progressive.	For one thing, [Williams] **says** he<u>'s finding</u> that blood pressure goes up when people are exposed to violence.
In the fifth example, the verb used to introduce the findings is in simple present while the verbs in the findings themselves are in the simple past because the findings refer to past events.	Most centenarians, but not all, **report** that they <u>had</u> at least one parent who <u>lived</u> to a "ripe old age" for their generation.

REPORTING VERBS + *THAT* + NOUN CLAUSES

Reporting verbs are frequently followed by noun clauses. *That* can follow certain verbs to create noun clauses. *That* connects a complete sentence to the verb. These noun clauses are the direct objects of the main verb. The reporting verb is in bold. The *that* clause is in brackets and *that* is italicized.	A World Health Organization (WHO) study of older people's working capacity recently gathered together the biological facts and **concluded** *that* [physical performance, at a peak in the early 20s, declines gradually thereafter.]
That noun clauses are frequent in academic writing, especially when a writer is reporting the ideas or research of other researchers or authors.	A study by Dr. Murray Mittleman and his colleagues at Harvard Medical School **suggests** *that* [an angry outburst can more than double the risk of a heart attack in some people.]
Writers can also use reporting verbs to introduce a quotation. *That* is not used when direct quotations are given.	Not long ago, letting rage out was, well, all the rage. Now, studies **suggest** *that* venting may up the heart attack risk. "You have to effectively understand your feelings," he **suggests,** "and find a means of calming yourself down."

STEPS TO EDIT REPORTING VERBS

STEP 1: Underline all the reporting verbs that you have used. STEP 2: Check to make sure that you used a variety of different types of reporting verbs. STEP 3: Check a dictionary to make sure that each reporting verb expresses the meaning you want to convey. STEP 4: Bracket the noun phrase or *that* clause that follows each reporting verb. Check a dictionary to see what types of grammatical structures can follow this reporting verb (e.g., *that* clauses, noun phrases). You can usually find this information in an English-English dictionary.	"The 120 Year Man," an article that was written in September 1991 by Darva Sobel, <u>shows</u> [different methods for extending one's life span]. According to James Mold, "genetic background is the key factor in determining how long a person can be expected to live. He ~~tells~~ <u>believes</u> [that hereditary factors allow people to get away with harmful behaviors and still live a long life]. After scientists had investigated a small village in Russia, they <u>concluded</u> [that the people living there had a genetic predisposition to reach an old age]. As a result, Professor Walford <u>thinks</u> [he can do the same thing for humans that he did for animals in laboratory tests].

4C   Citing Sources

TWO FORMATS FOR CITING SOURCES

There are many formats in which references and in-text citations appear, but only the two most common formats will be given here: those prescribed by the Modern Language Association (MLA) and the American Psychological Association (APA). These two styles are commonly used in the humanities and social sciences. Other disciplines and publications use other formats. Be sure to find out which reference format system your instructors want you to use in your papers and use publication manuals to guide your decisions.

Publication Manual of the American Psychological Association. (4th edition.) (1993). Washington, DC: American Psychological Association.

Achtert, Walter S. & Gibaldi, Joseph. (1985). *The MLA Style Manual.* New York: Modern Language Association of America.

APA FORMAT FOR IN-TEXT CITATIONS AND REFERENCES

In-Text or Parenthetical Citations	
These are used with any quotation, paraphrase, or summary of someone else's ideas, words, or research. Each parenthetical citation corresponds to a full reference list at the end of the paper. Place the parenthetical citation right after the material that you are quoting, summarizing, or paraphrasing.	
Author Named in a Sentence	As Savory (1959) put the matter, "Of course to interpret the thoughts, or their equivalent, which determine an animal's behavior is difficult, but this is no reason for not making the attempt to do so" (p. 78).
Author Named in an In-Text Citation	One study has found that older workers are as good at making decisions as younger workers (Jones, 1996).
Personal Communication This is for personal letters, interviews, e-mail correspondence, or other communication that you have quoted, paraphrased, or summarized.	Billy Earley (personal communication, September 3, 1988) reports that, at age 105, she still travels at least twice a year.

Continued

Bibliography and References
This is the list of references that appears at the end of the paper. All references are listed in alphabetical order according to the author's last name.

Book by One Author	Tavris, C. (1989). *Anger: The Misunderstood Emotion.* New York: Touchstone/Simon Schuster.
Book by Two or More Authors	Carlson, J.G. & Hatfield, E. (1992). *Psychology of Emotion.* New York: Harcourt, Brace, Jovanovich.
Article in an Edited Book	Griffin, D.R. (1993). Animal thinking. In P.W. Sherman & J. Alcock (Eds.), *Exploring Animal Behavior: Readings from American Scientist.* (pp. 49–55). Sunderland, MA.: Sinauer Associates Inc., Publishers.
Article in a Magazine	Mann, B. (1997, April). Stopping you watching me. *Internet World,* 42–46.
Article in a Newspaper	Talan, J. (1995, September 19). The anger factor. *The Los Angeles Times,* p. E3.
Article from the Internet The format for citing information from the Internet has not been standardized yet since this is such a new technology. The guidelines suggested come from Dawn Rodrigues, *The research paper and the World Wide Web* (Upper Saddle River, NJ: Prentice Hall, 1997).	Lewis, J. (1997, July 11). Mars on a shoestring. *L.A. Weekly* [Online Edition, 10 paragraphs]. Available: http.//www.laweekly.com:80/ink/archives/97/news-7.11.97-4.html

MLA FORMAT FOR IN-TEXT CITATIONS AND REFERENCES

In-Text or Parenthetical Citations
Notice that MLA format has different punctuation and does not use *pp.* to represent page numbers.

Author Named in a Sentence Unlike the APA, the date of publication of the source does not appear in parentheses after the author's name. Also, page numbers appear in parentheses after the quotation, paraphrase, or summary with no *pp.* before them.	As Savory put the matter, "Of course to interpret the thoughts, or their equivalent, which determine an animal's behavior is difficult, but this is no reason for not making the attempt to do so. If it were not difficult, there would be very little interest in the study of animal behavior, and very few books about it" (78).
Author Named in an In-Text Citation When the author's name is not mentioned in a sentence that signals the quotation or paraphrase, it appears in parentheses immediately followed by the page numbers. There is no comma separating the name and the page numbers.	One study has found that older workers are as good at making decisions as younger workers (Jones 35).
Personal Communication In your sentence, give some type of information that indicates the source and where readers can find it in your list of references.	Billy Earley, *in a personal interview,* reports that, at 105, she still takes at least two major trips a year.

Bibliography and References
Note that MLA format spells out the author's first name and puts the date of publication at the end of the citation. It also uses some punctuation and information order that is different from APA format.

Book by One Author	Tavris, Carol. *Anger: The Misunderstood Emotion.* New York: Touchstone/Simon Schuster, 1989.
Book by Two or More Authors	Carlson, John G. & Hatfield, Elaine. *Psychology of Emotion.* New York: Harcourt, Brace, Jovanovich, 1992.

Continued

Article in an Edited Book	Griffin, Donald R. "Animal Thinking." *Exploring Animal Behavior: Readings from American Scientist.* Eds. P.W. Sherman & J. Alcock. Sunderland, MA: Sinauer Associates Inc., Publishers, 1993. 49–55.
Article in a Magazine	Mann, Bill. "Stopping You Watching Me." *Internet Magazine,* April 1997. 42–46.
Article in a Newspaper	Talan, Jamie. "The Anger Factor." *The Los Angeles Times,* 19 September 1995. E3.
Article from the Internet	Lewis, Judith. "Mars on a Shoestring." *L.A. Weekly* 11 July, 1997: 10 paragraphs. [Online Edition]. Available: http.//www.laweekly.com:80/ink/ archives/97/news-7.11.97-4.html.

Section 5 Writing to Persuade

5A   Overview of Writing to Persuade

All writing is persuasive in some way. Whether writers are giving a definition, explaining the causes of an event, or giving reasons that their opinion is correct, they are all trying to convince readers to take them seriously, to believe that their ideas are correct and important.

Being persuasive in academic writing does not mean being more aggressive or screaming louder than your opponent, as it might in a debate or an argument. Persuasive academic writing has several features, all of which work together to create writing that can convince an academic audience. It: • presents enough evidence to support any generalization. • contains adverbs and modal auxiliaries to control the strength of general statements and claims. • acknowledges that some readers may have a different view or interpretation. This is done by using concessive statements. • contains *if* sentences to present the conditions under which certain problems will arise or certain solutions will work.	**Example** Let us consider, first, the position taken by some critics of TNCs: that business **ought to be conducted** in the same way the world over with no double standards. In particular, United States corporations **ought to follow** domestic law and single code of conduct in their business dealings everywhere. This position **might be expressed** as, "When in Rome or anywhere else, do as you would at home." A little reflection is enough to show that this high level of conduct is not morally required of TNCs in all instances and that they **should not be faulted** for every departure from home country standards in doing business abroad. Good reasons **can be advanced** to show that different practices in different parts of the world are, *in some instances,* morally justified. First, the conditions in other parts of the world are different in morally important ways from those in the United States and other developed countries. (*If*)Rome is a *significantly* different place, then standards that are appropriate at home do *not necessarily* apply there.) Drug laws in the developed world, for example, are very stringent, reflecting greater affluence and better overall health. The standards in these laws are *not always* appropriate in poorer, less developed countries with fewer medical resources and more severe health problems. In the United States, the risk of prescribing an antidiarrhea drug such as Lomotil to children is not worth taking. (*But*)a physician in Central America, where children frequently die of untreated diarrhea, **might evaluate** the risk differently. Second, the fact that a drug has not been approved in the home country of a transnational does *not automatically* mean that it is unsafe or ineffective. A drug for a tropical disease **might never have been submitted** for approval, since there is no market for it in the country where it is manufactured. Other drugs **might not be approved** because of concerns that are unfounded or open to question.

5B   Modal Auxiliaries

Modals add special meaning to the verbs they are used with. These meanings include: ability, permission, obligation, possibility. Modals present difficulties for readers and writers because the same form may have more than one meaning. It is important to understand the meaning of the paragraph in which the modal occurs to recognize which meaning the modal expresses.

THE BASIC GRAMMAR OF MODALS

In their basic form, modals combine with the simple form of a verb without *to* in front of it.	Although there's nothing illegal about requiring you to register with a site, you <u>should realize</u> that the registration information usually goes into a marketing database that is sold to just about anyone willing to pay for it.
Modals have one form and do not agree with their subjects.	<u>A sports-oriented site</u> <u>might sell[~~s~~]</u> its list of subscribers to a sports magazine, which may use it for an e-mail ad campaign.
Two modals cannot be used together.	Although there's nothing illegal about requiring you to register with a site, you <u>should ~~must~~ realize</u> that the registration information usually goes into a marketing database that is sold to just about anyone willing to pay for it.

THE BASIC GRAMMAR OF SEMI-MODALS

Since semi-modals are different from modals, each has its own grammatical form:

Be able to is like the modal *can* in its meaning. However, it has three major differences in grammar in that it: 1. requires subject-verb agreement 2. also uses the word *to* 3. can combine with other basic modals	When <u>they</u> <u>were not able</u> **to aggress,** their blood pressures and heart rates remained high. <u>Upjohn,</u> for example, <u>was able to</u> **manufacture** Depo-Provera legally by shifting production to plants in Belgium. And even if your company didn't have the right, it certainly has the ability—and <u>you</u> <u>would</u> likely never <u>be able to prove</u> that you were passed up for promotion because of the things you said about your boss via e-mail to a friend.
Ought to is like *should* in meaning. *Ought to* is different in grammar because it requires the word *to*.	In particular, United States corporations <u>ought to follow</u> domestic law and a single code of conduct in their business dealings everywhere.
Have to and *must* express necessities and requirements in present tense generalizations, and future time meanings. *Have to* is grammatically different from must in these ways: 1. It requires subject-verb agreement. 2. It uses the word *to*. 3. It can combine with other basic modals. 4. It has a past tense form. *Had to* refers to past time necessities.	<u>The issue of retirement</u> <u>has to be</u> carefully <u>examined</u> as people live longer and longer. Experts differentiate the recent rash of corporate downsizing from earlier cutbacks and the massive restructuring of companies such as <u>General Motors and IBM,</u> which <u>had to restructure</u> after they had lost huge amounts of money. "The age of retirement <u>will have to go up</u>," says Winfried Schmahl, an expert on work for older people at Bremen University.

THE BASIC GRAMMAR AND MEANING OF MODALS AND PAST TIME

Could and Would with Past Time Meaning
Only *could* and *would* have past time meanings when combined with a simple form of the verb. *Could* + verb and *would* + verb can be used to refer to past time abilities or habits that are no longer true in the present.

To create a modal with a past time meaning, combine the basic **modal + *have* + past participle.** These express two different meanings:

1) things not done or things done in an unexpected way *(could have, should have, would have)*
2) guesses/conclusions about past events *(may have, might have, could have, must have)*

To aid in establishing this deception, the students were asked to count backward from 100 to 0 by twos, as quickly as they <u>could.</u>

"We <u>would camp</u> along the way," Louis continues. "My parents slept in a tent at night with the baby. My sister and I slept in the wagon."

There <u>could have been</u> an invasion of cold Arctic air into the heart of Asia as part of this new pattern of climate.

A drug for a tropical disease <u>might never have been submitted</u> for approval, since there is no market for it in the country where it is manufactured.

THE MEANING AND USES OF *CAN* AND *COULD*

Can and *could* appear frequently in academic writing. Often writers use these words to mean the ability to do something, but sometimes they use them to signal other meanings. Here are some ways that writers use *can*.

Modal	Semi-Modal	Definition	Example
can	*be able to*	ability	Combining the information about the sites you visit, where you live, and the registration information many sites require, anyone with a sense of logic <u>can build</u> a quick and accurate profile on you.
		possibility	The first step in protecting yourself is to learn how your privacy <u>can be violated.</u>
		to express a judgment or evaluation with moderate strength	The practice of selling free drug samples <u>can still be considered</u> as morally wrong even though it is condoned by the local medical community.

Continued

		to express options the reader has	There are several steps you <u>can take</u> to protect yourself. With an anonymous remailer, you <u>can send</u> messages anonymously, but not receive responses.
		to indicate not only ability, but power	Only Congress <u>can impose</u> confidentiality laws governing interstate computer networks and prohibiting the disclosure of medical information without a patient's consent.
could	*was able to*	past time ability	To aid in establishing this deception, the students were asked to count backward from 100 to 0 by twos, as quickly as they <u>could.</u>
		present time possibility	Some recent scientific studies have shown that venting hostility can stir up stress hormones in your body in a way that, ultimately, <u>could damage</u> your heart.
		past time possibility	There <u>could have been</u> an invasion of cold Arctic air into the heart of Asia as part of this new pattern of climate.

MODALS IN ACADEMIC WRITING

Academic writers use modals such as *should, must, might,* and *may* to vary the strength of the general statements they make. They do this in order to more precisely relay the strength of their conclusions or recommendations or to give the reader room to have a different opinion.

USING MODALS TO VARY THE STRENGTH OF ADVICE, RECOMMENDATIONS, AND JUDGMENTS

Because they are used to give advice or offer solutions or make recommendations, modals vary the strength of the solutions or advice they give.

opportunity or choice *weaker*	Writers use *can* to offer readers options or choices. The recommendation leaves the choice up to the reader.	There are several steps you <u>can take</u> to protect yourself. With an anonymous remailer, you <u>can send</u> messages anonymously, but not receive responses.
suggestion or recommen-dation *weaker*	Using *could* or *might* is a polite way for writers to express suggestions or offer solutions.	Companies <u>might consider</u> rewriting their e-mail privacy policy once a month and communicating this to all employees.
strong recom-mendation *strong*	Writers use *should* when they are quite sure about the solution they are offering and want the solution to be adopted.	A company's e-mail privacy policy <u>should be updated</u> regularly and communicated to all employees.
strong recom-mendation *stronger*	*Must* or *have to* expresses a very strong recommendation or solution. The writer implies that ignoring the advice may have serious consequences.	A company <u>must have</u> a clear and unambiguous policy about e-mail privacy.

USING MODALS TO VARY THE STRENGTH OF GENERALIZATIONS, EXPLANATIONS, OR CONCLUSIONS

Writers often use modals to give possible explanations for unclear situations, events or actions, or to draw conclusions. They use different modals to signal the strength of their belief in their explanation or conclusion.

Possibility or chance less certain *weaker*	*Could, may,* or *might* express a possibility or a possible explanation, but their use also leaves room for other explanations.	Everyone has a right to subsistence, for example, but a TNC <u>may be</u> under no obligation to feed the hungry in a country where it operates. What principles <u>might serve</u> to justify the minimal duties or obligations of corporations engaged in international business? Scientists began suggesting that global warming <u>could cause</u> the world's oceans to rise by several meters.
possibility or chance more certain *stronger*	*Can* also expresses a possibility, but indicates that the writer is more certain about the possibility than with *may, might,* or *could.*	Often it is this conflict about anger rules, not the rules per se, that <u>can stir up</u> trouble.

USING MODALS TO VARY THE STRENGTH OF AN EVALUATION OR JUDGMENT

In addition to using modals to vary the strength of solutions, writers use modals such as *can, should/ought to,* and *must* to vary the strength of judgments that they make about an issue or practice, past or present.

judgment or evaluation *strong*	*Should* or *ought to* is used to express a judgment. Writers use *should* or *ought to* when they are sure of their evaluation.	Some critics of transnational companies believe that business <u>ought to be conducted</u> in the same way the world over with no double standards. TNCs <u>should not be faulted</u> for every departure from home country standards in doing business abroad.
judgment or evaluation *moderate strength*	*Can* also expresses a judgment, but implies a weaker evaluation. Writers use this when they want to leave the reader room for his/her own evaluation.	The practice of selling free drug samples <u>can still be considered</u> as morally wrong even though it is condoned by the local medical community.

5C   Adverbs: Function and Placement in Academic Writing

Writers use adverbs to add clarity and precision to sentences. Adverbs not only give information about *how, when, where,* and *why* things happen, they also control the strength of general statements. Writers who use adverbs well are very aware of their audience and the types of general statements or claims they will accept and the types they will need to limit in some way. Notice the different meaning between the two examples—all because of the strategic placement of one adverb.	Centenarians <u>represent</u> the most resilient genetic strain within each generation. Centenarians **probably** <u>represent</u> the most resilient genetic strain within each generation.

Writers need to consider three important things when choosing and using adverbs:

- whether the audience will accept the general statement without some limits or whether adverbs will be needed to control the strength of the generalization
- the kind of information the adverb adds to a sentence. Typically, *how* (adverbs of manner), *when* (adverbs of time), *where* (adverbs of place), or *how much* (adverbs of degree or intensifiers)
- where to place an adverb in a sentence

The following charts provide some examples of types of adverbs commonly found in academic writing and their placement in a sentence.

ADVERBS OF MANNER

Adverbs of manner are typically formed by adding *ly* to the adjective form of a word (neat-*ly*, quick-*ly*, general-*ly*). They usually modify the verb or the whole sentence. Some common adverbs in this category: *generally, typically, actually, rapidly, potentially, probably, (not) necessarily, substantially,* and *widely.*

Before the main verb	Centenarians **probably** <u>represent</u> the most resilient genetic strain. For this reason, they *actually* <u>tend</u> to be healthier than some people thirty years younger than they are.
Between the auxiliary and the main verb	Men and women <u>were</u> **randomly** <u>assigned</u> to one of the three different conditions. Some subjects had a chance to verbally aggress. Other subjects had to physically aggress against him. In the no-aggression group, subjects had no chance to agress against the experimenter
After the main verb (emphasizes the adverb rather than the verb)	During the experiment, heart rate <u>was monitored</u> **continuously,** and blood pressure was measured every two minutes.
At the beginning of the sentence	**Actually,** they are not only *not* natural, they are not even very common, worldwide.

ADVERBS OF DEGREE

Adverbs of degree add information that tells *how much* or *how complete*. Some adverbs of degree modify adverbs and adjectives. Others, like *for the most part,* can modify an entire sentence. Adverbs of degree that add information about *how complete* (completely) modify adjectives. Some even modify nouns.

Adverbs	What They Modify	Examples
for the most part	entire sentence	And employees **for the most part** accepted eagerly.
to some extent	entire sentence	**To some extent,** older workers can compensate for their slower reactions by experience.

Continued

| *Partly* | adjectives, adverbs, verbs | The prediction that there will be one million centenarians worldwide <u>is based</u> **partly** on the fact that several people now reach 100 every month. |
| *Relatively* | adjectives, adverbs | For example, it was once believed that those who achieved the age of 100 would tend to be calm, serene "Type B" personalities who had led **relatively** <u>stress-free</u> lives. |

EMPHASIZING ADVERBS

These adverbs emphasize particular words or grammatical constructions. They appear immediately before the words or constructions they modify. In the examples, the adverb is in italics and the element in the sentence that each adverb modifies is underlined.

Adverbs	Examples
only	These cardiovascular changes occur **only** <u>when people are watching violence carried out by someone of the same sex,</u> suggesting that they identify more with the character.
simply	But more difficulties arise for the catharsis hypothesis than **simply** <u>that it has limitations.</u>
merely	In the No-frustration group, the experimenter **merely** <u>praised</u> students when they reached 0.
just	For one thing, he says he's finding that blood pressure goes up when people are exposed to violence—not **just** <u>to the real-life kind</u> that's known to cause fight-or-flight hormones to surge, but also to "Rambo"-style movies.
even	**Not even** <u>a war</u> seems to purge a people's aggressive feelings.
really	Since that day, I've had the feeling that nothing <u>can</u> **really** <u>harm</u> me and have lived completely without fear.
actually	Centenarians **actually** <u>lived</u> through many of the historical events or social changes that most of us know only from history books.

TIME ADVERBS

These adverbs add information about the time or frequency with which something happens. Some of the most common time adverbs include *frequently, regularly, rarely, recently, currently, newly,* and *suddenly.*

Beginning of the sentence	**Recently,** studies of longevity have pointed to the keys to a long life.
Before the verb or between the auxiliary and the participle	She **frequently** <u>travels,</u> going to two or three places each year.

5D   Concessives: Using Coordination, Subordination, and Transition Words to Persuade Readers

Conjunctions, subordinators, and transition words do not only signal logical relationships between ideas in clauses and sentences. They also are used to persuade readers.

SIGNALING CONTRASTING RELATIONSHIPS

Writers not only use contrast words like *but, while,* and *although* to indicate the logical relationships between sentences (see pages 261–271 in Section 1), they also use them to persuade readers. Writers do this by putting two sentences or two clauses together. One sentence or clause expresses the writer's opinion or idea; the second expresses something that the audience thinks, knows, or believes to be true.

> **While** having some kind of e-mail guideline is better than having none, a poorly written policy can create new problems.

Acknowledging or stating a perspective that is different from the writer's makes the writer seem more reasonable and believable. This quality is very persuasive in academic writing. Here are some typical examples of concessive sentences.

Contrasting Word	Concessive Meaning
but	Many historians mention bad weather in passing when describing the events of these centuries, **but** few acknowledge the possibility that the deterioration in climate played a key role in the deterioration of civilization.

Meaning: The writer connects the two sentences with *but.* The first sentence acknowledges information or a point of view that differs from the writer's; the sentence after *but* gives the writer's idea or opinion.

Function: These types of sentences occur frequently in academic writing. A writer uses them in order not to appear "one-sided" and to acknowledge that other information or points of view exist about a topic; the writer then indicates that she or he has different information or a different opinion about the topic.

Contrasting Word	Concessive Meaning
although	**Although** the Norse were the people who seem to have taken fullest advantage of the opportunities provided by the period of medieval warming known as *the little optimum,* it would be wrong to leave you with the impression that the benefits bypassed the rest of Europe entirely.

Meaning: The writer connects the two clauses with *although.* The first sentence acknowledges a piece of background information that readers probably know and the second sentence makes the writer's point: that other countries besides Norway benefited historically from the warming period.

Function: Writers use sentences that begin with *although* to recognize readers' background knowledge. *Although* clauses allow writers to meet readers where they are and then give them new information.

Contrasting Word	Concessive Meaning
however	This act contained a little-publicized provision asking health care providers to build a national database of patients' medical records. Americans have much to gain from such a database. There are no federal laws, **however,** ensuring that medical records will be limited to professional hands like these. The Kennedy-Kassebaum Act gave Congress until late 1999 to devise a plan for ensuring medical confidentiality. Present dangers, **however,** demand action that is more prompt.

Meaning: The writer connects the two sentences with *however.* The first sentence presents one perspective or opinion on a topic. The sentence containing *however* presents an opposing or different perspective which the writer wishes to emphasize.

Function: Writers use *however* to connect sentences that present advantages and disadvantages or two opposing perspectives on some topic. The first sentence usually contains the perspective that the writer does not agree with. The sentence after the *however* contains the perspective the writer will emphasize and probably agrees with.

5E   Conditional and Hypothetical Sentences

When writers use conditional sentences, or sentences that contain *if*, they want to show that one thing is necessary to cause something else to happen.

Conditional and hypothetical sentences consist of two clauses. The condition is stated in the dependent clause that begins with *if, unless, when, given something*, or *suppose*. The result is stated in the independent clause.

Condition Word	Dependent Clause	Independent Clause
If	they can show that they need the information to make medical insurance contributions,	companies are allowed to see the medical records of their employees.
Unless	Congress acts promptly against inappropriate access,	Americans stand to lose as much as they will gain from the ongoing computerization of medical records.

Writers use different types of conditional and hypothetical sentences to convey distinct meanings. Some occur more frequently than others in academic writing.

CONDITIONAL SENTENCES

Time Reference	Form
present	Your company <u>has</u> the right to read whatever e-mail messages you send and receive if it <u>has informed</u> you of its right to do so in the employee handbook.
	If there <u>are</u> misconceptions that can easily be made plausible, amusing, or sensational, then the media <u>will use</u> them.

    Meaning: The writer is certain that the result will occur when the condition is met.

    Function: These types of conditional sentences occur frequently in academic writing. Writers use them when they want to convey "under these conditions" or "when" certain general statements will occur or are true.

Hypothetical Sentences

Time Reference	Form
present	If the greenhouse effect <u>were</u> to warm the south polar region by just five degrees Celsius, the floating ice shelves surrounding the West Antarctic ice sheet <u>would begin</u> to disappear.

If combination antibiotics <u>were not sold,</u> many doctors <u>would continue</u> to issue prescriptions for several different drugs to be taken simultaneously, very possibly in the wrong proportions. |

Meaning: The writer is not certain that the condition will be met, but is fairly certain that, if the condition were met, the result would occur.

Function: This type of conditional sentence allows the writer to speculate or wonder "what if" about a present situation or problem. Sometimes, as in sentence 1 above, the writer is speculating about what hasn't happened yet, but what might happen in the future. In sentence 2, the writer is saying "This is not true now, but isn't it interesting to think about?"

Time Reference	Form
past	If the writers of this textbook <u>had found</u> examples of this type of conditional sentence in the readings, they <u>would have written</u> them here.

Meaning: The writer knows that the condition can't be met because the situation is in the past; therefore, both the condition and the result are unchangeable.

Function: This type of conditional sentence allows the writer to speculate or wonder "what if" about past situations. This type of conditional is not the most common in academic writing. It is found, however, when writers speculate about "what might have been" if things had occurred differently in the past.

Section 6 Interactive Communication in Writing

6A   Overview of Interactive Grammar

Conversations are successful because people look at each other, read each other's body language and facial expressions, use intonation to relay subtle (or not so subtle) messages, share background knowledge, and keep talking until they reach some kind of understanding. In conversation, we ask questions, refer to the other people in the conversation as *you,* and talk about *I* and *we.* We also give short answers to questions. (These short answers might be considered incomplete sentences or fragments in academic writing.) Finally, we use informal vocabulary including colloquial expressions, slang, and contractions *(can't, won't).* (Contractions are not dealt with in this book, but writers should be aware that contractions signal a more informal writing style. Check with your instructors to find out whether contractions are appropriate for particular writing assignments.)

Writers can't count on any of these non-verbal or informal expressions to make their communication successful. They cannot ask their readers questions, so they must predict the background knowledge of their readers and provide whatever information is missing. They must rely on grammar and vocabulary, rather than on body language, facial expressions, and their voices, to convey attitude and emotions. Writers also must choose their vocabulary and certain grammatical structures carefully to convey exactly what they mean since they have no chance to restate their message if readers don't understand.

Because of these differences, the language of speaking and that of writing are often quite different. But the two are not distinct. Depending on purpose and audience, the language and style of certain pieces of writing may contain elements of conversational language: *fragments; I, you,* or *we* to address the reader more directly; indications of the *writer's voice, tone,* and *attitude;* and some *informal vocabulary.* For other audiences and purposes, writers will focus on the topic, but not address the reader, and have very few elements of conversational style in the writing. The three samples below vary in their use of elements of spoken language.

Sample 1 (quite a few elements of spoken language) • The writer addresses the reader as *you.* • The second sentence is a **fragment.** • **You** is the focus; the topic, privacy on the Internet, is introduced gradually. In the example, all mentions of the topic—lack of privacy—are underlined.	**Sample 1:** Someone is watching **you.** (Likely, several someones are—anyone from your boss to a nighttime employee at your Internet service provider, and possibly someone from the government.) From the moment you connect to the Net, **you** <u>are leaking information to the world about who you are, what *you* do,</u> and <u>what *you* are interested in. As private a pastime</u> as surfing the Internet might seem, <u>it's not.</u> The computers that make up the Net monitor and <u>often record everything *you* do while online.</u>
Sample 2 (one element of spoken language) • The writer focuses on the topic: the effects of the medieval warming period on European civilization. • All sentences are complete. The sentences are quite long and complex. • The writers address the readers once as **you.**	**Sample 2:** Although the Norse were the people who seem to have taken fullest advantage of the opportunities provided by the period of medieval warming known as *the little optimum,* it would be wrong to leave **you** with the impression that the benefits by-passed the rest of Europe entirely. The warmth in Europe seems to have continued until about 1300, a little later than in Greenland, and to have coincided with the awakening of the form of European civilization that has continued to the present day.
Sample 3 (no elements of spoken language) • The writer never addresses the reader, and focuses only on the topic: benefits of a national medical information database. • All sentences are complete. Some are long and complex; others are shorter and simple.	**Sample 3:** Last year, the U.S. Congress passed the Kennedy-Kassebaum Health Insurance Portability and Accountability Act. This act contained a little-publicized provision asking health care providers to build a national database of patients' medical records. Americans have much to gain from such a database. With it, emergency room doctors could review the medical history of an unconscious accident victim before deciding on a method to revive him.

6B   *I, You,* and *We*

UsING *I* IN ACADEMIC WRITING

Some writers believe that they should never use the pronoun **I** (or **me, my, mine**) in academic writing. This is not accurate. Depending on the audience and purpose of the academic task, academic writing might encourage the use of personal opinions and evidence. Other academic tasks might encourage a greater focus on the information, and therefore, a more impersonal style. One of the secrets of persuasive writing is to determine the style expected for particular writing tasks. Here are some examples taken from readings or student essays in this book to show how writers use **I** in academic writing.

The writer of this essay was asked to compare her experiences with anger with generalizations about anger presented by different authors. In this case, it is appropriate for the writer to express her opinions by using the pronoun **I.**	In *The Anger Factor,* the author reports that angry people can almost double the risk of heart attack. **I** agree with this statement. When **I** get angry, **I** can hear my heart pulsating like a nail being driven into a wall. **I** also experience shortness of breath and my face turns red. **I** believe these symptoms can lead to physical harm, such as a heart attack.
The writer of the investigative report this excerpt comes from chose to include personal information in her report. She therefore used the pronoun **my.**	Not only does Russia have this special case, but this phenomena has happened in **my** family too. All of **my** grandparents and their siblings have lived to be very old. **My** grandfather is 84 years old and he told **me** that his parents lived to be 92 and 87.

Using *You* in Academic and Published Writing

You has very limited uses in academic writing, but is used more broadly in published writing. **You** is used in academic writing to draw the reader into a very abstract topic or to outline the steps in a process that the writer must follow. When it is used, **you** creates a conversational tone in writing. This style may not always be appropriate, so writers need to look carefully at models of the types of writing they will do. Here are some examples when **you** is used in published writing for a non-academic audience.

This excerpt comes from the beginning of an article written about privacy issues related to using the Internet. It is clear that the writer's purpose in using the pronoun **you** is to establish a more personal, conversational style. This serves to make the information more directly relevant to the reader.	Someone is watching **you**. Likely, several someones are—anyone from **your** boss to a nighttime employee at **your** Internet service provider, and possibly someone from the government. From the moment **you** connect to the Net, **you** are leaking information to the world about who **you** are, what **you** do, and what **you** are interested in.
When giving advice, writers often use the pronoun **you** to speak directly to the reader.	Now that **you** know how snoops can invade **your** privacy online, what can **you** do about it? There are several steps you can take to protect **yourself**. Some are more cumbersome than others, and only **you** can decide when to make the trade-off of convenience for security.

Here is an example of when **you** is used in an academic textbook. The excerpt is taken from an introductory textbook in biology, and the writers are trying to tell readers directly what they will learn throughout the more than 1,000-page textbook. Other writers of academic texts often use **you** when they are telling readers about a procedure to follow.

As **you** proceed through this course, what **you** learn at one stage will give **you** tools to tackle the next. In the following chapter we will examine some simple chemistry. **You** are not subjected to chemistry first to torture **you,** but rather to make what comes later easier to comprehend. To understand lions and tigers and bears, **you** first need to know the basic chemistry that makes them tick, for they are chemical machines, as are **you.**

Source: P. H. Raven and G. B. Johnson, *Biology,* 2nd Ed. (St. Louis. MO: Times Mirror/Mosby College Publishing, 1989, 18).

USING *WE* IN ACADEMIC WRITING

We is also used in academic writing. It allows the writer to accomplish several things as these examples from academic writing show.

Function	Example
To indicate that the article was written by more than one person or that more than one person was involved in doing research. The writers of this example could have also used the passive voice to focus on the research, rather than on their work.	During the past several years, research into supporting database applications has established that one of the most important features that current database systems do not provide is the ability to define and manipulate complex objects and configurations of complex objects. During the past two years, **we** have studied the properties of complex objects and configurations, and explored implementation techniques for them. In particular, **we** have defined what **we** consider a complete set of meaningful operations on them and specified a language called DL/CAD for defining, traversing, and manipulating complex objects. This paper is a compendium of the results of **our work** on complex objects and configurations. Source: Won Kim et al. Operations and implementation of complex objects, *IEEE Transactions on Software Engineering,* 1988, Vol. 14, 985–995.
To get readers involved in a topic and convey enthusiasm for it.	Literature offers **us** an escape from life, but also provides **us** with new equipment for **our** inevitable return. It offers **us** an "imitation" of life. It helps **us** understand life, and life helps us understand fiction. **We** recognize aspects of ourselves and **our** situations in the more ordered perspectives of fiction, and **we** also see ideal and debased extremes of existence. Source: R. Scholes et al. *Elements of Literature,* 4th Ed. (New York: Oxford University Press, 1991, 124).
To connect with the reader. Writers often use **we** in this way when they want to point out a serious problem without pointing the finger directly at the individual reader.	**We** are at a critical turning point. **We** have spent billions to send a handful of people to the moon, only to learn the importance of protecting the diversity of life on the beautiful blue planet that is home. While technological optimists promise a life of abundance for everyone, conservationists and environmentalists warn that the earth's life-support systems are being strained and degraded. **We** face a complex mix of interrelated problems. One is population growth: World population has almost doubled—from 2.5 billion in 1950 to 5.2 billion in 1989. Another problem is the way **we** use resources. Source: G. T. Miller, Jr., *Living in the Environment: An Introduction to Environmental Science* (Belmont, CA.: Wadsworth Publishing Co., 1990, 2).

6C   Fragments

See Chapter 1, Academic Reading and Writing, for information, examples, and exercises on this topic.

6D   Questions in Academic Writing

At their most basic level, a question in any piece of writing helps the writer interact more with readers. See pages 28–29 in Chapter 1 for an explanation of the functions of questions in academic writing. Here are some examples of how writers employ questions.

This writer uses a number of questions. The first three questions serve to introduce the topic and raise readers' interest. The last question raises the key question or point that will be answered in the rest of the essay.	*What is it like to be an animal? What do monkeys, dolphins, crows, sunfishes, bees, and ants think about?* **Or do nonhuman animals experience any thoughts and subjective feelings at all?** Very few biologists or psychologists have discussed animal thoughts and feelings. While they do not deny their existence, they emphasize that it is extremely difficult, perhaps impossible, to learn anything at all about the subjective experiences of another species. But the difficulties do not justify a refusal to face up to the issue. As Savory (1959) put the matter, "Of course to interpret the thoughts, or their equivalent, which determine an animal's behavior is difficult, but this is no reason for not making the attempt to do so. If it were not difficult, there would be very little interest in the study of animal behavior, and very few books about it" (p. 78). **Just what is it about some kinds of behavior that leads us to feel that it is accompanied by conscious thinking?**

Section 7 Common Terminology

These are words that students and teachers often use when they talk with each other about the grammar of student writing. These charts provide an overview of the uses of these grammar structures in sentences. The charts do not teach you how to use the grammar but provide examples of the uses of the basic vocabulary for talking about English grammar. The topics are presented in alphabetical order. Only the terms most likely to be used by teachers or textbooks are given here.

7A   Adjectives

Adjectives are words like *good, useful, reliable, efficient, global, technological,* and many others. **Adjectives** are usually used with nouns in noun phrases.	a *rare* event *good* health a *new, older* age a *common physical* impairment
Adjectives can be used in the complement of a sentence.	subject verb complement This stereotype is *obsolete* for today's older people.
In addition to adjectives like *good, useful,* and *reliable,* there are two other types of adjectives that can be made from the past and present participles of verbs. These are called **participial adjectives** and **adjective compounds with participles.**	participial adjective Centenarians are a *growing* age group in the U.S. population. participial adjective with pres. participle adjective compound *Lifesaving* drugs and *life-prolonging* devices such as organ transplants and heart pacemakers have also helped people live longer lives. When centenarians are interviewed, they participial adjective with past participle often dispel society's *long-held* beliefs about the aged.
Most adjectives have **comparative** and **superlative** forms. Depending on pronunciation, comparatives are made with *er* or *more: happier* or *more effective.* Depending on pronunciation, superlatives are made with *est* or *most: happiest* and *most effective. Good* has the irregular forms *better* and *best.*	People are realizing that they are able to influence life-style factors that can lead to a *healthier* and *longer* life. This stereotype is *as obsolete as* is the arbitrary age of 65 for retirement. Billy Earley is *the happiest* and *most energetic* centenarian we interviewed. Continued

| Another name for the **relative clause** is **adjective clause** because it is like an adjective in its work. | relative/adjective clause
The good health *that makes longevity possible,* has been enhanced by medical discoveries such as antibiotics and other lifesaving drugs. |

7B   Adverbs and Adverbials

Adverbs give information about time, place, manner, purpose, etc. They answer questions such as *when, where, why,* or *how.* The adverbial can be a single word, a phrase, or a clause.

A single word adverb can be used.	Centenarians *probably* represent the most resilient genetic strain within each generation.
Groups of words can also do the same work as a single-word adverb. These are called **adverbials.** In this example, **a prepositional phrase** that answers the question *when* is an adverbial.	*At the time of the Samurai knights,* strict rules about anger had considerable survival value because a Samurai could execute anyone who was disrespectful to him.
A whole clause can give the same information as a single-word adverb. In this sentence, the adverbial is **a dependent clause** that answers the question *why.*	*Since centenarians represent the most resilient genetic strain within each generation,* they tend to be healthier than many people decades younger.

7C   Articles and Determiners

Several types of words precede nouns and noun phrases. These words specify the noun phrase in some way. **Articles** are the words *a, an,* (also called *indefinite articles*) and *the* (also called the *definite article*). **Determiners** are a larger group: *this/that, these/those, each, much, no, another, some, such,* etc.	**Articles** *an* intensive study *the* small village *a* redefinition of work	**Determiners** *this* notion *these* types of animals *such* problems *another* issue *each* author
Personal pronouns *(my, your, his, her, our, their)* can also precede nouns. They can also be called **determiners.**	Someone is watching you. Likely, several someones are—anyone from **your** boss to a nighttime employee at **your** Internet service provider, and possibly someone from the government. In this case, as in many others, producer David O. Selznick sacrificed accuracy to suit **his** larger goals.	
The words *this/that* and *these/those* are sometimes called **determiners** and sometimes called **demonstrative pronouns.**	*Gone with the Wind* still reflects historians' inaccurate view of the African-American experience, portraying happy-go-lucky "darkies" loyal to benevolent masters. **This** view dominated the study of U.S. history during the first half of this century. None of **these** gangsters is representative of the larger ethnic groups from which they happened to originate.	

7D   Auxiliary Verbs

English verbs are either simple single words, or they combine two or more words to make the verb. For example, present and past progressive verb tenses combine a form of *be* with the *ing* form of the verb. In this situation *be* is called the **auxiliary verb.** Sometimes you will hear the term **helping verb**—that is just another name for the auxiliary verb.	simple present tense (two forms) **study or studies** simple past tense **studied** auxiliary verb + main verb (present progressive) **is studying**	auxiliary verb + main verb (present perfect) **has studied** auxiliary verb + auxiliary verb + main verb (present perfect + progressive) **has been studying** auxiliary verb + main verb (a passive verb) **is required**
Questions and negatives can also require *do, does,* or *did* as an auxiliary verb.	*do* as auxiliary verb and *think* as main verb What <u>do</u> animals <u>think</u> about? Interestingly, many centenarians say they *do* as auxiliary verb and *feel* as main verb <u>don't feel</u> old.	
Modal auxiliary verb or **modal** is the name for the words *will, would, can, could, may, might, must, shall, should.* They combine with main verbs to create verb phrases.	People are realizing that they <u>can influence</u> lifestyle factors that <u>might lead</u> to a healthier and longer life. Students <u>will have</u> the rest of their lives to own an automobile and pay expenses.	

7E   Comma Splices

A comma splice is an error that occurs when a compound sentence has a comma but not a coordinating conjunction. A comma <u>cannot</u> be used alone to make a compound sentence. Here is an example of a comma splice. Many teachers consider this a very serious error.	*Small departments have been under attack, this new restructuring will protect these types of departments. (Incorrect)
To correct a comma splice, you can separate the clauses and make independent sentences.	Small departments have been under attack. This new restructuring will protect these types of departments.

Continued

You can add a semicolon.	Small departments have been under attack; this new restructuring will protect these types of departments.
You can add a coordinating conjunction or transition word, depending on the logical relationship between the two sentences. Sometimes, both a transition word and a coordinating conjunction can be used.	Small departments have been under attack. **Thus,** this new restructuring will protect these types of departments. Small departments have been under attack, **and, as a result,** this new restructuring will protect these types of departments.
You can use subordination. This method might require other changes in the sentences to get exactly the right meaning.	Because small departments have been under attack, this new restructuring will help protect our department.

7F   Complements

| Complements are often nouns, noun phrases, or adjectives. The complement describes or renames the subject of the sentence. | verb + noun complement
David O. Selznick <u>was</u> *the director of Gone with the Wind.* |
| The verb *be* and other **linking verbs** like *become, seem, taste,* and several others connect the subject to the complement. In the following example, the verb *be* links the subject to an **adjective complement.** | Business conditions in other parts of the world

verb + adjective complement
<u>are</u> *different* in morally important ways from those in the United States. |

7G   Conjunctions

The two most frequently used kinds of conjunctions are **coordinating conjunctions** and **subordinating conjunctions.** (See http://www.gsu.edu/~wwwesl/egw/bryson.htm for more details on conjunctions.)

Coordinating conjunctions *for, and, nor, but, or, yet,* and *so* are used to combine words and phrases. They are also used to make compound sentences and compound-complex sentences. The most common are *and, but, so,* and *or.*	*and* used to connect two nouns for the subject Family **and** friends help with decisions. *and* used to make a compound sentence Layoffs win points for corporate CEO's with Wall Street, **and** many companies are pursuing this policy.
Subordinating conjunctions are used to make complex sentences and compound-complex sentences. Subordinating conjunctions create units that are called **subordinate clauses** or **dependent clauses.**	At the time of the Samurai knights, strict rules about anger had considerable survival value **because** a Samurai could execute anyone who was disrespectful to him.
Transition words such as *thus, however, consequently, nevertheless, on the other hand,* and others are used to connect two independent sentences logically.	Marketing executives are less interested in your personal information than what you buy. **Moreover,** there are laws and regulations designed to make sure it stays that way.

7H   Infinitives

An **infinitive** is the combination of *to* + base form of the verb. Infinitives are used in four major ways: as direct objects, adverbials, with nouns, and with adjectives.	*infinitive as the direct object* People tend **to fear unusual weather patterns.** *infinitive as an adverbial to tell how* Centenarians know how **to cope with old age successfully.** *adjective + infinitive* It is **startling to see** how good one can look after 100 years of living. *Noun + infinitive* a **desire to live a long life.**
Notice that infinitives can have objects—and sometimes very long objects. The objects are in bold type.	to influence **life-style factors** to desire **a long life**

7I   Nouns and Noun Phrases

A noun is a word or phrase like *student, computer, grammar,* or *conscious thought.* Nouns refer to people, places, things, and concepts. They are used in sentences as subjects, objects, complements, and a few other functions.

	Singular Count Nouns	Plural Count Nouns	Noncount Nouns (have only one form)
Count nouns have *singular* and *plural* forms. **Regular count nouns** form their plurals by adding *s*. **Irregular count nouns** have several ways to form their plural. In the examples *woman/women* and *person/people* are irregular count nouns. **Noncount nouns** have only one form. They cannot be used with *a* or *an; s* is not added to make the word plural.	a woman a person a cat	women people cats	value justice ethnicity *Continued*

Noun phrases are a group of words that, together, function as a noun. They can function as subjects or objects of sentences—just like a one-word noun does. A **complex noun phrase** is a noun phrase that is long and complicated with words attached to the central noun.	**Noun Phrases** an intensive study the small Bedfordshire village hormone levels animal thoughts and feelings	**Complex Noun Phrases** an intensive study of cats a redefinition of work anyone who is disrespectful to him the classic assertion of American industry that was voiced by Alfred P. Sloan, the former chairman of General Motors

7J   Objects

The word **object** is used for two different types of grammar structures. Verbs can have objects. Prepositions have objects.

A transitive verb must have a **direct object.** Sometimes this direct object is just called the object of the verb. The direct objects are in italics in these examples.	<u>The climate</u> <u>is undergoing</u> *a permanent change.* <u>Scientists</u> <u>identify</u> *long-term climate changes and the natural and human causes behind such changes.*
Some transitive verbs can have another object called the **indirect object.** The indirect object "receives" the direct object. You cannot have an indirect object unless you also have a direct object.	subject verb indirect object <u>Many parents</u> <u>give</u> *their children* direct object *money* to make up for their absence at home.
Prepositions have objects. The combination of a preposition with its object is called a **prepositional phrase.**	preposition + object = prepositional phrase **in** *average conditions* **for** *economic development*

7K   Participles

The **present participle** is used to form present and past progressive verb tenses.	present progressive tense The climate regime <u>is</u> not just <u>**varying**</u> on some relatively short time scale. past progressive tense The earth <u>was</u> <u>**sliding**</u> toward the next ice age.
Past participle: In regular verbs, the past participle is formed by adding *ed* *(walked)* to the verb; irregular verbs have irregular past participles *(go → gone)*. This form of the verb combines with the auxiliary verb *have* to create the present and past perfect tenses and the auxiliary *be* to create the passive voice.	present perfect tense Very few biologists <u>have</u> <u>**discussed**</u> animal thoughts and feelings. past perfect tense Hay production in Iceland <u>had</u> <u>**dropped**</u> by 25 percent because of cooler temperatures. passive An intensive study of cats <u>was</u> <u>**undertaken**</u> in the small Bedfordshire village.

7L   Phrases and Clauses

| A **phrase** is a group of words that work together as a single unit. It cannot stand alone as a complete sentence. It must be connected to an independent clause to be a complete sentence. There are several types of phrases and each type of phrase can have various functions within a sentence:

• **noun phrases**
• **verb phrases**
• **prepositional phrases** | At the time of the Samurai knights,
noun phrase/subject of the sentence
strict rules about anger had considerable
noun phrase/direct object of the verb
survival value because a Samurai could execute anyone who was disrespectful to him.

At the time of the Samurai knights, strict rules about anger had considerable survival value
verb phrase/main verb
because a Samurai **could execute** anyone who was disrespectful to him.

prepositional phrase/time adverbial
At the time of the Samurai knights, strict rules about anger had considerable survival value because a Samurai could execute anyone who was disrespectful to him.

Continued |

A **clause** is a sentence that has been changed in some way to be used as part of another sentence. A clause is different from a phrase because a clause has a subject and a verb. Here are four important types of clauses:

1) **dependent clause** (also called a subordinate clause). These usually function as **adverbial clauses** and answer such questions as *why* and *when*.
2) **independent clause** (also called a main clause). An independent clause is just another name for a simple sentence, a sentence that can stand alone.
3) **relative clause.** This adds information to a noun.
4) **noun clause.** This usually follows verbs like *suggest, know, say, conclude,* and *that.*

At the time of the Samurai,

independent clause

<u>strict rules about anger had considerable survival value</u>

dependent clause

<u>because a Samurai could execute anyone</u>

relative clause

[<u>who was disrespectful to him</u>].

A World Health Organization (WHO) study <u>concluded</u> ***that***

noun clause

physical performance, at a peak in the early 20s, declines gradually in older people.

7M Prepositions

Prepositions are words like *on, by, from,* and many others. A related structure is the **prepositional phrase.** This term refers to the combination of a preposition with its object. Prepositional phrases are often used as adverbials to tell *when, where, why, about what,* and so forth.

Several books were published

prepositional phrase as an adverbial to tell *about what*

on the topic of extreme climate change.
In some regions, half the population was

prepositional phrase as an adverbial to tell *how*

wiped out **by these plagues.**

Prepositional phrases are also often attached to nouns in complex noun phrases. Research has shown that this combination is more common than the combination of a noun plus a relative clause.

- these adolescents **from Hong Kong**
- experts **at the DC Office on Aging in Washington**
- the search **for longevity**
- the emergence **of preventive medicine**

Continued

Prepositions are also closely tied to some verbs and need to be learned as part of the structure of particular verbs. (See Appendix A on Vocabulary in Academic Writing for a list of these prepositional verbs; also, consult the World Wide Web at http://www.gsu.edu/~wwwesl/egw/verbprep.html)	*refer to*	Climatologists <u>refer to</u> any factor that influences the climate as a forcing function.
	rely on	Climatologists <u>rely on</u> scientific data and people's stories about the weather.

7N   Pronouns

Pronouns are words like *I/me, you, we/us, he/him, she/her, it.* These are also called **personal pronouns.**	personal pronouns *we* If **we** look at the problem of "parachute kids" as an educational problem or as a racial problem, **we** may overlook the part that family structure plays in the issue.
Other words are also called **pronouns.** These include the following types: 1. **demonstrative pronouns** (*this/that* and *these/those*). (These are sometimes called determiners—see page 336.) 2. **relative pronouns** (*who, whom, that, which,* and some others). 3. **interrogative pronouns** (*who, whom, whose, why, how,* and some others) for making questions.	There could have been an invasion of cold demonstrative pronoun *this* Arctic air into Asia as part of **this** new pattern of climate. relative pronoun at the beginning of a relative clause Armadillos *that* had migrated as far north as Kansas were moving southward. interrogative pronoun *what* **What** do animals think about?

70 Sentences

A **sentence** is a complete unit that contains at least a **subject** and a **verb.** Sometimes the verb requires a **direct object** or an **indirect object,** or both. Sometimes the verb requires a **complement.** Sentences can also have **adverbials.**

subject   verb
<u>Bad deeds</u> <u>escalate.</u>

subject   verb   direct object
<u>Good manners</u> <u>melt</u> resentment.

Business conditions in other parts of the

verb + complement
world <u>are</u> *different* in morally important ways from those in the United States.

indirect object   direct object
The doctor <u>gave</u> **the people** *the drug Lomotil* at no cost.

subject   verb   adverbial
<u>Americans</u> <u>express</u> their anger *little by little.*

Verbs can be followed by :
1) a **direct object.** Direct objects are nouns, pronouns, and other words that complete the meaning of the verb. Verbs that require a direct object are called **transitive** verbs.
2) an **indirect object.**
3) a **complement.** Complements can be nouns, pronouns, or adjectives. This kind of verb is called a **linking verb** because it links the subject to the information in the complement. (A list of linking verbs is on the WWW at http://www.gsu.edu/~wwwesl/egw/vanassch.htm.)
4) neither a **direct object,** an **indirect object,** or a **complement.** These are called **intransitive** verbs. Such verbs are not followed by direct or indirect objects. But, they can be followed by adverbials.

transitive verb   direct object
Good manners <u>melt</u> **resentment.**

transitive verb   indirect object/direct object
The doctor <u>gave</u> **the people** *the drug Lomotil* at no cost.

Business conditions in other parts of the

verb + complement
world <u>are</u> *different* in morally important ways from those in the United States.

intransitive verb
Bad deeds <u>escalate</u> /quickly/.

7P   Subjects of a Sentence

Subjects can be single nouns, longer noun phrases, really complicated complex noun phrases, pronouns, and other combinations of words that can be used like nouns. In these examples, the subjects in these sentences are underlined with one line.

subject: single noun

<u>Armadillos</u> were migrating southward.

subject: pronoun

<u>You</u> are ultimately the only one who can safeguard your e-mail privacy.

subject: two-word noun phrase

<u>Climate change</u> can be considered objectively and subjectively.

subject: two nouns combined with *and*

<u>Climate change and its causes</u> are the subject of this essay.

complex noun phrase as subject

<u>Human's fear of nature</u> makes them so concerned about the weather and climate change.

relative clause as subject

<u>The criteria that are applied to non-profit companies</u> are very loose.

7Q   Verbs in Sentences: Verb Form; Verb Tense; Passive vs. Active; Modal Auxiliaries

Verbs play an important role in sentences. Since they convey the action in the sentence, readers get important information from them. Each sentence must have a subject and a verb. The verb in a sentence is often called the **verb phrase.**

Verb Forms
Verbs have several forms:

1) **infinitive:** This is also called **the base form** of the verb. The infinitive form usually follows the preposition *to*.

2) **main verb:** A verb in this form shows verb tense and agrees with a subject in the present tense. This is also called **subject-verb agreement.**

3) **past participle:** In regular verbs, the past participle is formed by adding *ed (walked)* to the verb; irregular verbs have irregular past participles *(go → gone)*. This form of the verb combines with the auxiliary verb *have* to create the present and past perfect tenses and the auxiliary *be* to create the passive voice.

4) **present participle:** This is formed by adding *ing* to the verb *(walking)*. It combines with the auxiliary *be* to create the present and past progressive tenses.

5) **gerund:** This is formed by adding *ing* to the verb *(walking)*. This functions *not* as a verb, but as a noun and can even be the subject of a sentence.

Americans <u>tend **to get**</u> angry *slowly.*

As Ford Motor Company learned, <u>achieving high performance</u> <u>requires</u> a redefinition of work and of the relationships among <u>people</u> who <u>work</u> together. <u>These companies</u> **know** that they must respect their workers.

past participle

Very few biologists <u>have **discussed**</u> animal thoughts and feelings.

There are an estimated 25,000 centenarians in the United States, and their numbers, it

present participle

seems, <u>are</u> rapidly **increasing**.

<u>Achieving high performance</u> <u>requires</u> a redefinition of work and of the relationships among people who work together.

Continued

Verb Tense

Verbs indicate the time of the action and whether the action is complete or ongoing. This is called **verb tense.** Here are some of the most important verb tenses: *simple present, present progressive, present perfect, simple past, past progressive,* and *past perfect.*

simple present

Achieving high performance <u>requires</u> a redefinition of work and of the relationships among people who work together. The health problems of the elderly

present   progressive

<u>are</u> rapidly <u>increasing</u>.

present perfect

Very few biologists <u>have discussed</u> animal thoughts and feelings.

simple past

The scientists also <u>drew</u> blood to test stress hormone levels.

past progressive

"I <u>was burning up</u> with fever and couldn't move or speak."

past perfect

By the 1970s, ethnicity <u>had become</u> a subject of popular interest.

Active vs. Passive Verbs

Depending on their form, verbs indicate who/what does the action expressed in the verb. In **active voice,** the subject of the main verb is the doer of the action. In **passive voice,** the subject of the main verb receives the action.

active verb

<u>Several scientists</u> <u>undertook</u> an intensive study in the small Bedfordshire village.

passive verb

An intensive study of cats <u>was undertaken</u> in the small Bedfordshire village.

Modal Auxiliaries

Depending on their form, verbs can also indicate shades of meaning such as *ability, permission, obligation, possibility.* These special meanings are added to verbs by **modal auxiliaries. Modals** are words such as *will, would, can, could, should, may, might,* and *must.*

modal auxiliary

A Samurai *could* <u>execute</u> anyone who was disrespectful to him.

APPENDIX A: BASIC FEATURES OF ACADEMIC WRITING

A   Introductions

An introduction to an essay is similar to the first impression that we get of someone who we meet: It lasts and it may determine how the rest of our experience with that person will go. The introduction must accomplish a great deal:

- familiarize the reader with the topic and provide background information
- arouse the reader's interest in the topic
- explain the writer's focus, argument, or main idea
- make the purpose of the piece clear

PROVIDING BACKGROUND INFORMATION

Writing a good introduction requires you to know your audience. It is important to know your readers' knowledge, interests, and expectations about your topic. You don't want to provide so much information or such basic information that your readers will be bored. On the other hand, you don't want to assume that they have so much background information that you say too little. Your job is, without seeing your readers, to predict the experience with or information about the topic that they already have.

The background information in the introduction not only provides information on the topic, but also arouses the interest of your readers. That means that, even if you are telling your readers something they already know, if you sound interested in your topic, probably the readers will be, too.

WRITING A THESIS STATEMENT

Writing a good introduction also requires you to be precise. Precision comes in the form of a thesis statement, a clear, concise statement of the paper's central idea or argument. Some teachers call the thesis your "promise" to the reader because it tells readers what the paper will give them, and after reading it, they can determine whether the writer has kept the promise. The thesis is also a helpful guideline for the writer, keeping the paper on topic and focused.

You may have learned that the thesis should always be the last sentence of the introduction. While this is a useful and often logical place to put the thesis, there is no absolute rule about where the thesis must appear. When writing in-class essays or papers for large classes, putting the thesis at or near the end of the introduction helps the professor find your main idea and read the paper more quickly and accurately.

Below are three sample introductions. The **central idea** or **central question that the essay or article will answer** is in **boldface**. The examples continue on the next page.

Example #1	Example #2	Example #3
The following introduction comes from an essay written by a community college student about the problem of garbage. Melissa Castro's introduction provides both a general background about the problem and a clear statement of the problem with evidence of it. Her thesis statement contains her proposed solution to the problem.	This introduction, written by Donald R. Griffin, comes from an article on animal thinking in an academic book. In his introduction he raises several questions that engage the reader in the topic of animal thinking. The last question is the central question that sets the direction of his article. Each subsection provides parts of the answer to the central question.	You might notice that this introduction, taken from a student essay by Yumiko Okamoto on the problems of nonprofit organizations, is longer than the other two. It has been included here to remind you that there is no set formula for the number of paragraphs in an introduction. Just remember that you should provide your readers with the amount of background they need to understand your essay.
Day by day, societies all over the world consume more and more stuff. They follow the example of first world nations, thus making the same mistakes. Garbage is the biggest of them all. It is known that the richer the country, the more waste it produces. The United States alone produces about 209 million tons of municipal waste per year, which is more than four pounds per person per day (Discover magazine, June 1997). This extends from harmless candy	What is it like to be an animal? What do monkeys, dolphins, crows, sunfishes, bees, and ants think about? Or do non-human animals experience any thoughts and subjective feelings at all? Very few biologists or psychologists have discussed animal thoughts and feelings. While they do not deny their existence, they emphasize that it is extremely difficult, perhaps impossible, to learn anything at all about the subjective experiences of another	Whenever we hear the word "nonprofit organization," we assume that they are some kind of public benefit organizations with a genuine intention of doing good. This is a misconception. **Today, nonprofit organizations look and act like normal companies— running businesses and making money. Yet, somehow, they maintain a tax-free status, thereby enriching their executives.** Across America, 1.1 million organizations claim tax-exempt status.

Continued

wrappings to giant sites where toxic wastes are dumped.

Garbage is our worst enemy. In countries like the U.S., to open a snack package shows one of the infinite reasons why we have so much waste. First there is a regular carton. Then there is the plastic wrapping. And after that, you will still find a plastic or paper tray before you can actually reach your snack. **It would be much easier for us and especially for mother nature if that same snack came in only a plastic or paper wrapping or even in a reusable package. That is why recycling is essential for our society.**

species. But the difficulties do not justify a refusal to face up to the issue. As Savory (1959) put the matter, "Of course to interpret the thoughts, or their equivalent, which determine an animal's behavior is difficult, but this is no reason for not making the attempt to do so. If it were not difficult, there would be very little interest in the study of animal behavior, and very few books about it" (p. 78). **Just what is it about some kinds of behavior that leads us to feel that it is accompanied by conscious thinking?**

Many of them are able to pay their executives millions of dollars while providing little charity and doing no research. In fact, they are so busy making money that they do not have time to do their presumably core mission. The National Geographic, a scientific and educational nonprofit institution, made $459.6 million in 1993, but contributed less than 5% to geography education in American schools. The Institute for Advanced Studies in Medicine, another nonprofit, applied only $3,373 to research out of the $792,000 it raised in funds.

Don't all the numbers bother you? We should be asking, "Why are they 'nonprofit'?" "Why aren't they paying taxes?" Actually, the reason these companies don't pay taxes is because of the lack of clarity in the tax code.

B   Conclusions

Just like introductions, conclusions perform many functions in academic writing. A good conclusion should:

- remind readers of the main focus and ideas/arguments covered in the piece of writing
- tie together the key arguments or ideas that have been presented in the paper
- **not** introduce ideas that are unrelated to the paper's main focus

Depending on the type of writing, audience, and purpose, the conclusion might also:

- leave the reader with something to think about
- explain the meaning of the ideas/arguments covered in the piece of writing

Many writers find the conclusion the most challenging piece to write because they may feel they have already said it all. A useful approach to conclusions is to consider them as "matching" the introduction. If you ask a question in the introduction, you can use the conclusion to answer it. If you discuss a problem in the introduction, you might use the conclusion to discuss a solution or summarize solutions that you have written about.

The example from a student's essay below shows how introductions and conclusions work together. In the introduction, Trang Bui successfully introduces her readers to the topic of her investigative essay about factors that affect longevity. Her thesis statement, in boldface, lets them know what she aims to cover in the body. Based on her thesis statement, readers of Trang's essay can expect to learn about several factors that contribute to long life.

Notice that the information contained in her concluding paragraph matches what she has said in her introduction. She tells readers she has delivered the promised information about the factors that contribute to an extended life.

Introduction	Conclusion
"The 120 Year Man," an article that was written in September 1991 by Dava Sobel, shows how people could have a long life. The term "longevity," for most people, was thought to be an impossible thing to achieve not very long ago. Scientists all over the world have been trying to do research in order to help peoples' dreams come true. They have to face many problems, which seem impossible to solve, and the public questions what they are doing. Fortunately, scientists' endeavors have not been wasted because finally they have a big improvement that is very important on the way to achieving their goal. Having a long life as we wish is really possible. **There are several factors that contribute to extending the life of elderly people.**	In conclusion, one of the fantastic dreams of the humanity has become true. People who used to think that life span cannot be extended are now changing their "big mental block." Elderly people can still enjoy healthy lives. Although the explorations of Professor Roy Walford and some other scientists do not get to the final answer yet, those factors bring happiness to a lot of people. Getting good results mobilizes other people who persevere at this hard job. **Having a good genetic background and following a calorie-restricted diet are the basic factors for us to open a new horizon of the extended life.**

C   Body Paragraphs: Topic Sentences and Supporting Information

Because academic writing presents complex information that is logically connected, writers have a special responsibility to create paragraphs between the introduction and conclusion that help readers understand both the ideas and the logical relationship between the ideas. Paragraphs help the writer order the ideas in the essay and make sure they are focused. The sentences in paragraphs usually move between general statements and more specific information.

TOPIC SENTENCES OR IDEAS

Most paragraphs are focused on one idea that explains or elaborates on some part of the paper's main idea or argument. This idea is stated in a *topic sentence*. But sometimes writers use several sentences to express the topic of the paragraph. The topic sentence is usually a general statement, not an example.

SUPPORTING INFORMATION

The purpose of supporting information is to provide more detail and depth to the general statement expressed in the topic sentence. Supporting ideas are sentences that present details, examples, facts, or quotations that explain or give evidence for the topic. Sentences containing supporting information are often more specific and give more detail than the topic sentence. This supporting information is sometimes called *paragraph development*. In comments about your paper, when teachers ask you to *develop* your ideas, they usually want you to add more details, examples, or facts that elaborate on, explain, or provide evidence for the topic idea.

Below are two examples of how topic sentences are supported. In both examples, the topic sentences are in boldface.

The first excerpt comes from the article "Beware of Well-Fed Felines" by Churcher and Lawton. The following paragraphs taken from the article connect to the boldfaced question in the first paragraph, **"What makes a cat a good hunter?"** A factor is introduced in each paragraph, in the form of a topic sentence. These are in **bold** and *italicized*. Following each topic sentence are supporting details.

What makes a cat a good hunter? ***Part of the answer is its age.*** Old cats get lazy; the younger the cat, the more animals it catches. Although we looked only at catches of birds and mammals, several owners reported that their kittens practiced their hunting skills on frogs or butterflies, but only a few of them persisted with these types of prey into adulthood. Sex and neutering did not appear to have a marked effect on hunting success.	central question *topic sentence* **evidence of how age affects hunting & other factors**
Where the cats lived did affect both the type and number of prey brought home. Cats in the middle of the village, without easy access to open ground, caught fewer items in total and proportionally fewer small mammals and more birds. This pattern was reversed for cats living at the edge of the village. The density of the cats themselves seemed to have a slight effect on catching success, with cats in areas with more competition for prey catching fewer items.	*topic sentence* **evidence of where cats hunted**

This next example comes from Atsuko Otani's essay, "What Affects Our Life Span?" The topic of her essay is in the form of a question: **"Why do some people live longer than others?"** The controlling idea or thesis of her essay is in the first paragraph and in **bold** and *italics*.

The two paragraphs that follow the introduction both discuss factors that affect longevity, or answer the initial question raised in the first paragraph. The topic sentence of each paragraph is in **bold** and *italicized*. These are followed by details that support the paragraph's main idea.

Why do some people live longer than others? Many scholars and specialists have tried to find the answer by research and statistics. ***According to those studies, a person's gender is an important factor in how old they live to be.***	central question *topic sentence*
Women live longer than men, and this is partly due to men's lifestyle and habits. According to a New York Times' survey, "the life expectancy of American men is on average seven years shorter than that of American women" (1994). They say one reason is men's smoking, drinking, and reckless behavior. Most people who smoke at least one package of cigarettes a day and go to bars after work often and know the best medicine to take for hangovers is men. Men have lots stress at work, and they try to get rid of it by diversion. However, the way of diversion is a shortcut to heaven.	*topic sentence* **evidence from a survey, facts**
Another reason for the difference of life span between men and women is that "men hate going to the doctor" (*New York Times,* 1994). To explain the reason for that, Andy Kimbrell, a co-founder of the men's network, explains that "in their earlier 20s they are too strong to need a doctor, in their 30s they are too busy, and in their 40s they are too scared" (*New York Times,* 1994). As a result of this behavior, many companies are concerned about their employees' health. In Japan, company managers know that their employees hate going to the doctor, so they bring the doctor to them. Most Japanese companies give workers a chance to undergo a medical checkup once a year. On the day of the medical checkup, a doctor and some assistants visit the company's office with medical equipment.	*topic sentence* **quotation from an expert, evidence of men's fear of the doctor, example of a Japanese company that brings doctors to their male employees**

To develop the supporting information in your paragraphs, it might be useful to ask yourself questions that you think the audience will have as they read your paragraphs. This may be difficult to do on the first draft because often you are just getting familiar with your ideas about the topic. If you use the questioning technique as you revise your paper, you can often think of more ideas and go into more depth in each paragraph.

D   Coherence

One of the most important qualities of a good piece of writing is coherence; that is, every paragraph builds on, helps to explain, or relates to the paper's main idea or argument. Since most academic writing presents complex ideas, coherence helps the reader understand the writer's ideas clearly and easily.

Coherence is something that writers build or create in several ways.

- They make sure that every paragraph relates to the main idea or central question that they are answering in their piece of writing.
- They write a topic sentence that clearly expresses how the ideas in the paragraph relate to the central question. In academic writing, topic sentences usually show the logical relationship between the ideas in every paragraph. For this reason, some topic sentences may express main ideas that answer the central question and others will express sub-points that further support or explain these main ideas.
- They use specific language that signals to the reader that all of the ideas are related. This is called *coherence.* Writers create coherence by repeating key words and phrases, replacing nouns with pronouns, and using transition expressions and subordination and coordination.
- They use entire sentences called *transition sentences* to signal that they are moving from one idea to the next and to show something about the logical relationship between those ideas. Sometimes the transition sentences are the same as the topic sentences.

Sometimes rereading your entire essay and attempting to outline or summarize it can help you determine whether every paragraph relates to the paper's main idea or argument. As with idea development, it is best to do this rereading several hours or a day after you have written a draft of the paper.

Read the following excerpt from *Manners, Emotions, and the American Way* by Carol Tavris (1989). This particular excerpt comes from a chapter that asks the central question: *"Why do people from different cultures seem to show their anger in different ways and as a result misunderstand one another's behavior?"*

The reading is marked to show all the ways that the writer has made the passage coherent.

A culture's rules of anger are not arbitrary; they evolve along with its history and structure.* The Japanese <u>practice of emotional restraint,</u> for example, dates back many centuries, when all aspects of demeanor were carefully regulated: facial expressions, breathing, manner of sitting and standing, style of walking. Not only were all <u>emotions</u>—anger, grief, pain, even great happiness—<u>to be suppressed</u> in the presence of one's superiors, but also regulations specified that a person submit to any order with a pleasant smile and a properly happy tone of voice. At the time of the Samurai knights, these rules had considerable survival value, because a Samurai could legally execute anyone who he thought was not respectful enough.	*topic sentence #1*
Even today in Japan, an individual who feels very angry is likely to show it by excessive politeness and a neutral expression instead of by furious words and signs. <u>A Japanese</u> who shows anger the Western way is admitting that he has lost control, and therefore lost face; <u>he</u> is thus at the extreme end of a negotiation or debate. In other cultures, though, showing anger may simply mark the beginning of an exchange, perhaps to show that the negotiator is serious; <u>a man</u> may lose face if <u>he</u> does not show anger when it is appropriate and "manly" for <u>him</u> to do so.	*topic sentence #2* **builds on the previous paragraph's idea**
Psychotherapy, of course, takes place within a culture and is deeply embedded in cultural rules. Arthur Kleinman, himself both an anthropologist and <u>psychiatrist,</u> tells of a psychiatrist in south-central China who was treating a <u>patient</u> who had become depressed and anxious ever since <u>her</u> demanding mother-in-law had moved in. "She is your family member. It is your responsibility to care for an old mother-in-law," <u>the Chinese psychiatrist</u> said. "You must contain your anger. You know the old adage: 'Be deaf and dumb! Swallow the seeds of the bitter melon! Don't speak out!'"	*topic sentence #3* **new idea that relates to the central question**

E   Transition Sentences

Transition sentences act as "bridges" between the ideas in two paragraphs. Unlike topic sentences, which state the main idea of a paragraph, transition sentences do more than just indicate the paragraph's main idea. They act as "glue" and do these three things:

- *summarize* briefly the ideas in a previous paragraph or part of the paper
- *introduce* a new idea
- *signal the logical relationship* between the previous ideas and the new idea

Because of all the work they do, writing clear transition sentences can be tricky. Sometimes a simple transition word, such as *nevertheless, first,* or *on the other hand*, followed by a simple sentence is enough to link the ideas in two paragraphs. When the logical relationship between two paragraphs is more complicated, writers often use a sentence that has two clauses connected by subordination or coordination. A transition sentence can serve as a topic sentence also, but paragraphs may contain both a transition sentence and a topic sentence.

Read the first two paragraphs of the editorial article, "Threat to Confidentiality of Personal Medical Records." The first paragraph explains an act of the U.S. Congress allowing the creation of a computer database with the medical records of all U.S. citizens and tells the reader the benefits of the action. The author makes a transition in the second paragraph to discuss the dangers of creating such a database. The transitional sentence linking the first and second paragraphs has been underlined and bolded.

Last year, the U.S. Congress passed the Kennedy-Kassebaum Health Insurance Portability and Accountability Act. This act contained a little-publicized provision asking health care providers to build a national database of patients' medical records. ***Americans have much to gain from such a database.*** With it, emergency room doctors could review the medical history of an unconscious accident victim before deciding on a method to revive him. Or researchers could try to determine whether medication given to pregnant women was associated with diseases in their children years later.	INTRODUCTION *topic sentence for ¶ 1*
<u>**There are no federal laws, however, ensuring that medical records will be limited to professional hands like these.**</u> And so ***unless Congress acts promptly against inappropriate access, Americans stand to lose as much as they will gain from the ongoing computerization of medical records.*** Now many doctors are thinking twice about what information they include in patient records, for fear it could be used against a patient's best interest.	TRANSITION SENTENCE *topic sentence for ¶ 2*

The transition sentence above restates the idea in paragraph 1 with the words "medical records." The writer repeats these key words to create coherence. The transition sentence also contains the word "however" to signal that contrasting information will be presented. Finally, the writer adds new information about the old idea of "medical records" by stating that not only medical professionals will have access to this computerized information. The transition sentence in this example is typical of those found in persuasive writing.

The following example shows the difference between topic sentences and transition sentences. The writer has divided the analysis into two categories: 1) a definition of climate change, and 2) factors that cause climate change. The boldface and underlined sentences act as transition sentences that signal to the readers each new category. Other transition sentences show the logical relationship between paragraphs. This writer does not use transition sentences between all paragraphs. Sometimes, the writer simply uses a topic sentence to state the main idea of the paragraph and does not directly restate ideas from previous paragraphs or the logical relationship between paragraphs. If the writer had used only topic sentences without transition sentences, the logical relationships between the ideas would not have been as clear.

[1] **Climate change can be considered objectively and subjectively.** *Objectively, it can be defined as variability, fluctuations, and change in the strictest sense of the word.* Variability describes changes on a relatively short time scale, followed by a return to an average condition. Fluctuations represent nonpermanent changes that take place over decades. The strictest definition refers to longer-term changes over many decades or centuries, followed by a return to some expected average condition, or to a permanent change in average conditions prevailing for some period of time. Most policy makers today are concerned about this definition of climate change when they refer to global warming. The fear is that the climate regime is not just varying on some relatively short time scale but, in fact, is undergoing a permanent change.	CATEGORY 1 *topic sentence/ paragraph 1*
[2] *Climate change can also be defined according to human perceptions.* Humans tend to think in terms of shorter time scales, such as years and decades. Even if cooler or warmer years were to occur, people might view them as a permanent change in climate and not as variability or fluctuation.	*topic sentence &* **transition sentence**
[5] **Several factors can bring about climate change.** Scientists call them *forcing functions* because they make the climate system alter its behavior. They can be divided into internal and external factors: The former are inherent to the climate system; the latter are external to it. External forcing functions include solar activity, variations of earth's orbit over very long time scales, and random	CATEGORY 2 **transition sentence**

Continued

volcanic activity. Global climate changes over the past thousand years have been attributed rightly or wrongly to one or a combination of these functions.	
[6] ***Many people believe that the number of sunspots (as a measure of solar activity) influences our climate.*** The sunspot cycle of 11 and 22 years is a prime example of a belief in this particular forcing function. Sunspots go through periods when they are numerous or relatively few, and people searching for some explanation of weather variations have resorted to linking the two phenomena. Using solar activity as an indicator, they try to forecast rainfall amounts in the agricultural heartland of the United States—the Great Plains—or estimate grain prices in the world marketplace as a result of drought that may be sunspot-related.	*topic sentence*
[7] ***Although many scientists are skeptical of the linkage, people who look for cycles in nature believe that every 20 to 22 years or so drought returns to the Great Plains.*** They use the 1930s Dust Bowl as ground zero and step off 20-year intervals from there in both directions: Droughts plagued the midsection of the United States during the 1870s, 1890s, 1910s, 1930s, 1950s, 1970s, and most recently the mid-1990s. Today there is renewed interest in the scientific community about the influence of solar activity on climate and weather.	***transition sentence & topic sentence***

APPENDIX B: VOCABULARY IN ACADEMIC WRITING

This appendix provides reference materials that can be used by academic writers to compose and revise their work. Academic writers need to be aware of the kinds of specialized vocabulary used in various types of academic writing. These lists can be expanded by writers to include other vocabulary often used in the fields they are studying. In addition, writers can use *The Newbury House Dictionary* to get definitions and see words used in context. The dictionary is available on the World Wide Web at http://nhd.heinle.com.

A   Denotation and Connotation of Verbs That Link Causes and Results

In Chapter 5, page 167, we discussed verbs that express causes and consequences. Some of the verbs may have a negative meaning. Some have a positive meaning. Others can have either a negative or a positive meaning, depending on the noun phrase that follows the verb. To find out the connotations of these verbs, (1) ask a native speaker, and (2) look them up in *The Newbury House Dictionary* on the World Wide Web at http://nhd.heinle.com.

Verbs That Express Results or Consequences	Positive Meaning	Negative Meaning	Either Meaning
breed		√	
achieve	√		
undermine		√	
create			√
increase			√
cause			√
result in			√
contribute to			√
bring about			√

B   Varying Word Choice in Academic Writing

When we speak, we tend to use a small number of verbs. In academic writing, there are synonyms for some of these common verbs. Below is a list of common verbs and their synonyms that you can use in academic writing. There is space left for you to add other words when you find them in the readings in this book or in readings for your other courses.

Common Verbs	Synonyms for Common Verbs
do *(business/research)*	engage in
(problems) happen	*(problems)* arise
cause	give rise to
decide	determine
show	illustrate
give *(good reasons)*	*(good reasons)* are/can be advanced
make	bring about
use	employ
carry out	accomplish
deal with	address
try	attempt
look at	focus on
choose	opt
leave out	overlook
understand	recognize
give up	sacrifice
stand for	symbolize
see	witness
ask us to do something	encourage

C   Learning the Grammar of New Verbs

Learning vocabulary helps readers understand what they read better. But if you want to use the new words you encounter, you must also learn <u>how</u> to use them, and this means you have to understand a bit about grammar. Verbs usually are followed by certain types of grammar structures. It is important to learn this information when you learn the new word. The verbs below can be followed by a noun or a clause.

noun/noun phrase
Some biologists <u>interpret</u> **the meaning of animal behavior.**

clause
Most pet owners <u>have determined</u> **that their animals have emotions.**

Verb	Synonym	Can be followed by:	
		noun or noun phrase	*that* **clause**
determine	set establish condition	The factors that **determine** <u>an animal's behavior.</u>	
determine	conclude prove		Biologists have **determined** <u>that animals are capable of conscious thought.</u>
emphasize	stress	Biologists **emphasize** <u>the importance of observing animals in nature.</u>	Biologists **emphasize** <u>that it is extremely difficult to learn anything about the subjective experiences of another species.</u>
observe	watch discover	Janes (1976) **observed** <u>nesting ravens.</u>	Janes **observed** that <u>nesting ravens use rocks to drive predators away.</u>
infer (make inferences about)	arrive at a conclusion guess	Some scientists **make inferences about** <u>animals' emotions.</u>	We can **infer** <u>that this intelligent bird was anxious to chase the human intruders away from its nest.</u>

Continued

| reveal | show | Communication can **reveal** <u>information about the conscious thinking of the communicator.</u> | Our research **revealed** <u>that animals are capable of conscious thought.</u> |
| stress | emphasize | Biologists **stress** <u>the importance of observing animals in their natural habitats.</u> | Biologists **stress** <u>that it is difficult to learn about animal thinking.</u> |

D Reporting Verbs: Selecting Exactly the Right Word to Convey Your Meaning

Writers are very careful when they choose reporting verbs to select the one that will convey to readers how to interpret the reported information.

Verb	Example from Readings	Notes on the Meaning	Neutral	Evaluation	Weakens Information
agree	Gerd Naegele, a gerontologist, **agrees** that businesses will need time to adjust to an older retirement age.	*agree* signals that an opinion will follow and that more than one person thinks this opinion is right		√	
argue	Genevieve Reday-Mulvey, of the International Association for the Study of Insurance Economics **argues** strongly that people should not be forced to retire.	*argue* signals that the reported information is an opinion and controversial. Notice the contrast with *say* or *states*.		√	

Continued

Verb	Example from Readings	Notes on the Meaning	Neutral	Evaluation	Weakens Information
believe	80% of respondents—of all ages—**believed** that older workers were discriminated against in job recruitment.	*believe* signals that the reported information is an opinion and that it is considered to be true by the subject of the reporting verb		√	
claim	Critics **claimed** that the company's decision to close its factory was unjust toward the community because it was violating a contract made 31 years ago when it began operations there.	*claim* signals that an argument will follow and that the writer probably doubts the reported argument		√	
conclude	A World Health Organization (WHO) study of older people's working capacity recently **concluded** that "the definition of an aging worker could be considered to apply from 45 years."	*conclude* signals that the reported information is a generalization that is usually based on research	√		

Continued

find	A World Health Organization (WHO) study of older people's working capacity **found** that older workers make decisions as well as younger workers do.	*find* signals that the reported information is a generalization based on research or some finding from a research study	√		
indicate	A World Health Organization (WHO) study of older people's working capacity **indicates** that older workers may be as good at making decisions as younger workers.	*indicate* signals that what follows is a conclusion (usually from research), but that it is not 100% sure. Compare with *show* and *find*.			√
note	Many employers **have noted** the importance of employee loyalty.	*note* means to *call attention to* and is followed by a generalization	√		
predict	The Census Bureau now **predicts** that by the year 2050 there will be one million American centenarians.	*predict* is followed by an educated guess or hypothesis about what will happen in the future			√
propose	Many experts on aging **propose** that countries should increase the age of mandatory retirement.	*propose* indicates that what follows is a possible plan or course of action (there may be other plans or solutions)			√

Continued

Verb	Example from Readings	Notes on the Meaning	Neutral	Evaluation	Weakens Information
report	Many centenarians **report** staying active and optimistic.	*report* signals that what follows is based on observation or interviews	√		
say	"The age of retirement will have to go up," **says** Winfried Schmähl, an expert on work for older people at Bremen University.	*says* usually precedes a quotation from an expert or an interviewee	√		
show	A World Health Organization (WHO) study of older people's working capacity **shows** that older workers are as useful as younger workers, in their own way.	*show* signals that the reported information is a generalization based on research or some finding from a research study	√		
suggest	One study **suggests** that drinking one glass of wine per day can reduce the risk of heart attack.	*suggest* signals that what follows is a conclusion, but that it is not 100% sure.			√
think	80% of respondents—of all ages—**thought** that older workers were discriminated against in job recruitment.	*think* signals that the reported information is an opinion		√	

E   Verb + Preposition Combinations

Many verbs commonly found in academic writing are really verb + preposition combinations. That is, certain verbs combine with a preposition to form a unit.

Verb + preposition combinations are often confused with phrasal verbs (verb + particle) such as *hand in, hang up,* or *leave out.* Phrasal verbs are different from verb + prepositions because adding the particle (preposition) to the verb often changes the meaning of the original verb to create an idiomatic expression. For example, look at the difference between *hang* and *hang up* or *leave* and *leave out.* The prepositions in verb + preposition combinations, however, do not change the meaning of the verb. They are just part of the grammar of the verb. Here are a few examples: *adapt to, rely on,* and *participate in.*

Phrasal verbs and verb + preposition combinations also differ in their grammar. The "particle" that is attached to the phrasal verb can move around in a sentence, but the preposition in verb + preposition combinations cannot move. For example, if a sentence with a phrasal verb contains a direct object, the particle can come either before or after the object. When the direct object is a pronoun, the particle must come after it.

direct object   direct object   pronoun as direct object

I <u>turned on</u> **the light.**   OR   I <u>turned</u> **the light** <u>on.</u>   BUT   I <u>turned</u> **it** <u>on.</u>

The preposition in verb + preposition combinations must always appear before its direct object, whether it is a pronoun or a noun. The third sentence in the example is wrong.

I <u>adjusted to</u> **the new computer** very quickly.

I <u>adjusted to</u> **it** very quickly.

*I <u>adjusted</u> **the new computer** <u>to</u> very quickly. (incorrect)

Verb + preposition combinations are very common in English. When you learn new verbs, it is important for you also to find out if they are part of a verb + preposition combination. The following list is from the readings in this book. For a more complete list, consult the World Wide Web at http://www.gsu.edu/~wwwesl/egw/verbprep.htm.

Verb	Preposition
account	for
adapt	to
adjust	to
attribute *(something)*	to *(something/someone)*
be concerned	about
comment	on Continued

communicate	with
consist	of
contribute	to
define *(something)*	as
depend	on
divide *(something)*	into *(something)*
have an influence	on
link *(something)*	with *(something)*
participate	in
prefer	to
prevent *(someone)*	from
refer	to
rely	on
resort	to
search	for
succeed	in
view *(something)*	as

$\mathscr{C}$redits

Chapter 1: Page 5: R. Williams and V. Williams, *Anger Kills: Seventeen Strategies for Controlling the Hostility That Can Harm Your Health.* (New York: Harper Perennial, 1993).
Page 13: Jamie Talan, "The Anger Factor," *Los Angeles Times,* September 19, 1995. ©1995. Newsday/Jamie Talan.
Page 19: Excerpt adapted from John G. Carlson and Elaine Hatfield, *Psychology of Emotion* (Ft. Worth, TX: Harcourt, Brace, and Jovanovich, 1992).©1992 by Holt, Rinehart and Winston. Reprinted by permission of the publisher.
Page 24: Carol Tavris, *Anger: The Misunderstood Emotion* (New York: Touchstone/Simon Schuster, 1989). Reprinted with the permission of Simon & Schuster. ©1982, 1989 by Carol Tavris.

Chapter 2: Page 48: P. B. Churcher and J. H. Lawton, "Beware of Well-Fed Felines," *Natural History,* July 1989, 40–47. With permission. ©1989 the American Museum of Natural History.
Page 51: (Diagram) J. Alcock, *Animal Behavior: An Evolutionary Approach,* Fifth Ed. (Sunderland, MA: Sinauer and Associates, Inc., 1993).
Page 52: W. K. Purves, G. H. Orians, and H. C. Heller, *Life: The Science of Biology,* Fifth Edition. (Sunderland, MA: Sinauer and Associates, Inc., 1998; NY: W. H. Freeman and Company, 1998).
Page 52: (Diagram) J. Alcock, *Animal Behavior: An Evolutional Approach,* Fifth Ed. (Sunderland, MA: Sinauer and Associates, Inc., 1993).
Page 53: (Diagram) W. K. Purves, G. H. Orians, and H. C. Heller, *Life: The Science of Biology,* Fourth Ed. (Sunderland, MA: Sinauer and Associates, Inc., and New York: W. H. Freeman and Co. 1995).
Page 55: Two cartoons: *The Far Side* ©1987 Far Words, Inc. Used by permission of Universal Press Syndicate. All rights reserved.
Page 56: Jeffrey Moussaieff Masson and Susan McCarthy, *When Elephants Weep* (New York: Delta Publishing, 1995). ©1995 by Jeffrey Masson and Susan McCarthy. Used by permission of Delacorte Press, a division of Doubleday Dell Publishing Group, Inc. All rights reserved.
Page 62: Paul W. Sherman and John Alcock, *Exploring Animal Behavior: Readings from American Scientist* (Sunderland, MA: Sinauer Associates Inc., Publishers, 1993). Reprinted by permission of *American Scientist,* magazine of Sigma Xi, the Scientific Research Society. Donald R. Griffin, *Animal Minds* (Chicago: University of Chicago Press, 1992). ©1992 by the University of Chicago Press. All rights reserved.
Page 72: Donald R. Griffin, "Animal Thinking" in Paul W. Sherman & John Alcock, *Exploring Animal Behavior: Readings from American Scientist.*
Page 75: Charles Walcott, "Show me the way you go home," *Natural History,* November 1989, 43–46.

Chapter 3: Page 96: Lynn Peters Adler, *Centenarians: The Bonus Years* (Santa Fe, NM: Health Press, 1995. ©1995, Health Press.
Page 104: A Gradual Goodbye in "All our tomorrows: A survey of the economics of aging," *The Economist,* January 27, 1996. ©1996 The Economist Newspaper Group, Inc. Reprinted with permission. Further reproduction prohibited.

Index